Multimedia

Multimedia

Texts and Contexts

Anne Cranny-Francis

SAGE Publications
London ● Thousand Oaks ● New Delhi

First published 2005

SAGE Publications Ltd
1 Oliver's Yard
55 City Road
London EC1Y 1SP

SAGE Publications Inc.
2455 Teller Road
Thousand Oaks, California 91320

SAGE Publications India Pvt Ltd
B-42, Panchsheel Enclave
Post Box 4109
New Delhi 110 017

British Library Cataloguing in Publication data

A catalogue record for this book is available
from the British Library

ISBN 0-7619-4994-1
ISBN 0-7619-4995-X (pbk)

Library of Congress Control Number available

Typeset by C&M Digitals (P) Ltd., Chennai, India
Printed in Great Britain by Cromwell Press Ltd, Trowbridge, Wiltshire

CONTENTS

PREFACE

This study of multimedia was written after several years' work as a consultant, analysing web sites. Its genesis was, therefore, in the practical need to communicate effectively with the users of information technology. My role was to analyse the ways in which the web sites made meanings available to users, and the kinds of meanings they offered. This meant exploring both the meaning-making practices of this new medium and the medium itself – how it positioned the individual user, and how users reciprocally influenced the development of the new technology and its textual practice.

The institutions and corporations represented by these web sites were often surprised, and sometimes alarmed, by the accuracy with which their web sites told their story to the public. Even when designed by an outside web consultant, the web sites betrayed the internal politics of the source in ways that seemed uncanny. On the other hand, the sites proved to be a rich and immediate source of communication with users – utilised to impart information, sell products, entertain, share thoughts and feelings.

So my involvement in these projects was very practical. It was about finding ways to talk about the meanings of this new genre of text, to enable designers and owners to assess their sites and also to create new and different meanings for their users. I worked with a colleague who conducted both on-line surveys and interviews with the users, which meant that I was able to check that my textual analyses accorded with the experiences of users. Through this hands-on experience I began to build up an understanding of how the different textual strategies available on a web site create meanings – or meaning-potentials – for users. Further, I also observed the development of the web site as a specific textual genre, with its own sub-genres and textual conventions. And I noted that the difference between the various types of sites was associated primarily with their social function – whether they were primarily about selling products or providing information or sharing interests. This function or purpose determined the meanings the sites were designed to convey and so their use of particular textual strategies; which also means being able to identify the meanings that the textual strategies available to multimedia texts can bring to the user's experience.

This book explores some of these meaning systems and concepts and how they contribute to the text: writing, visuals, sound, movement and space. The study works against their disciplinary pigeon-holing and, instead, suggests ways of appreciating the specific aspects of each, as well as the contribution of each to the overall meaning-potential of the text. This sometimes entails identifying forgotten or elided meanings associated with a meaning system and its textual strategies. We see this particularly with familiar meaning systems such as writing and visuals. At other times, it involves teasing out the meanings a particular system or concept and its strategic textual use can offer. Sound is equally familiar, but less often subject to analysis – and the same applies to movement and space, both of which are sometimes simply characterised as 'natural'. As this study shows, all of these meaning systems are culturally-specific and are created by their social uses and roles.

I have included examples of web site analysis as well as of other kinds of multimedia (though not always digitally multimedia) texts, including museum exhibitions and films. I have done this to acknowledge that many textual strategies have a cultural history of use that makes their meanings familiar to the users of the new digital medium. However, I also specifically address the digital environment since it generates its own constraints and possibilities.

I also discuss the connection that digital technology makes possible because, for good and for ill, it is one of its major capacities. It is this connectedness that has made us the posthuman subjects we now are – connected with each other, with technologies, and with other living beings in complex networks that make the autonomous and homogeneous humanist subject redundant. Now digital technologies (among others) extend the haptic capacity of human being and consciousness to operate beyond its skin boundaries – which is not to disavow the corporeality of individual consciousness, but rather to note its foundation in that extended corporeality.

At each point in the analysis it is essential to acknowledge the embodied user whose sensuous engagement, cultural preoccupations, social positionings, and political and ethical investments determine the extent to which she or he activates the meanings offered by the text. So the study of textual practice must be culturally-specific or located in order that the likely responses of particular users and audience can be predicted and explored.

This study now seems very introductory, yet I think it opens up many of the issues that must be addressed as multimedia becomes the standard literacy of the twenty-first century. No single chapter is complete; none is a complete grammar – and yet this is always the case with grammars. They are simply ways of introducing a temporary metastability to a system that is inherently ungovernable. Hopefully, this study is a contribution to that new digital literacy – and one that opens up its creative potential, rather than attempting to regulate it or close it down.

I want to thank my colleague, Patricia Gillard with whom I conducted the consultancies that were the genesis of this study. Her ethnographic studies of audiences and users complemented this cultural and textual analysis of multimedia and showed me that it worked, and her friendship was a great source of strength. I also want to thank Mary Macken-Horarik who shares my interest in sound, especially in science fiction film, and Bobbie Gledhill for quoting Tennyson and watching *Star Trek* with me.

Thanks are also due to my Macquarie University colleagues, especially Nick Mansfield and Joseph Pugliese, who were always supportive and encouraged me to finish this project. And finally I also thank Kiri for the coffee, my Mum and Dad for being there, and my two creative inspirations, Hamish and Conal Francis-Martin.

COPYRIGHT ACKNOWLEDGEMENTS

The author and the publisher would like to thank the following people for permission to use their images:

Figure 2.1 Barbara Kruger *Untitled (Your Gaze Hits the Side of my Face)*
Courtesy of: Mary Boone Gallery, New York

Figure 3.1 Amrit and Rabindra Singh, *Les Girls*
© The Singh Twins Amrit and Rabindra. www.singhtwins.co.uk

Figure 3.3 *Template Gothic*
Courtesy of: émigré.com

Figure 3.4 *The Sydney Morning Herald*, cover page Jan 17-18, 2004
Courtesy of: The Sydney Morning Herald

Figure 3.5 *Gothic Organic*
Courtesy of: Aree Cohen

Every effort has been made to trace the copyright holders but if any have been inadvertently overlooked the publishers will be pleased to make the necessary arrangement at the first opportunity.

ONE

INTRODUCTION

Jay David Bolter and Richard Grusin (1999) use the term 'remediation' to explore the changes to textuality that have accompanied the development of multimedia. They describe:

> ... a double logic of *remediation.* Our culture wants to both multiply its media and to erase all traces of mediation: ideally, it wants to erase its media in the very act of multiplying them. (Bolter and Grusin, 1999: 5)

For Bolter and Grusin one of the key issues involved in remediation is that of immediacy – the demand for erasure of the medium of the viewing experience: 'The medium itself should disappear and leave us in the presence of the thing represented: sitting in the race car or standing on a mountaintop' (1999: 6). Further, they argue, this immediacy 'depends on hypermediacy' (1999: 6), which they later define in the terms of William J. Mitchell as a visual style that 'privileges fragmentation, indeterminacy, and heterogeneity and ... emphasizes process or performance rather than the finished art object' (Mitchell (1995, quoted in Bolter and Grusin, 1999: 31).

Bolter and Grusin also trace a cultural history of both remediation and hypermediacy. Earlier visual artworks, they claim, often used linear perspective and naturalistic lighting effects to create the sense of immediacy for which late twentieth-century and early twenty-first-century multimedia artists have striven. And the logic of hypermediacy, so apparent now in web sites and the desktop interface, can be seen also in earlier text-forms such as illuminated manuscripts, medieval cathedrals and in the work of Dutch painters, such as Jan Vermeer, who were fascinated with the process of representation (Bolter and Grusin, 1991: 31–9).

Bolter and Grusin's work provides some fascinating insights into multimedia and this study accords with some of their insights, and challenges others. And in both cases the rationale for this response comes from the theoretical framework used here to explore multimedia texts – which is derived from the work of Russian linguist, Mikhail Bakhtin. From Bakhtin, for example, comes the notion that all texts are read in the context of a cultural history of textuality – so that a reader or viewer or listener understands a specific text by comparing and contrasting it with her or his experience of all other texts. Bakhtin explained this when writing of the novel:

> For the prose writer the object [the text] is a focal point for heteroglot voices among which his own voice must also sound; these voices create the background necessary for his own voice, outside which his artistic prose nuances cannot be perceived, and without which they 'do not sound'. (Bakhtin, 1981: 278)

Bakhtin called this cultural mix of voices, heteroglossia; Julia Kristeva later translated the concept as 'intertextuality'. In both cases it is used to understand the ways in which readers mobilise the meanings in a specific text – by locating it intertextually; that is, in relation to the heteroglossia of other texts (voices) in, to and through which it speaks. So a contemporary painting of a female nude speaks or has meaning not only in relation to other contemporary representations of the female nude, but also in relation to the cultural history of the female nude which most viewers bring in some, often implicit, form to their viewing.

So, like Bolter and Grusin, this study understands the meaning of contemporary multimedia texts as generated not only by reference to other contemporary multimedia, but also in relation to the cultural history of textuality of which they are a part. It differs somewhat from their argument in that it does not see contemporary multimedia texts or audiences as wanting to erase the medium of a text; instead both texts and audiences seem often to play exuberantly with an intense awareness of the media used and their potential for meaning-making. Bolter and Grusin acknowledge this 'immediacy through hypermediacy' later in their book, where they associate it with the interactivity of video games (1999: 81). For this study, however, this interactivity with the text is a consistent feature of any reading or viewing or listening practice; part of the audience's mobilisation of intertextuality that creates the meanings of the text.

The notion of the active audience also crucially informs this study; the recognition that texts of all kinds only mean (that is, make meaning) because there is a reader or viewer or listener interacting with them. So it is not appropriate or useful or effective to entertain the concept sometimes heard in IT circles of the 'stupid user' – the user who cannot access a web site or use a program. If a web site or program is so difficult or inaccessible, it is most likely that it fails to acknowledge and mobilise the intertextual resources that its target audience(s) bring to it. In other words, the designer has not understood and used the cultural literacy of the audience in creating the product.

This study focuses on the kinds of cultural literacies employed in multimedia texts – whether they are digitally-generated multimedia (such as web sites and computer games) or composite forms of multimedia texts (such as films, museum exhibitions, performance art). Both forms are essentially multi-modal in that they employ different modalities of text – writing, visuals, sound, movement, spatiality – in their construction and meaning-making. The cultural meanings of each of these different modalities is explored for what it brings – historically and culturally – to the design and reading of contemporary multimedia. And in each case, also, we consider the ways in which this different mode of communication positions the user as a contemporary (multimedia) subject.

Chapter 2 explores writing in the age of multimedia. We start by exploring the historical significance of writing – its role as a guarantor of authority and truth (the written contract, the word of God) – in order to understand the kinds of cultural echoes it brings to any text. But we also consider the role of writing as a technology, something our familiarity with written texts can lead us to overlook. How does it operate as a technology? What kinds of meanings does the very 'look' of writing generate? We consider the changing relationship between visuality and writing and whether the visual has now superseded the written word, as well as the visuality of writing itself – an aspect of writing we again tend to overlook (Ong, 1982). Chapter 2 also addresses the issue of digital literacy, the specific literacy demands of the digital era, and ends by exploring the ways that this new literacy is shaping us as contemporary subjects.

Chapter 3 begins by examining some fascinating recent visual work by artists Amrit and Rabindra Kaur Singh, and H.R. Giger, for the kinds of meanings they generate about contemporary society and culture. For the Singhs, this is an overt political practice; for Giger, an implicit element in his work. Yet, both produce beautiful and affecting art. We look at the visuality of a typeface and how this, too, generates a specific cultural experience. And we look at a complex, multimedia (hypermediated) text – the front page of a newspaper – for the complex meanings it offers readers and casual viewers. In each case we are looking at the ways that visuality articulates cultural (and social and political) meanings. We consider also some of the ways we might use to access these meanings, some of the critical terms that are useful for exploring visual texts. We then mobilise these terms to analyse a specific multimedia genre, the web site. We explore the web site as a specific visual genre: how it can be described and what functions it performs. We analyse a particular site (*HistoryWired*, operated by the Smithsonian Museum in Washington, USA) for the ways it uses visuals to perform its role as a particular kind of web site (institutional, educational) and how it positions users. In the course of that analysis we also explore some of the concepts and practices that can be used specifically to analyse visuality.

Chapter 4, 'Sound' begins with a series of scenarios in which sound is a major factor. These range from the pumped-up bass track of the Dolby Sound System used with *Star Wars* films to the writer who takes a laptop to a busy, noisy café to work. In each case we explore the contemporary sound theory that enables us to understand the different deployments of sound in these scenarios – whether it is sound as an imperialist practice that inter-pellates the listener into a particular transaction or exchange or narrative, or the personal stereo used to individuate the soundscape and protect the user from forms of social regulation. We consider the different concepts and ideas we can use to understand and analyse sound as a form of communication and as an embodied practice (we feel, as well as hear, sound). And we explore the terms that have been developed in several disciplines (including film studies, media, linguistics) to discuss the meanings of sound. The chapter concludes with an example of sound analysis in a section of film, which attempts to show how sound elements such as music, sound effects, and voice quality work together to generate a particular story and its (social and political) meanings.

Chapter 5 explores movement as another of the modalities used in multimedia texts. Like writing, visuality, and sound, movement is a culturally- and historically-specific practice – as the work of Marcel Mauss in the early twentieth century made clear. Mauss looked at the ways people move and discovered associations between styles of walking and individuals from specific cultures (both between and within countries or nations). The Chapter investigates the historical and social meanings of movement; how under- standings of movement have changed in the West over the last several hundred years and the significance of those changes for textuality. We look specifically at the significance of movement in relation to digital technologies, including how metaphors of movement articulate the power and practice of the technology (for example, in the hyperlink that characterises many digital texts). Several 'moving' texts are analysed for how the movement contributes to their meanings (socially, culturally, politically). And we also consider the relationship between movement and embodiment, and how that may effect the meaning- making practice of the multimedia text – as well as how specific movements define the multimedia subject(ivity). Finally, we discuss how the movements generated by conventional layout diagrams map the common narrative of Western societies.

In Chapter 6 we examine the last of the modalities that we associate with the practice of multimedia, which is spatiality. Again, we explore the socio- historical significance of this modality beginning with the redefinition of space in the early twentieth century as (a component of) space-time; that is, as inseparable from time as a parameter of human existence and experience. We trace the ramifications of this new understanding of space in the social theory of the later twentieth century, which theorises space as generated by particular actions and activities. In particular, we consider the creation of 'cyberspace' as the metaphor that enables many of our interactions with digital technologies. We also look at the proliferation of spatial metaphors in the work of theorists such as Deleuze and Guattari, used so often by multimedia theorists. Our concern is with how these spatial metaphors con- figure both contemporary textuality and subjectivity. Finally, we consider how metaphors of space inform our understandings of memory, and how they distinguish human and machine memory; which also inscribes under- standings of spatiality into our understanding of the difference between information and knowledge.

Chapter 7 addresses the issue of connection, which is one of the defining features of digital technologies. Allucquére Rosanne Stone describes the connection between humans and their technologies in a way that is both enabling and unnerving: 'Since in a deep sense they are languages, it's hard to *see* what they do, because what they do is structure seeing. They act on the systems – social, cultural, neurological – by which we make meaning. Their implicit messages change us' (1995: 167–8). With this in mind we consider Martin Heidegger's important work, 'The Question Concerning Technology', for its conception of this connection between technology and the human; particularly for the possibility of reflexivity that Heidegger locates in our uses of technology. This leads to a study of the work of two theorists – Bruno Latour and Donna Haraway – who, from very different perspectives, explore our relationship with technology and how that reflects our current understanding of the connection between mind and body – which, for both theorists, generates new conceptions of hybridity and of connectedness. We trace a grounded example of this new connectedness in the use of digital technology to create new kinds of relationships between people, new intimacies, and the reflexivity they can promote. Finally, we consider one of the major theorists of this field, Jean Baudrillard, and how his work can inform our understanding of the relationship between the user and the multimedia text.

In all of these chapters the guiding principle is that we are dealing with a specific mode of communication that multimedia audiences or users encounter in a variety of different textual practices or locations. Our concern is with how users mobilise their understandings of these earlier encounters in their readings of multimedia texts. This follows the same logic as Susan McClary when she writes of a Mozart piano concerto:

> ... the Mozart piano concerto movement with which we are concerned neither makes up its own rules nor derives them from some abstract, absolute, transcendental source. Rather it depends heavily on conventions of eighteenth-century harmonic syntax, formal procedure, genre type, rhythmic propriety, gestural vocabulary, and associations. All of these conventions have histories: social histories marked with national, economic, class and gender – that is, political – interests. (1986: 53)

To understand the politics – the meanings – of a text of any kind, including multimedia, involves understanding the politics/meanings of its conventions – another Bakhtinian principle (Bakhtin, 1981; Jameson, 1981; Todorov, 1984). And understanding the meaning of any text involves both its poetics and its politics – whether we are looking at a contemporary web site or listening to a Mozart concerto.

This cultural knowledge is the subject of this book. It is the raw material, if you like, from which users, readers, viewers and listeners generate their own specific textual readings/meanings. Those readings are a combination of contemporary literacies and idiosyncratic experience that situate the text within a specific user's life experience and knowledge.

None of this exploration of meaning potential is prescriptive; rather it is a mapping exercise. The object is to explore the cartography of contemporary meaning-making; how different techniques and strategies make meanings for users, readers, viewers and listeners, and what those meanings are. It is intended as a resource – a way of developing a language about these strategies that might enable authors and designers to talk more explicitly about their work; users to talk about their readings. And it might also provide a way of conceptualising the relationships between these strategies and the politics of the text. This includes both the meanings these strategies make within a particular configuration (in the specific text) and the significance of the specific text as an example of contemporary multimedia.

TWO

WRITING

When the first series of *Star Trek* graced television screens in 1966 viewers were shown a vision of the possible future of human (or, more accurately, US) society. The women wore micro-mini skirts and some of the men flaunted 'Beatle' haircuts – but one of the most striking features of the programme was its view of technology. The producers of *Star Trek*, led by the visionary Gene Roddenberry, rejected the hokey technology of its more successful rival programme, *Lost in Space* for a credible extrapolation of 1960s technology. The starship, *Enterprise*, was controlled by a computer that was accessed either by direct voice-command or by patterns of lights. Science officer, Mr Spock, was frequently shown playing his hand over a bridge console to activate light patterns that communicated with the computer, and then translating those patterns into verbal information when the computer responded to his commands. There were no screens of verbal data on the *Enterprise*. The later *Star Trek* series added minimal verbal icons to the coloured patterns but communication with the computer remained basically non-written – either direct verbal interaction or patterned displays of icons or lights. The written text was somehow not appropriate to this future vision. And, in fact, when it appears, it does so as a charming antique – as in Spock's gift to his captain, James T. Kirk, of a copy of Charles Dickens's *A Tale of Two Cities*.[1]

Written communication is now both central to our lives and not so dominant as it once was. That apparent contradiction is evident in current multimedia texts. As Bolter and Grusin (1999) note, however, there have always been multi-modal texts. Many medieval paintings employed verbal and visual modes. Later, printed books included printed words and woodblock or woodcut images. In more recent times, newspapers and magazines, film, television, books and video use a mix of modalities in their texts – words, images, voice, sound, music. So contemporary users have a history of consumption of multimodal, multimedia texts and have developed ways of understanding their (potential) meanings and of incorporating those meanings into their everyday lives.

The change produced by digitisation is that it not only became possible to generate multimedia texts, but also that it placed the possibility of multimedia production in the hands of the everyday user. Just as word-processing made it much easier for individuals to edit their work (who can remember the days, not so long past, of typewriters and tippex?), now programs found on most computers (such as Microsoft Word) enable users to generate texts that combine words and images – and without much more expertise to include animation and sound. This increased availability of multimedia production signals a change in the significance or value of different modes of communication. Writing still has a major social and cultural role, but it is not as dominant as it was in the nineteenth century soon after the steam-powered printing press took newspapers, pamphlets and, eventually, books into the homes of all but the poorest members of the community; or when 'universal' (verbal) literacy became the basis of educational policy. The ability to read and write soon became not only the hallmark of a civilised person, but also an essential requirement for men, women and children inside the home and without. We now have a technology that is equally transformative. With the possibility of generating multimedia texts placed in the hands of so many users, multi-modality is becoming the new literacy.

This chapter deals with writing as a communication mode in an age of multimedia. As with the other chapters on the textual strategies of multimedia, the aim of this chapter is not to be prescriptive about the use of writing, but rather to open up the possibilities it offers. This discussion begins with an acknowledgment of the power of writing in our society; of its function as a technology that establishes and maintains authority and 'truth'. This is followed by a study of the relationship between writing and visuality: how it has changed over recent years, and the meanings of those changes. The visuality of writing is also explored, with emphasis on what we have learned not to see and how those elements contribute to its communicative power. This discussion leads to a consideration of 'digital literacy', and of the demands that the immediacy of writing on-line make on individual users. Finally, we consider the relationship between writing and subjectivity and how it enables us to understand the contemporary multimedia subject(ivity).

The technology of writing

In *Of Grammatology* (1974) Jacques Derrida explores the meaning of writing, noting of the printed text:

> The idea of the book, which always refers to a natural totality, is profoundly alien to the sense of writing. It is the encyclopaedic protection of theology and of logocentrism against the disruption of writing, against its aphoristic energy, and ... against difference in general. (1974: 18)

In this way Derrida draws attention to the distinction between writing as a communicative practice and a way of thinking, and the printed word, which is a technology for specifying the politics of a situation or an event or act. In Derrida's formulation the printed work closes down the disruptive potential of writing to challenge ways of thinking and acting – through the slippages and elisions that make its meaning undecidable. Derrida points instead to the history of what he calls 'writing in the common sense, the dead letter' (1974: 17) as a means of asserting and maintaining authority.

Early forms of the written word were associated with authority, either as religious texts (handwritten by monks and other religious orders) or as official state chronicles. These early written texts were rare: literacy was limited to scholars, religious orders, state officials and the upper classes (many individuals occupying several of those roles or identities simultaneously); paper and inks were expensive. Many of these texts, interestingly, were multimedia in that they featured beautiful visual elements such as illuminated letters that were more than just illustrations of the verbal texts. Sometimes, the illuminations added other layers of meaning to the verbal text, visually expanding on the subject-matter of the verbal text; at other times, they chronicled the life of the illuminator and his community. In either form the preciousness, beauty and expense of the manuscript immediately associated it with those in positions of power and authority (Church or State (regal)) – and the written word itself became a sign or guarantor of authority. In this sense it literally enacted the concept of the divine word in Judaic and Christian doctrine: the godhead manifest in the word – 'I am the Word.'

The spread of commerce in the West and the development of secular power bases were effected through the medium of the written word. The written word was used to record commercial exchanges that formed the power base of the middle classes. The written word maintained its authority through official documents or bills of lading; it was accepted as a guarantee that an action had taken place, or that it should. The word still carried the same semi-divine authority it always had.

Equally crucial to this dominance of the written word in western societies was its role in the development of western science. In fact, the written word might be seen as *an* – or even, *the* – essential technology of science; that is, the written record of scientific observation and experimentation became the fundamental precondition and guarantor of scientific authority, which that scientific episteme constructed as 'truth'. In her essay, 'Modest_Witness @Second_Millennium' (1997), Donna Haraway writes about the development of the scientific method. She refers particularly to the study by Steven Shapin and Simon Schaffer of the chemist, Robert Boyle, whose work came to define the scientific method. Haraway records that in their study, *Leviathan and the Air-Pump: Hobbes, Boyle, and the Scientific Life* (1985), Shapin and Schaffer (quoted in Haraway, 1985) note that three different technologies come into play when a new life-form (the scientific method) is generated: a material technology, a literary technology, and a social technology (a formulation that applies equally to the study of contemporary information and communication technologies).[2] The literary technology of the scientific method was a written report by a supposedly neutral observer[3] who objectively recorded observations and experimentation that tested an hypothesis and so reached value-free conclusions ('truth'). Without this written documentation and presentation of results the scientific method – and western science – does not exist. For a contemporary scientist the guarantor of the value and validity of her work is its publication in an internationally-recognised, peer-reviewed journal. The written word operates as guarantor of authority and as a source of truth.

One striking example of this power of the written word is given in an exchange between an obstetrician and his patient, recorded by British child-birth educator, Sheila Kitzinger:

Doctor: [*reading case notes*] Ah, I see you've got a boy and a girl.
Patient: No, two girls.
Doctor: Really, are you sure? I thought it said … [*checks in case notes*] Oh, no, you are quite right, two girls. (1988: 145)

Kitzinger uses this example to demonstrate how traditional Western medicine positions the patient as powerless and as totally lacking in authority. However, the more striking feature of this exchange is that *both* doctor *and* patient are subordinate to the case notes (and the basis for this can be found in the literary technology of science, discussed above). In fact it is the doctor's own subjection to the case notes that leads him to make this extraordinary challenge to his female patient about her knowledge of the gender of her own children. Of course, other factors no doubt intersect here – the power relationship between doctor and patient, and conservative gender relations that position the male as authority figure. Yet, it is the power of the written word that enables an exchange that is more than simply unequal; it is preposterous.

Similarly it is interesting to note that the so-called 'killer ap' of the late twentieth-century technological revolution was not the web site generator but e-mail, a very basic form of writing. E-mail has transformed contemporary western lives in a way that only the development of the first postal and rail systems did. Business is conducted at a faster turn-around time; arrangements (for travel, purchase, co-productions) are made at the speed of a modem or cable; people chat to strangers in different parts of the globe about their interests, their love lives, their hopes and aspirations for the future. And it works so effectively because writing maintains its authority.

Derrida's challenge to the logocentrism of writing is one of the fundamentals of mid- to late twentieth-century philosophy (Derrida, 1978), and had far-reaching consequences in a range of disciplines – from Literary Studies to Cultural Studies, History to Sociology. However, the challenge to the authority of writing also comes from those who have been excluded from the position of 'modest witness', sometimes because their literacy skills are inadequate, at other times because their accounts are not held to be sufficiently objective or well enough documented. A striking example of the latter occurred in some responses to the *Bringing Them Home* report on the State-sanctioned abduction of indigenous children from their families in Australia (National Inquiry, 1997). The first-person narratives of survivors of this abuse were challenged by some respondents as insufficiently objective or as undocumented – accusations that seem as preposterous as the example above of the doctor–patient interaction. For those respondents the written word is the only proof of an event, a guarantor of its veracity. Such respondents have not understood or accepted the need to situate the mechanism of authority; that this mechanism of authority (the written word) is culturally-, socially-, and politically-specific.

The poststructuralist interrogation of epistemology in the latter half of the twentieth century, inspired by theorists such as Roland Barthes and Jacques Derrida, focused on the role of writing as a technology of 'truth'. In exploring the assumptions encoded in writing and subsequently established by the written word as 'truth', poststructuralist critics both acknowledged the social, cultural and political power of writing and opened it up to critical challenge.

The written word has had a tempestuous history. It both retains its power and has that power under challenge. Or rather, perhaps we might say that what is under challenge is the situation of the word: whose written word is it? Why is it regarded by some people to be the only guarantor of truth? Which people make that claim? In a time of such flux, of questioning and debate rather than unquestioned obedience to authority (whose authority?), the written word has multiple possibilities of use in any text. It can be used for simple information delivery – but then its authority is under challenge, so will that information be accepted? It can be used to suggest this very complexity, and so can operate both literally and interrogatively, or ironically, in the same text. And this is particularly evident in texts that combine writing and other modes of communication, such as the visual.

Writing and visuality

In his essay, 'Visual and verbal modes of representation in electronically mediated communication: the potentials of new forms of text'[4] (1997), Gunther Kress argues that the relative status of the verbal and the visual as a mode of information delivery has been changing over many decades. Kress examines two school science textbooks, from 1936 and 1988, and notes a crucial difference in their use of visual material. In the earlier book the graphics illustrate the written text; their relationship to the written text is one of redundancy. In the more recent book, however, there is no redundancy between verbal text and graphics. Instead the graphics convey information that is not contained in the verbal text, so that the verbal and visual material in the book work in a complementary, not redundant, fashion. This important change signals a new status not only for the visual (considered in more detail in the following chapter) but also for the verbal. The written word is no longer the sole source of (scientific and other) information.

At the same time the written word starts to take on a new role in art and design. Postmodern artworks mix modes of representation, so that visual works appear with words written across them. In fact, a blend of writing and visuality has become a kind of postmodern cliché. This mix of modalities signifies the end of an older reading and viewing practice in which the visual was surveyed for its possible meanings and then a verbal translation was attempted.

FIGURE 2.1 Barbara Kruger, *Untitled (Your gaze hits the side of my face)*
(1981), viewed at www.usc.edu/schools/annneberg/asc/projects/
comm544/library/images/541.html

Instead the verbal and visual are interrelated to generate meanings. For example, Barbara Kruger's 1981 collage, *Untitled (Your gaze hits the side of my face)*, features an image of a classic carved female bust with the words 'Your gaze hits the side of my face' pasted down the side of the image, as a series of cut-outs (see Figure 2.1).

One obvious reading – literally – of the work is that it directs the viewer to the ways in which the gaze has objectified the feminine, with the essential violence of that objectification conveyed by the verbal pun on 'hits'. Another reading, however, focuses on the relationship of the verbal and the visual in that reading practice and, instead, sees the whole work as about ways of reading. Kruger's cut-outs indicate that reading is a construct, and in so doing begs the questions of who speaks here and what is the status of that speech. One answer is that this is a female voice (of which the classical female image is a visual metaphor) – in an art-world dominated by masculine voices, as both artists and critics. A second answer is that this voice is active in the artwork, rendering it a political as well as an aesthetic practice; that is, the inclusion of this marked voice – marked because it is female, not the (supposedly) politically 'neutral' male[5] – makes the point that all art is political and that the aesthetic is a fundamentally political practice. It deconstructs the 'neutrality' of both the masculine and the aesthetic.

Kruger's work not only constructed a new voice (making an unfamiliar, feminist reading of a classic work), but it also located the voice, rather than assigning it the transparency of neutral observer status. Kruger's work is not only a criticism of the masculinised world of the gaze, but also a deconstruction of the masculinised voice of authority – as it operates in the art world, in disciplines such as philosophy (and aesthetics), and in everyday life.

The use of the written word in postmodern artworks is often a way of examining the status and power of the written word. As noted earlier, however, this interrelation of the verbal and the visual has now become almost a cliché, which underscores just how central this critique has been to contemporary understandings of textuality and, specifically, of writing. It does not devalue the power of writing but instead demonstrates its continuing role as a social, cultural and political technology.

Gunther Kress argues that writing has lost its dominance and that verbal literacy is now less important than it once was. Alternatively, verbal literacy can be seen as even more necessary than ever, with internet users processing vast amounts of writing with greater speed than ever before. Furthermore, users need to be alert to many aspects of writing that have become invisible through familiarity – like the use of fonts, the layout of a page – for their role in the creation of meaning.

The visuality of writing

Whether as an element in a postmodern artwork or on a web site, writing now has to be considered not as a transparent carrier of meanings, but as a feature of the design. So the visuality of the written text once again becomes visible. As everyday multimedia users we know, for example, that a text printed in Times New Roman looks vastly different from a text printed in Sand font – and will be perceived differently; it will mean different things. This pervasiveness of writing in multimedia led designer, Matthew Butterick, to note in an essay on typography:

> The sole bit of good news is that [written] text rules the digital frontier, because it is compact to load, easy to create, familiar to use, and compatible with all computing platforms. The popularity of the World Wide Web has shown that text is still a vital medium, and though it's less flashy than pictures, sound, and video, it offers the best bang for the bandwidth. (2001: 39)

Most e-mail is conducted in either Times New Roman or Courier font, prompting Butterick to write that 'Internet users look like the most fertile new group of type consumers: a giant new demographic suffering from an acute case of dreadful typography' (2001: 40). Though as Butterick goes on to note: 'the language of Internet typography (HTML) allows for no explicit typeface choices, and only a handful of different sizes' (2001: 40) – a provocative thought for the technologically-gifted typographer.

In exploring the ways in which the visuality of writing can be used to construct complex, multiply-significant texts it may be useful to consider an example. In 2000 the National Archives of Australia (www.naa.gov.au) launched a web site called *Documenting a Democracy* (www.foundingdocs.

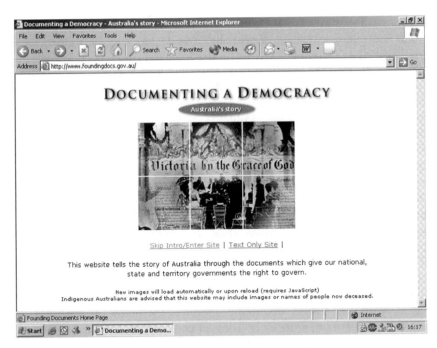

FIGURE 2.2   *Documenting a Democracy* home page, viewed at
www.foundingdocs.gov.au

gov.au) that shows visitors some of the founding documents of Australian democracy – which is to say, white Australian settler society. These documents include the Letters Patent that established many of the separate Australian States as well as the documents that declare the Federation of Australia. The site features some beautiful graphics and the virtual presence of those powerful documents has produced an awed response in more than one visitor.[6] However, equally impressive is the site's interrogation of the values that those documents seem at first glance to confirm unquestioningly. And it is the web author's use of the written word that is the major channel of this critique.

On its home page (see Figure 2.2) the web site features a splash screen: a mosaic of images of white settlement (or invasion, depending on point of view) overlaid with samples of copperplate handwriting and some typed material that the user assumes are from the documents recorded at the site.

At a most literal level this juxtaposition of verbal and visual material refers the user/visitor to the site's role in presenting the documents of Australia's white history. However, the superposition of writing over the images suggests another meaning, which is that the document precedes the event. In other words, the written document is not a simple recording of material events – which is the most commonplace understanding; instead, the implication is that the document actually enabled or caused the event. This is a very powerful statement about the power of the written word. It can be read as the site's acknowledgment of the episteme discussed above, whereby the written history is the valid history – the 'truth'.

Yet, as all Australians now know, this is just one version of the history of white Australian settlement. Essentially, it is the story of the victors; those who claimed by force the power to speak for all and whose documentary history is proclaimed the true history of Australia. And this, too, is shown on a number of pages at the site, including the splash page. The images over which the writing appears constitute a visual history of white–indigenous relations: from paintings of the First Fleet sailing along the coast and amicable meetings between English and indigenous Australian people, to the famous image of Prime Minister Gough Whitlam returning land to Aboriginal activist, Vincent Lingiari, by symbolically pouring dirt into his hands. Juxtaposing the documents (represented by the writing) with this history that Australians know to have been a bloody one, and one still fraught with injustice, immediately suggests the equivocal role of these documents in establishing what the victors now label a 'democracy'; that is, these documents that apparently offer a guarantee of equality and liberty were based on bloody conflict, the destruction of the liberty of indigenous Australians and the denial of their equality (they were not classified as Australian citizens until a referendum in 1967 changed the Australian constitution to enable this). This deconstructive reading of Australian history essentially questions the nature of history itself, and the role of written documentation in constructing the narrative that is accepted as history. This is arguably a crucial role for a web site that has professional historians as its major clients.

So the *Documenting a Democracy* site mobilises the visual representation of the written word to produce a web site that is not only a major source of information for historians, but which also engages historians – and potentially all users – in a fundamental questioning of the nature of history and subsequently of the meanings of terms like 'democracy'. And thus the site makes a major contribution to the development of the democracy – Australian society – which the recorded documents establish as a geopolitical construct.

In this example, debates about the written word, about the nature of documentation and about the history it produces discursively have a particular relevance. Nevertheless, it is impressive that the web authors do not rely on written argumentation to make this point. In fact, it may well be that on a government-sponsored site it would be very difficult to make this kind of argument directly. Rather, it is made in a number of different ways, including the reproduction of a map of indigenous languages (making the point that 'Australia' is not a monocultural construct, no matter who gets to write the history) and the inclusion of contextualising commentary with many of the documents – at times acknowledging their profoundly undemocratic nature. For example, on the Timeline page, the 1869 Aboriginal Protection Act (Victoria) is described as 'Democracy in reverse'. Yet, the most subtle and insistent argument comes from the splash screens and their interrelation of writing and visual images. And again the major point here is that the design employs the image of written word rather than its content to make this argument. It is the writing's implicit evocation of documentary materials, of written history and of the producers of that history – their power and status – that generates the argument.

This example also raises two issues about writing as a mode of communication. Firstly, it confirms the power of writing through its ongoing involvement in debates about the nature of power. Secondly, it raises the issue of the visuality of the written text. What is it about the visuality of the written word that has been obscured by its power as a medium? What do we elide in our explication of the meaning of the written word?

Seeing the written word: reading the design

It could be argued that visual elements of writing (such as font, layout, spacing) are fundamental, communicative properties that we tend not to notice overtly – or, at least, not to subject to critical interrogation. In the second half of the twentieth century, however, there were attempts to draw attention specifically to the visuality of writing. Concrete poetry, for example, employed the materiality of the written word in the production of meaning, for example as in Eugen Gomringer's *Silencio*: the word 'silencio' (silence) printed in three columns, with five words in columns one and three and four words (omitting the middle word) in column two. In other words, it is the empty space at the centre of this block of words that constitutes the poem, 'Silencio' is nothing – silencio. The concrete poets utilised elements of the written text that had been ignored in the fetishisation of words; they explicitly evoked meanings that were generated not by words but by their arrangement in time and space.

Consider how much visual elements contribute to our understanding of written text. A particular spacing of lines indicates that we are dealing with a lyric – either poetry or song. Words arranged in columns most often appear in newspapers and magazines. So, spacing of words enables us to locate the genre of a work and also its medium:

Words in lines
Which end in rhymes
Tell us tales
Of grief or passion.
Words in columns and prose
More or less verbose
Are journalistic and factitious
And debate our world in a political fashion.

A lyric poem written without its conventional spacing would be very difficult to process, and would most likely seem the most mawkish or overblown prose. A newspaper or magazine article written across a page, without columns, would read quite differently. On-line versions of newspaper stories commonly do appear without columns in their printer-friendly form and the result is often that the impact of the piece is lost. This is because the journalist has written the story in a form that enables her or him to create salience in particular ways, by the use of grabs or by an arrangement of short and long paragraphs that highlights a particular statement. In transforming the piece for a printer, this layout is lost – and so is the writer's emphasis, which is a major part of the meaning-making practice of the text.

Using the written word in any medium, therefore requires an awareness not only of the dictionary-derived meanings of the words but also of how their deployment in different forms and configurations may impact on those literal meanings. And this is not simply a matter of an individual aesthetic choice by author or user. The very fact that a choice can be made which is pleasing or disturbing for many users indicates that the choice is not a matter of individual taste, but is based in shared, cultural values and meanings. To utilise those meanings in the richest sense, then, an author needs to understand those configurations and their meanings – because they are part of the implicit cultural environment of users. Those users may not be able to articulate the meanings they read in exact historical and cultural detail, but they do see, read and hear those meanings. The informed designer or author adds to her or his palette, aesthetically, culturally and politically, by understanding the history of the modality. It enables the author to make complex meanings, to layer meanings, to add irony without need for laboured verbal or written explication.

In 'Designing Hate: Is there a Graphic Language of Vile Emotion?' Steven Heller (2001a) asks whether a particular typography can be evil – that is, whether the very look or shape of a word can be evil. His conclusion is that the connotation of evil comes from context, not from any implicit quality. So Heller writes that the swastika had no evil connotation before it was used by the Nazis; in fact, it was used by a US infantry unit in the First World War to signify courage. The swastika is an ancient symbol, signifying power. Because of its use by the Nazis, however, its meaning has changed forever: now it can only mean great evil. Visual artists employ the symbol in this way. Heller continues:

What typeface says 'nigger'? What logo denotes kike, spic, or wop? Are there design conventions for expressing racism? Can hate be well designed? (2001a: 42)

He concludes that the type font used in Nazi propaganda – a German Fraktur type – now connotes brutality and savagery, not because of some essential quality in the font, but because of its cultural deployment. Of course, this begs the question of whether it was used originally by the Nazis because it already suggested some of these qualities. The answer is in the writer's analogy with the swastika. The font may have had some (culturally) accrued meanings to do with power, but it was a particular historical, social, political, cultural mobilisation of those meanings – in the genocidal attacks on Jews, gays, the disabled, and others not acceptable to the Nazi regime (such as gypsies) – that have given the Fraktur font its (evil) meanings for contemporary readers.

An interesting supplement to this argument by Heller comes from a web site (wordiq.com), which records an interesting twist to this story of the Nazi font:

> Fraktur went out of fashion during the early 20th century because of the obvious communication problems with non-native German speakers. However, in an attempt to deliberately differentiate Germany from the rest of the Western world, it was reinforced by Nazi Germany (1933–1945), which pronounced that Antiqua typefaces were not Aryan. During that time, new, more artificial Fraktur typefaces were designed … . This policy was officially held up until January 3, 1941, when Martin Bormann issued a circular letter to all public offices which suddenly declared Fraktur to be Judenlettern (Jewish letters) and prohibited further use. It has been speculated that the regime had realized that Fraktur would inhibit communication in the territories occupied during World War II as well.
>
> Despite being an old German tradition, the use of Fraktur still has a strong Nazi connotation to many, who are unaware of the Nazi decree of 1941 actually outlawing Fraktur. Consequently, Fraktur is today used merely for decorative typesetting; for example, a number of traditional German newspapers still print their name in Fraktur on the first page.
>
> (Heller at www.wordiq.com/definition/Fraktur, accessed 27/08/2004)

The interesting point of this discussion is that the significance of the Fraktur typeface is seen in terms of its cultural history, even where that cultural history is essentially a fanciful construct – as in Bormann's response to the typeface as 'Jewish'.

Heller's conclusion argues for a designer who is culturally-aware – able to understand the relation between design and meaning. Most particularly what this means is that design is understood not as individual choice and not as neutrally 'aesthetic', but as culturally formed and shared – and as culturally-specific. Heller notes, for example, that right-wing groups can deploy design elements associated with leftist groups to avoid being identified immediately with hate propaganda. The multimedia author has the plasticity of the word to work with – the fact that it can be made in a variety of ways, with different fonts, in different spatial arrangements, in combination with visual and other modalities (sound, movement, touch). But each use has its own history of meanings that users implicitly understand (to varying degrees, according to their own cultural backgrounds) and deploy in their construction of meaning – and that authors and designers therefore need to explore and understand. Let us look at the following examples of Bang: the word,

- **Bang!**
- *Bang!*
- B a n g!
- Bang!

Despite our fetishisation of the literal meaning of the word, readers/users have many different ways of interpreting the meaning of a word in context – or of creating the context of the word (and hence its possible meanings) as it appears in different forms or fonts. It is not difficult for example, to determine appropriate contexts and therefore possible meanings for the expression 'bang!' printed in the above fonts:

- **Arial Black Bang** – an adventure story bang, with lots of boofy blokes shooting at each other
- *Apple Chancery Bang* – an extremely genteel bang – probably a door blown shut in a gentle breeze
- **Sand Bang** – a children's cartoon bang
- **Techno Bang** – a constipated, uptight, Keanu in tight leather bang

We can predict the meanings of these fonts through our common cultural experience because we are exposed to the use of fonts to make meanings through their visual appearance. One industry and context in which this has a major role and function is, of course, advertising – but the same principles apply to all uses of the written word. Its appearance is always meaningful, even if that meaning is to convey transparency (like the neutral observer of scientific discourse).

It might even be that an author could choose a design such as that on the *Documenting a Democracy* web site without any further critical thought. And yet it was a choice. The author may have chosen only to engage with a contemporary mode of representation, the juxtaposition of verbal and visual text – but a critically- and culturally-aware author would know that this mode of representation signified more than an attractive arrangement of shapes. And, of course, we could argue that an author who is unable to artic-ulate verbally this self-reflexive practice is nevertheless enacting an awareness of it through her or his visual skills. So the choice of design is a critical prac-tice. It is worth noting even so that an author who knows why she or he makes such a choice is inevitably in a stronger position to make complex and interesting choices in the development of a text.

Breaking the rules

Stone wrote in *The War of Desire and Technology at the End of the Machine Age* that: 'Before breaking rules it is necessary to understand them, so I have written and continue to write, academic articles that are quite mainstream in character' (1995: 166). This statement might be amended. It may not be necessary to understand rules in order to break them. However, to break rules and understand the significance of both the break and the text it generates, it is necessary to understand the rules in the first place; which is to say, one has to know how these rules work textually (what meanings they make as a com-ponent of the text, their diegetic function) and how they work culturally (what meanings they make for particular readers at a particular place and time).

As I noted earlier, this study does not follow the rule-governed approach of some handbooks on multimedia that argues for a set number of words per page or line, or that denigrates particular kinds of design, or even particular fonts. Instead, it argues that usability is a feature of the cultures of users – literacies, subject positionings, social status – and that authors and designers can predict those cultures by an understanding of their users. It also argues for a textually- and culturally-aware author/designer who is able to articulate her or his design choices for clients and collaborators; and to articulate this not only in aesthetic terms but also as meaningful (meaning-filled) choices.

Screen-reading

Having argued for a non-prescriptive, culturally-sensitive response to the notion of usability it is, nevertheless, important to note that there are features of web-based uses of writing that may be technological, rather than cultural, artefacts. I use the word 'may' because it may also be that these features have a cultural component.

Analysts such as Nielsen make some important points about usability and writing even if they tend to do this in a rather prescriptive way. So, for example, they note that the font size should be easily readable on screen. This seems an obvious point – but it is apparently not obvious to designers of many institutional sites. All those columns of ten-point type are irritating because even if they contain information sought by the user, they are too small for most users to read. What kind of thinking has produced a web site that offers information but puts it in a format that is so hard to read? The obvious answer is: one that is not attuned to the needs of users. A brief survey of government web sites shows that this is a common failing. Rather than operating as a point of communication with the public, the site operates as a point of reference for the institution – categorising its functions, without any apparent awareness of the need to make these functions accessible to the public.

Challenged about this, one response from designers has been that there is a lot of information about the organisation to convey, and that this can only be done by reducing the font and displaying as much information as possible on the front page. A contrary view is that this approach does not acknowledge the primary function of the site as communication, and the need to present information in an accessible form.

This is why many analysts argue that the verbal text on a web site should be limited and not too conceptually dense. Too many words on a screen are difficult to read and a complex argument on a screen is very difficult to digest. One limitation of the rigid screen monitor is that moving back and forward (as one often needs to do in order to understand a complex argument) tends to be jumpy – and everyone has experienced the frustration of finding the line you wanted somehow lost in the click from page to page. The older technology of the printed book or journal enables the user to move easily from page to page or even to hold several pages open at once. At this point, this difficulty of movement seems to be a feature of the technology – yet it may not always be so. Furthermore, it is worth considering whether the limitation is also primarily a perception of readers trained to read a different (printed) technology. When children interact with a screen – for example, reading information for homework assignments – they do not seem to experience the same kind of frustration with the limits of the screen. Is this perhaps because they do not have a long history of interacting with a different technology?

Even if this limitation is mostly cultural (generational), it must still be acknowledged by the contemporary multimedia author. Contemporary adult users may feel constrained in their reading of written text on-screen. They have a habit of being able to interact physically with a written text – touch it, write on it, underline or highlight it, physically manipulate the text in order to assert their own control of it. They want to refer back to earlier parts of the text physically, not virtually. As a result it is necessary to present written text on-screen differently from the way it is presented in printed form. The material cannot be as dense conceptually, but that does not mean it cannot be conceptually rich. Writing on-screen can be complex so long as users are able to interact with it in such a way that they can incorporate it into their understandings of themselves and the world; that is, so that they can use it to generate knowledge(s) – less on the model of monastic scholarship, more on the model of interactive play.

Digital literacy

The cultures of users are cited as critical knowledge for the author who needs to understand how to deploy the meaning-making resources available to her or him in constructing an on-line or multimedia text. The discussion has not yet considered how this on-screen engagement affects the user.

Stone wrote:

> Ubiquitous technology, which is definitive of the virtual age, is far more subtle [than computers]. It doesn't tell us anything. It rearranges our thinking apparatus so that different thinking just *is*. (1995: 168, italics in original)

Stone's vision of the subtle, transformative effect of technology on individual subjects is evocative and provocative. It is Heidegger's argument in 'The Question Concerning Technology' in more user-friendly language. And it suggests why it is so important to understand the relationship between users and technology – because this too is part of understanding how users process an on-line text.

The brief study of writing with which this chapter started did not deal at length with the changes in the technology of writing. Yet, writing has always been associated with technology; we conceptualise it technologically. Paul Gilster in his study, *Digital Literacy* (1997), notes the significance of changes to the technology of writing: for example, from scrolls of parchment to books in codex form. As Gilster notes, when verbal text was presented in (codex) book form, it first became possible to cross-reference easily, to perform that backward and forward movement that some users feel is lost on-screen,[7] and to develop a system of page numbering and of indexing (Gilster, 1997: 25). The development of the printing press by Johannes Gutenberg in the mid-fifteenth century made books, newspapers and pamphlets more available than ever before, at least to the developing middle-classes. People were exposed to new ideas – about the nature of divinity, the role of church and state, and the relationship between individuals and each of these institutions. Not only did this have a major effect on the development of new secular institutions, but it also presented a great inducement to literacy – for all individuals who wanted to participate in social and cultural change. And this was accelerated in the nineteenth century by the development of the steam-powered press which further decreased the cost of printing. By the time the cheap paperback format was developed in the 1890s, universal literacy was an educational standard (if not practice) throughout western societies.

Understanding how a text came to be is part of understanding how meaning operates in a society; how information is transformed into knowledge; how your own textual production is socially and culturally positioned and how you might intervene in that positioning. Further, as Paul Gilster argues in *Digital Literacy,* it is more than ever now an essential skill. He bases this assessment on how current technology has impacted on information and communication delivery:

> Acquiring digital literacy for Internet use involves mastering a set of core competencies. The most essential of these is the ability to make informed judgments about what you find on-line, for unlike conventional media, much of the Net is unfiltered by editors and open to the contributions of all. This art of critical thinking governs how you use what you find on-line, for with the tools of electronic publishing dispersed globally, the Net is a study in the myriad uses of rhetoric. Forming a balanced assessment by distinguishing between content and its presentation is the key. (Gilster 1997: 2–3)

Gilster notes that users must learn techniques for assessing the authority and/or reliability of what they access on-line, and concludes: 'Developing the habit of critical thinking and using network tools to reinforce it is the most significant of the network's core competencies' (1997: 33).

To argue for a change from critique to design, as does Gunther Kress (1997), seems to undervalue both critique (as a contextualised practice that impacts on both everyday life and text production) and design (as a specialist practice that interrelates textual practice and meaning). On the other hand, critics and designers are now, perhaps more than ever, positioned to learn from each other – to interrelate their skills and abilities in order to (co-)produce text. It is significant, therefore, that contemporary design educators are writing of the need for designers to develop ways of working collaboratively, which means being able to articulate their abilities and to explain how their design works as a communicative practice:

> New principles of interaction, information architecture, and collaboration must be folded in, while traditional principles of perception, conceptual thinking, and design processes are adapted to tomorrow's tools. (Fried, 2001: 11)

> Students must be taught to see themselves as contributors to the design process, as essential members of a team effort, and not just as 'visualizers' of the concepts generated by others. (Niederhelman, 2001: 16)

So just at the time that literacy educators such as Kress are arguing that critique must give way to design, design educators are arguing that design must move beyond its 'visualizing' practice to a more conceptual (and, therefore, critical) role.

Digital literacy involves a critical understanding of the social, cultural and political function of writing as a practice, and as a technology of everyday life. Like all technologies, writing powerfully influences how we think. Writing on-line has its own practices and protocols, which again contribute to the production of contemporary knowledges and understandings of our world and ourselves.

Being on-screen: subjectivity on-line

Paul Gilster writes that digital literacy is 'partly about awareness of other people and our expanded ability to contact them to discuss issues and get help' (1997: 31). This statement locates interpersonal communication as one of the key features of this new medium. He goes on to note: 'But it is also an awareness of the way the Internet blends older forms of communication to create a different kind of content' (Gilster, 1997: 31). It is significant that Gilster brings these two different aspects of on-line experience together – the experience of new possibilities of interpersonal communication and of new forms of textuality based, as we have noted elsewhere, in the reconfiguration of older forms. Both kinds of experience are related in that they impact on the individual's understanding of themselves and their world – their renegotiation of subjectivity and formations of identity.

One basic assumption of this work, and of all recent work on textuality, is that reading participates in the individual's negotiation of subjectivity. Users encounter a range of values and attitudes in the process of reading, viewing and listening that they negotiate by reference to their own cultural history and values. The result may be a reinforcement of the individual's fundamental beliefs and values – and corresponding feelings and actions – or some modification of them. In either case the individual's subject positioning is renegotiated in this transaction: values confirmed or challenged; attitudes reinforced or undermined; corresponding emotional responses reinforced or constrained; potential actions confirmed or opened to question.

Referring back to the *Documenting a Democracy* web site, let us consider the ways that different readings might contribute to the negotiation of subjectivity. For example, a user who has not grappled with the concrete realities of Australian history might read the site relatively naively as a simple cataloguing and description of powerful documents. For this user the site confirms a belief in the value of democracy and a patriotic engagement with Australia as a western democracy. So the site reinforces the user's basic sense of self – their understanding of themselves and their own history, their relationships with others and with society as a whole. However, another user, who is more historically-aware, might read the site as problematising the nature of democracy and the notion of nationhood. For this user reading the site may mean the generation of understandings about democracy, nationhood, justice and equality that modify earlier ideas. This reader may be confronted with a new understanding that their own position within the society is based on conflicts that resulted in the dispossession of others, and on-going injustices and inequalities afflicting those dispossessed peoples. This reader reaches a new understanding of self, of others and of social relations as a result of their experience of the site. Both users have renegotiated their subjectivity as result of the interaction with the site; however, in the first case, the renegotiation results in no substantial change while in the second case the user's subjectivity is altered – a new sense of self is formed.

As noted above, this process is not unique to on-line reading but is a feature of all reading practices. For the on-line reader the concern is to be aware of how the elements that are specific to the medium influence the readings of written text. Gilster describes this as a historical awareness of the different modalities and of their new possibilities. With writing it means a heightened awareness of its elided visual elements that, in some on-line genres such as web sites, contribute substantially to the meanings. It also means being aware of how other textual strategies such as use of image and sound synergise with the written text to generate meanings. In other words, the literacy demands described above are important in the exploration of subjectivity because they enable the user to understand how they are being positioned by the text to accept particular values, attitudes and ideas. So the renegotiation of subjectivity is more self-aware; the individual is able to intervene consciously in the process.

Writing (for) your life

As noted earlier, e-mail is the most common and effective mode of on-line communication – and it is a writing genre. One of the most common ways of discussing how writing to others on-line affects individuals is through the notion of identity. Without physical representation a fifty-year-old man may represent himself as a teenage girl; a young woman as an eighty-year-old man. For some this raises the possibility of freedom from oppressive stereotypes they may encounter in everyday life. For others it may be a way of exploring aspects of identity that are normally closed to them – by adopting an on-line gender different from their own, for example, and noting how others react to them on this basis (though, of course, those others may also not be themselves, so to speak!).

There have been some celebrated cases of individuals adopting identities very different from their own and then having to deal with the fall-out when that difference is revealed. This possibility of formulating an on-line identity opens up for the individual the whole issue of identity. It raises issues about how much of identity is inherent in the individual and how much is generated by others' reactions to that individual. Michele Everard has discussed how exchanges between school children on a local area network (LAN) seemed to have been facilitated by the lack of bodily engagement. Not having to negotiate the bodily presence of interlocutors freed the exchanges from the usual gendered problems: 'Some of the stereotypical behavior did exist in my project, but many of the children went far beyond what might be considered gender boundaries on the net' (Everard, 1996: 201). She adds that, 'the gender participation levels were clearly different from those on Usenet', which she began by noting is dominated by male voices (Everard, 1996: 201). Everard's reading of this situation is that internet communication has been male-dominated because more men than women were using the technology early in its development. Everard suggests that involving both boys and girls in the development of the LAN has helped diminish stereotyped gendered responses. However, she is not so sure that the same situation would pertain with adolescents, who are more critically involved in the formulation of identity (gendered and otherwise). Conversely, it might be that on-line communication challenges stereotypes because it reveals the ways in which those stereotypes are used. For example, in formulating on-line identities, how often do users employ just those kinds of stereotypes? Game-players and chat-room frequenters report how prevalent conservative stereotypes are – that is, individuals may choose to be a different identity, but that identity is itself often a stereotype (a muscle-bound hero, a buxom blonde, Lara Croft, a wizard, a dragon, and so on). This raises the issue of how much identity is invested with the notion of stereotype – and explains why the notion of identity itself has been rejected by many poststructuralist writers, queer theorists, and others.

The immediacy of e-mail – and of blogs, list servs and chat-rooms – means that individuals can be involved on an everyday basis in debating issues of concern and interest to them. So individuals arguably can be more involved in public debates about matters of professional or personal concern. They can obtain access to information easily and quickly and this can enable them to form a more fully contextualised view of their own position in the world, which may impact in all sorts of ways on their sense of selfhood and of identity.

A striking recent example of verbal sharing on-line is the work of the Iraqi blogger, known as Salam Pax.[8] By sharing his thoughts and experiences, fears and desires, whilst his country was invaded by foreign troops, Salam Pax opened up the possibility for understanding between very different peoples. In a sense, Pax's missives opened up a range of issues about subjectivity and identity that had to be negotiated by Western war propaganda. His writings revealed him to be 'not an alien' but a fairly ordinary, though in the context also courageous, person; someone to whom Western users/readers could relate. For Western users, negotiating their own subjective positioning with reference to that war, Pax's writings may have had a range of possible effects – from encouraging them to question Western strategy to sympathy with the people oppressed by their own social institutions and leaders.

Most on-line written communication is not of that nature, however. A lot of it is administrative material associated with people's jobs and there is now much more of this than ever before – because of the immediacy of e-mail. Some is from friends and it is a great joy to find that e-mail enables daily contact with friends in very distant places. This enables discussions and sharing of views on matters that are personal and political, professional and domestic. It also enables people to form new relationships and even to fall in love on-line. So e-mail is an activity in which the individual enacts a range of identities – professional and personal.

E-mail is the subject of much research by linguists and others because of its status, not quite writing, not quite spoken text. And it is the characteristic speed or immediacy of the communication that generates this ambiguous status. Because this written communication can be almost instantaneous, users write often; they join in debates; they dialogue on-line. As a result users developed a range of contractions (for example, OTOH – on the other hand) and shortened spellings (for example, you becomes 'u') to enable them to communicate more economically. Users also had to deal with the fact that written text can be read in a variety of ways by other users – which can be a major problem in on-line dialogue and debate. When there is a physical body present, bodily gestures are used to indicate intended meanings. In addition, if the text is a conventional written text, it is usually longer so that statements that might be ambiguous are clarified by the surrounding text. Here, one early solution that is still used at times is emoticons – syntactical characters used to create icons for emotion, for example, a smile as :) (which some computer interfaces routinely transform into the smiley icon). These textual characteristics developed for e-mail and other on-line genres are now exploding exponentially in popularity because of the introduction of text-messaging on mobile/cell phones – which have much smaller screens and require even greater economy of expression.

Each of the on-line written genres and sub-genres has subject positions that individuals must negotiate. The context of the communication determines the subject position and identity adopted by the user, which in turn governs the degree of formality used in the verbal text. So an on-line discussion of a fashionable area of study may include postings written in street-cred language, whilst a debate with the Dean/CEO/Chief Scientist about funding would be conducted in formal language. In each case the user employs language to construct an appropriate identity – fashionable scholar or fiscally prudent academic/manager/scientist. Both situations involve a high awareness of the medium in order to manipulate the text successfully – in order to produce the required identity. In other words, a high degree of literacy enables the user to generate the identity on-line that best suits his or her purpose at a particular time and place.

In conclusion ...

This chapter on multimedia writing has singled out a number of aspects of written text for discussion, such as the cultural history and power of writing, the visuality of writing, the new literacy demands of multimedia writing, and the negotiation of subjectivity and of identity in on-line writing. I have not described at length the principles of textual criticism since this is available elsewhere – in a whole range of textual and cultural criticism. This study uses concepts and ideas drawn from: the work on textual practice of Mikhail Bakhtin (1968, 1981, 1984, 1986); work on readership derived from the writings of Teresa de Lauretis (1986, 1987) and of Michel de Certau (1984) (exemplified in the work of John Fiske (1989); the work of Henry Jenkins (1991a, 1991b, 1992) and Constance Penley (1991, 1992)); Foucault's description of discourse (1977, 1980, 1981); and work on subjectivity derived from the works of Foucault and Heidegger (1977). The next chapter makes an argument for the analysis of the visual in the same terms, arguing the importance of this non-specialist (in the sense that it is not discipline-specific) terminology as a way of discussing texts that draw on the resources of more than one meaning-system (and disciplinary formation).

Notes

1   In the film *Star Trek II: The Wrath of Khan* (1982).
2   This study of multimedia is based on precisely this kind of understanding of the development of ITC – as a material technology (what we commonly understand as the technology of ITC), as a literary technology (both in its practice and in the volumes, including this one, that are devoted to understanding and locating its practice), and as a social technology (via its effect on individuals and on their lived social relations).
3   Haraway's particular interest in her article is the neutral status of the observer – who (i.e. which social subjects) were considered capable of this 'neutral' role, and the effect of this judgment not only on science but also on gender, class and race.
4   This title itself is an argument for the development of visual communication!
5   In a sense this is the artistic version of the neutral observer – the authoritative male artist or critic. His suitability for that role is signified by the lack of any gendered marker in descriptions of himself or his work – so that a male artist is never identified as male, nor are his works grouped together as 'male artists'. Similarly, the writings of male critics are not identified – except recently by gender-aware, often feminist critics – as generated from a masculine point of view. By contrast, women who practise in the arts are often referred to as 'female artists' and their works are grouped together in exhibitions for no other reason than their shared gender. And female critics are often themselves criticised for a perceived female 'bias'. In other words, to be female is not to be neutral or authoritative, not the 'modest witness'.
6   See the report of visitor studies in Gillard and Cranny-Francis (2002).
7   Note that the cross-referencing referred to here is that performed by the reader/user, not that of the author which is perhaps more easily available on-line as links.
8   See: dear_raed.blogspot.com and salampax.fotopages.com

THREE

VISUALS

In an episode of *StarTrek: Deep Space Nine* called 'Trials and Tribble-ations' (1996) the trill science officer, Jadzia Dax (played by statuesque, comedy actress, Terry Farrell) appears in the female uniform of a twenty-third century Federation officer (from the original *Star Trek* series) – the briefest of mini-skirts, skin-tight top and knee-high boots, accessorised with beehive hair-do. Like Captain Sisko, Doctor Bashir and Engineer O'Brien she is dressed for a time-leap mission back to the twenty-third century to save the original *Enterprise* captain, James Kirk, from a retrospectively arranged death. The three male officers are discussing the changes to their uniform colours, with Sisko noting that, 'In the old days operations officers wore red, command officers wore gold ...' when Dax appears, poses for effect, and quips: '... and women wore less.'

For the viewing audience this is a delightful moment. For the casual viewer it recalls the 1960s' television series, *Star Trek* that was the progenitor of *Deep Space Nine*. It also recalls a different time, signified by the clothing, when Western society was undergoing great change – away from the intense conservatism of the post-war 1950s. And for those audience members with an eye for irony, it also demonstrates the obtuseness of a time when women were seeking equality and when love was supposed to be 'free' and yet pro-fessional army officers conducted their duties dressed for rock'n'roll.[1]

The visuals in this scene conveyed multiple meanings to the viewing audience. It was simply funny for a relatively uncritical viewer with little knowledge of the *Star Trek* history. It had more meanings for the *Star Trek* viewer, who appre-ciated the flashback to an earlier programme history, and even more for the fans who had participated over the years in debates about this very issue. And it had more meanings still for the viewer who combined all those experiences with a critical eye to the development of Western gender relations.

So the visuals carried meanings that could only have been laboriously explained verbally. They were not simply decorative but contained layers of meanings about gendering – about how television operates as a 'technology of gender' in Teresa de Lauretis's terms (1987); about the ways that embod-iment articulates gendering; about the constitution of gender as a discourse, and how it operated at a specific historical moment.

This chapter deals with the ways that visuals operate to produce meaning – or potential meanings – in multimedia, multi-modal texts. Like verbal text, visual text engages viewers in ways that have been developed by a long viewing history. Visual art has always articulated contemporary attitudes and beliefs, fears and desires. And it has been a powerful medium for debate about these issues because it engages the senses, not just the brain. Verbal argumentation is powerful but can also be disengaged, relegated to the realm of the intellect. The visual arts engage viewers as embodied subjects, encouraging them to relate the meanings of the visual to their everyday lives. For example, Dante Rossetti's orgasmic studies such as *Beata Beatrix* (1864), and Ford Madox Brown's confrontational image of an abandoned mistress in *Take Your Son, Sir!* (1857) and his study of working-class labour and middle-class idleness in *Work* (1862–5) trace the lineaments of Victorian hypocrisy about gender, sexuality and class.

The first part of this chapter addresses this cultural (meaning-making) practice of visual texts, arguing for recognition of the visual as a meaning system that is just as discursively engaged – and so susceptible to critique – as writing. The work of several contemporary artists is considered for its engagement with critical social and cultural issues and ideas, while retaining its own artistic, visual integrity. This is followed by a study of the terminology used to discuss these visual texts and relate them to their contextual and intrinsic meanings. In particular, this discussion uses an analysis of the visual genre of the web site to explore contemporary visuality: the deployment of familiar visual conventions to generate new visual forms. In particular, the Smithsonian Museum web site, *HistoryWired* is analysed for its complex use of visuality – to fulfil the role of a specific institution, to operate as exemplar of a particular discipline (social history), and to generate a particular identity for the institution and for users.

Visual artists, visual texts

Amrit and Rabindra Kaur Singh

The paintings of Amrit and Rabindra Kaur Singh (see, for example, Figure 3.1) visually construct a complex, conceptually-rich critique of contemporary British society, from the perspective of the non-Anglo citizen. Their works have the clarity and jewel-like beauty of the Indian miniatures that provided their inspiration. And they are unquestionably modern in their use of contemporary iconography – from McDonald's to the late Princess Diana and the Beckham family. The life of contemporary Indian-British subjects is presented with humour, delight and compassion. The tensions between Anglo-British expectations and material realities on the one hand, and the religious and ethnic values, ideals and expectations of the Indian-British family on the other, map the everyday lives of these transcultural subjects.

The critique fashioned by the Singh twins does not need verbal explanation; it works visually. The paintings use iconic images of both Indian and Anglo-British culture that are accessible to most viewers. And it is the juxtaposition

FIGURE 3.1 Amrit and Rabindra Kaur Singh, *Les Girls*

of those images – traditional Indian dress with a child dressed as Batman – that generates the ideas and feelings in the paintings: the richness and tension of the lives of individuals whose family lives are constituted at least partly in terms of values, beliefs, and experiences that are very different from the mainstream culture where they live. And yet they do live in that culture and their presence is part of the remaking of that culture. Indian-British subjects contribute substantially to the culture and economy of contemporary Britain. So Britain can no longer be the monoculture it once attempted to be (when non-Anglo-British cultures were suppressed). And that raises many issues for Anglo-British culture as well as for all other constitutive British cultures (Welsh, Scottish, Irish).

The Singhs' paintings not only raise those issues, but also bring them into the viewers' everyday lives. They do this by reference to shared cultural icons such as Marilyn Monroe, McDonald's, soccer, Batman, Madonna. As that list indicates, these iconic images may not even be specifically British – which reinforces the Singhs' point, that cultural icons may be meaningful in a variety of different contexts. Many are originally US American icons that have accrued meanings within a British cultural context – the sexualised femininity of Monroe and Madonna, crusader masculinity of Batman, mass consumption of McDonald's, the cult of celebrity that creates the Beckham family as a new kind of 'royal family' in Britain. The use of US-derived icons confronts Anglo-British subjects with their own transcultural nature, now strongly influenced by the globalisation of US values, while the Beckham portrait challenges British notions of class and identity.

Interestingly, the twins' web site (www.twinstudio.supanet.com) displays their own verbal defence of the Beckham portrait against claims from some in the Sikh community that it offends traditional religious values by portraying the family as Hindu divinities. Their defence includes a detailed explanation of the painting, its sources and the generic and political history of other similar images:

> IT IS NOT SAYING THAT THE BECKHAMS ARE SPIRITUAL GODS. The painting was merely inspired by a traditional image of Shiva and Parvati – in terms of the general composition and artistic symbolic language used. In this respect we are following a long tradition in India of using an old and religious symbolic art language to deal with contemporary issues within a secular context. For example many of the posters produced by Hindu artists during the Freedom struggle were used as propaganda in the fight against injustice against British rule.
>
> (Singh, A. and R. www.twinstudio.supanet.com. Accessed 10/01/2004)

In answer to a particular question the Singhs state:

> No, we would not like it if Beckham were depicted as one of the Sikh Gurus or a Jewish prophet but, as we have explained above, we have not depicted the Beckhams as Hindu Gods, only as themselves – as secular icons in a secular world obsessed with the cult of celebrity.
>
> (Singh, A. and R. www.twinstudio.supanet.com. Accessed 10/01/2004)

The Singh twins' self-defence includes some of the principles that can be used to understand visuality. Visual texts are generated out of a long history of visuality, which includes earlier genres of visual text; in the Singh case, this included Indian miniatures. Contemporary visual texts re-situate their generic references by using them with new subjects or combining them with new genres. In the Singhs' paintings we see the miniature style used to depict the everyday realities of life in late twentieth-century Britain – soccer, backyard barbecues, Princess Diana, McDonald's, comic strips, film star icons. These older visual genres have meanings for the contemporary audience that they bring to their readings of the contemporary text. These meanings may not be the same as the meanings generated by the original audience, but are nevertheless significant. So, for example, some members of the Singhs' contemporary audience – part of the Indian-British community – will know the historical meanings associated with the miniature; others, including members of the Anglo-British community, may not understand the historical meanings of the genre but will understand the genre as non-Anglo-British and so as signifying an ethnicity different from that of the mainstream.

The last point refers to the meanings that often accrue to an artwork because of its cultural history, rather than its inherent subject. For example, black and white photographic images and film generate a particular 'feel' and meaning for the viewer, regardless of the subject-matter. Black and white images are often read as more artistic or poetic than colour images; black and white film as more honest or authentic than colour film. These readings are not necessarily related to the original development and use of the earlier media, but since contemporary audiences give them those meanings, then those are the meanings which contemporary artists and designers acknowledge in using them.

The same point might be made about references in a contemporary work to a canonical visual text. For example, reference to the work of a Renaissance master such as Michaelangelo or to a major Impressionist such as Monet may not be an attempt to engage with the issues and ideas that motivated those artists and their works, but rather a way of signifying 'quality' – value with which everyone can be assumed to agree. A contemporary artist may use such a reference directly or satirically to mobilise or challenge this sense of value. However, in either case the meaning generated by the reference is related not to the subject-matter of the work itself, but rather to the cultural and historical positioning of the work and the artist. This is one of the issues with which the Singh twins had to deal in defending their portrait of the Beckhams.

In the work of the Singh twins, then, we see artworks that mobilise a complex intertextuality in order to present a critique of contemporary Western society, as well as to articulate the position of a contemporary transcultural subject. The twins use the reference to an older painting genre, the miniature, to situate their work culturally and aesthetically – as not within the Anglo-British mainstream, as about everyday life. Through the images they use with/in that genre, they articulate the complexity, richness and tensions of life in a contemporary Western multi-ethnic society. And that articulation is both sensory and conceptual; of the mindbody in Hayles's terms (Hayles, 2002), not the fetishised, distanced mind.

H.R. Giger

H.R. Giger's work is very different from that of the Singhs. Giger is also a contemporary artist but his work engages very differently with the fears and desires of late twentieth- and early twenty-first-century Western society. Giger's work can also be seen on-line at www.HRGiger.com, www.HRGigerMuseum. com, www.HRGigerAgent.com, www.Giger.com and www. LittleGiger.com.

His work is perhaps best known to mass audiences from the *Alien* movies, for which he designed the aliens.

Giger's work is drawn from very different sources such as surrealism, European grotesque (including the work of Goya), and Gothic art. Giger is most widely known as a surrealist and fantasist, with an exhibition now permanently housed at the H.R. Giger Museum, in Gruyères, Switzerland. Giger's work also deals with the traditional preoccupations of Gothic – fear, desire, sex, death, torture, bodily mutilation, the extremity of the physical. And it uses conventional Gothic images and strategies – darkness, bodily fragmentation, bodies in extreme states (of pain or pleasure). However, it moves beyond most Gothic representations in its intimate focus on the body. The response of most viewers to Giger's work is shock; it produces a bodily response that mirrors its preoccupations.

When Ripley and her co-workers first encounter the alien spaceship designed by Giger for the film *Alien* (1978), viewers immediately know they are in for trouble. With its vaginal openings and sticky secretions the spaceship is a compendium of populist Freudian images of masculine fear and desire. The use of Freudian imagery aligns Giger's work with surrealism, but other elements of his work are more directly Gothic – the darkness of his images, their claustrophobia, the recurring labyrinthine structures that inhere in and enclose bodies, the eroticism of his images. Here, Giger gives a contemporary spin to Gothic's fundamental preoccupations with the nature of boundaries, of how we define 'the real', the systems of classification and categorisation that we use to establish 'this reality' and so our 'normality'. Gothic has traditionally mounted this challenge through nightmare scenarios and images that confront comforting 'normalising' assumptions – about gender, sexuality, class, ethnicity, ability, and so on. So, just as the nineteenth-century vampire challenged assumptions about sexuality (particularly 'proper' femininity) and class (through its barely concealed deconstruction of class hostilities between the bourgeoisie and the aristocracy), Giger's alien famously challenges contemporary fears of feminine sexual power – and, ultimately, social and cultural constructions of the feminine. From its penile 'face-hugger' stage through to full-grown state the alien is a monstrous projection of Western fears about sexuality – as penetrating and/or devouring. But it articulates most dramatically the fear of the feminine, as it deconstructs 'normal' masculine (hetero)sexuality.

Anthropologist, Mary Douglas wrote: 'the body is not a "being," but a variable boundary, a surface whose permeability is politically regulated, a signifying practice within a cultural field of gender hierarchy and compulsory heterosexuality ...' (Butler, 1990: 139). Accordingly, heteronormative discourse constructs a gender hierarchy in which the surface that is penetrated and permeable – the feminine – is weaker than that of the penetrating and supposedly impermeable – the masculine. This explains the devaluing of not only the feminine but also the penetrated, homosexual (or non-heterosexual) male. Giger's aliens routinely penetrate both male and female bodies; the first human to be penetrated is male, when Kane is penetrated by the face-hugger in *Alien*, an horrific fellatio. In other words, the aliens break through this discourse, indiscriminately penetrating masculine and feminine subjects – and in the process demonstrating that both feminine and masculine bodies are permeable. Conventional, heteronormative constructions of gender and sexuality are thereby challenged.

Physically the aliens 'look' this permeability. Humanoid in shape, they feature exposed musculature, bone matter, and organs; the skin boundary has disappeared. Their behaviour is transgressive, exposing the categories (permeable, impermeable; penetrated, penetrating) by which heterosexuality and (hetero)normative gendering is constituted. And so the aliens are exposed; heterosexual discourse – its fears and desires – laid bare: blood, guts, slime, ejaculate, muscle, bone, sinew, penis, vagina.

This is one element only of Giger's work, but it serves to make an important point in relation to the visual: visual texts articulate contemporary social and cultural debates, whether they formally construct a debate or not.

Template Gothic

Template Gothic (see Figure 3.2) is a relatively recent font that has attracted a lot of attention. It can be viewed at www.emigre.com/EF.php?fid=125 or at designer, Barry Deck's own web site, www.barrydeck.com. Deck describes its origins:

> There was a sign in the laundromat where I do my laundry. … The sign was done with lettering templates and it was exquisite. It had obviously been done by someone who was totally naive. A few months ago, it was replaced with a plastic sign painted by a skilled sign painter. I asked them if I could have the old sign, and they gladly handed it over to me. Now it's on the wall in my bedroom.

> (Accessed 10/01/2004)

The emigre web site concludes:

> Deck was thus inspired to design a face that looked as if it had suffered the distortive ravages of photo-mechanical reproduction. The resulting Template Gothic typeface reflects Deck's interest in type that is not perfect; type that reflects more truly the imperfect language of an imperfect world, inhabited by imperfect beings.

The association of the Gothic with an interrogation of the real continues in Deck's font design. The font, like Giger's aliens, challenges idealised images of the real by being self-consciously imperfect, stripped bare of the civilising effect of clothing – whether that clothing be skin or the perfection possible with digital reproduction.

In his essay 'A Brief History of Type'[2] Thomas Phinney quotes designer Carlos Segura: 'Typography is beyond letters. Some fonts are so decorative,

Template Gothic Regular

Template Gothic Bold

FIGURE 3.2   Template Gothic, viewed at at www.emigre.com/EF.php?fid=125

they almost become "visuals" and when put in text form, they tell a story beyond the words – a canvas is created by the personality of the collection of words on the page.' Another Deck font, Washout, makes this point (see www.barrydeck.com). Washout operates as a ghostly trace of itself, the memory of a font left behind on a blotter. Letters are barely there or are smudged where excess ink has gathered in loops and folds in the letterform. Again, Deck's font suggests the imperfections of human agency, of handwriting with a fountain pen. Visually the font predisposes the reader to find in the content the echoes of a more genteel time, the vagaries of romantic love, or the mystery of a Lord Peter Wimsey clue. However, it is not only strikingly decorative fonts that carry meaning; all fonts are significant. For example, use of 12 point Times font in an academic article might signify only that the author is aware of current conventions for academic text production – but that is significant. To test this, consider how an academic editor might read an article presented in Sand font. The editor would read the font as significant simply because it is unconventional. If no reason for the use of the font is found, the editor is likely to find the article problematic – since subsequent readers will not focus on the argument but on looking for the reasons that this font has been used. In other words, the font distracts the reader from the argument and so renders the article unfocused and unprofessional. Of course, the author might have a good reason for using the font but unless that emerges in the terms of the argument, the response will be negative.

Rick Poynor begins his article, 'American Gothic', by noting:

> The process by which particular typefaces come to embody the look, mood, and aspirations of a period is mysterious and fascinating. It cannot be predicted with any accuracy and no single designer can will it to happen, but somehow a typeface will look fresh, unexpected, precisely attuned to the moment – and a consensus emerges. (2001: 51)

In other words, meanings accrue to the font that the author may (and sometimes, may not) want to include as part of the meanings of the work. When we look at newspapers from the nineteenth century, for example, they are situated historically and culturally not just by their pictures (or lack thereof) nor just by the kind of language they employ, but by the look of the verbal text – the typefaces used. Those typefaces embody the nineteenth century just as the work of Barry Deck, Hat Nguyen and others embodies the late twentieth-century.[3]

In other words, visuality is not only the use of images; it is a function of all aspects of the 'look' of a text. Barry Deck's grunge font, 'Template Gothic', deconstructs the technical 'perfection' of digital media and so embodies the late twentieth-century ambivalence about the role of technology. This is also articulated in films such as *Terminator 2: Judgment Day* (1992) and *The Lord of the Rings: The Two Towers* (2002),[4] in the steady growth of Green movements and politics around the world, and in the preoccupation with viral contamination (digital and organic) that suffuses late twentieth-century and early twenty-first century life, work and cultural production. Not every viewer/reader might locate these specific meanings in the font. However, its use predisposes readers/viewers towards these meanings simply because it eschews the technical precision associated with – and visually representative of – mid- to late twentieth-century technology.

Thus, locating the meanings in a visual text involves more than reading images; it also means an awareness of visual conventions – and of the meanings associated with those conventions. This might be the complexity and sensual richness of an Indian miniature, the darkness and dankness of Gothic, or the play with line in typography.

Newspaper front page

The final example of visual text in this opening section is the front page of a newspaper (see Figure 3.3), a complex text that includes both images and writing.

If the paper is read above the fold-line (it is a broadsheet), then we find a debate about identity constituted visually that is only obliquely referred to in the written word. This discourse is constructed by a juxtaposition of texts:

- Title:
  - The Sydney Morning Herald
- Banner previews:
  - ALL HAT, NO CATTLE HOLMES A COURT DROPS OUT IN STYLE
  - CHILDREN WITH NO ROOM TO MOVE
  - OUR EDITED IDENTITY
  - LIVING TREASURES IN SEARCH OF NEW GREATS
- Headlines:
  - Push to train US troops in Australia
  - Caption: A century late, and five minutes early, it's the never-never express

FIGURE 3.3   *The Sydney Morning Herald*

The space also features a number of images:

- Banner:
  - A man in a hat (presumably Robert Holmes a Court)
  - A child wrapped in bubble-wrap
  - A face painted with tribal markings
  - A cheery female face

- A very large image, occupying three-quarters of the bottom half of the (half-)page of the train referred to in the caption (above).

The most striking feature of this folded page is the image of the train travelling through the desert. The desert is yellow/orange, dotted with scrub and the train is deep red, highlighted in black and white, and the carriages are decorated with Aboriginal images. The red, yellow and black of the image recall the colours of the Australian Aboriginal flag. The indigenous images on the train refer to the same (Aboriginal) identity – and all the debates in which it is implicated. While the debates themselves are recalled by the use of the term, 'never-never' – a description of the Australian outback used in nineteenth-century colonial Australia.[5] In other words, the picture of the train and its caption signify both contemporary Aboriginal identity and the colonialist society which attempted to eradicate that identity. That combination of meanings also recalls the active debates in contemporary Australian society about the nature of Australian identity, which is also recalled by the reference above to 'Our Edited Identity'. This header suggests that there are forces attempting to manipulate Australian identity, as well as referring to the prominent

Australian family, the Holmes a Courts, and to 'Living Treasures' – those Australians who are touchstones of Australianness. Situated next to this complex of references to identity is the headline about US troops training in Australia – which immediately evokes the concerns of many Australians about the nature of Australia's official relationship with the USA, and their fears (signified in the use of the word, 'push') that the USA is attempting (or able) to control Australian politics and policy.

So, in this juxtaposition of visuals and writing, which is the casual reader's introduction to this edition of the newspaper, we find a complex debate about the nature of contemporary Australian identity, which includes the relationship between indigenous and white Australians, the nature of colonial history in Australia, and concerns about the power of the USA to influence Australian domestic politics – and eventually the distinctive Australian identity itself.

In this example the verbal text alone carries a fragmented set of ideas about identity and about politics. However, the visuals – with their intertextual references to other iconic images (the Aboriginal flag) and to individual Australian citizens (the Holmes a Courts, the 'living treasures') – combine with the verbal references to construct the debate about identity. The 'meaning' of this (half-)page is constituted just as much by the visual, as the verbal, text – and the visual is not simply an illustration of the verbal; it combines with the verbal to constitute a debate that is not articulated verbally.

Visceral reading

Visual text is not decoration. It may comprise discrete images; it may be in the shape of a type-font or the layout of a page; it may be in the form of maps, graphs and tables. Or, it may be a combination of these. Some of these modes of visual text are more directly linked to affect than are others. Particular visual images or the shape of a font may generate a visceral response in the viewer – of sympathy or loathing, calm or disquiet, fear or desire. Others may position viewers to experience certain discourses, certain feelings and attitudes and values. Others may seem more dispassionate, presenting data for interpretation, and yet may strategically position viewers to perform that interpretation in line with particular discourses or ideologies.

Visceral reading seems an appropriate metaphor for this practice because it conveys the relationship between the text and the embodied practice of reading. Users do not simply view a multimedia text and file it in some form of neural filing cabinet. That kind of dispassionate removal from everyday life is not a feature of most people's lives, nor of their knowledge-making practice. Knowledge is constructed when abstract ideas or concepts are placed within an understanding of the practice of everyday life. If any form of human activity is isolated from the context in which it is practised, then the significance of that practice cannot be understood; it cannot be part of an individual's or a society's generation of knowledge. In the same way, a visual text is also not removed from the everyday; its significance is understood when it is positioned within the everyday; and it thereby becomes a part of knowledge production, individually and socially.

Accordingly, it is important to generate some principles by which to understand those visuals, much as we did for verbal text. This is a complex task since it calls on a visual literacy that is widespread but relatively uncodified. In contrast, verbal literacy has been a focus of Western education for some 150 years. Grammars have been written that codify the ways we read and speak. And, of course, grammars simply convey the current topography of a language; individuals manipulate and change the grammar so that this is a topography constantly in flux. In essence, an official grammar might spell out the official (institutional) view of how people should write, read and speak at a particular time and place, but it is people who communicate, not grammars. People constantly change and challenge the grammar so that it articulates what they want to say or write about their lives. So there is still fierce debate about how languages should be conceptualised and taught, and grammars are constantly reconceptualised and rewritten to capture the particular nuances of language use.

Visual literacy is far less developed as a field of study and education. We do not have the equivalent to verbal grammars to teach us how to 'read' a visual text. Even if what we mostly want to do is argue with the grammars. Up until recently visual literacy has been constituted as a number of separate disciplines: fine arts, design studies, art history, art theory, cinema studies, television studies, semiotics, architecture. Each contributed something to our understanding of how visual texts operate. However, each drew on a different set of technical languages, had different reference points, studied different kinds of texts in different ways.

In studying the multi-modal and multimedia texts that we live with daily, we are attempting to find ways of discussing their different modes, including the visual, which are accessible and easily applicable. And we also want these ways of discussing modalities to be flexible, open to change and challenge, as are grammars.[6] Because the concepts and ideas used for discussing the visual are drawn from so many different fields, there is no one line to be followed or theory propounded, but rather an eclectic mix of concepts and ideas that can be deployed where appropriate.

In the discussions above of specific texts we see some of the principles that might guide the use of visual strategies in texts – by authors, designers and users. We understand the paintings by the Singhs and by H.R. Giger as specific to a particular culture and time; they articulate particular meanings and ideas about their cultures now. Further, we read their work in relation to other texts. For the Singhs, the major referent is Indian miniature painting and its deployment in political art; for Giger we view his work in the context of fantastic art – surrealism, Gothic. But we also view these artworks within a broader intertextual understanding of late twentieth-century visual art and media, as well as of late twentieth-century readings of earlier art. Giger's work must also be seen within the context of other work for the cinema, other contemporary modes of exploring the body (new media art, performance, embodied art such as tattoo, the erotic), and earlier visual modalities to which his work refers (the paintings of Goya, early Gothic, the fantastic, religious art, the erotic). The Singhs' paintings must similarly be placed in the context of other contemporary attempts to deal with issues of transculturation and of difference, including the works of artists such as Renée Stout, Trigo Piula, Jim Logan, Tracey Moffatt and Fiona Foley, and television programmes such as *The Ali G Show* and *The Kumars at Number 42*, as well as the decorative arts and their cultural history, and the history of Orientalism in the arts.

We are not thereby claiming that every viewer sees each of these references or appreciates every nuance that the paintings may suggest. Instead, this is a way of mapping the possibilities opened up by these images for a range of different viewers. It is equally important to acknowledge the choices made by the author in generating the text, however that text is subsequently processed by its reproduction, distribution and marketing. For example, it is critical to understanding the power and meanings (or potential meanings) for the audience of Peter Jackson's films of *The Lord of the Rings* (2001, 2002, 2003) to study, among other things, the visions of other cultures used in that film. How are they delineated (dress, skin colouring, language, manner)? What are their intertextual referents, and what meanings might those referents have for the contemporary viewing audience(s)? What is the visual effect of such an accumulation of rich detail? How does the incorporation of an animated character (a *simulacrum*) affect the representation of intercultural and interpersonal relations? How is the *simulacrum* constructed (generically, intertextually)? Since Peter Jackson went to all this trouble in the production of the films, he must have thought it was essential to the finished text – in order for the audience to have the experience he wanted them to have; in which case it seems essential to an understanding of the literacy (or literacies) mobilised in the films, and hence of the audience responses to them, to explore those choices.

Furthermore, this discussion suggests another principle essential to an understanding of visual texts: do not underestimate the visual skill and knowledge of the author/designer. And I make that statement even while acknowledging that the author/designer may have very different ways of understanding her or his choices. That does not preclude us from pursuing the meanings of those choices in terms that we may find equally appropriate. As noted in the opening chapter, textual strategies can generate a range of meanings for a range of audiences; it is neither possible nor desirable to attempt to lock down the meaning potential of a text.

For example, we may locate meanings in *The Lord of the Rings* films that Peter Jackson may not have predicted, but which, nevertheless, are appropriate to their understanding – both diegetically (how they tell the story) and discursively (the kinds of values, attitudes, beliefs and feelings they articulate and mobilise). For example, some viewers were disturbed by the fact that the second film was subtitled *The Two Towers* because for them the name recalled not Tolkien's work but the twin towers of the World Trade Center in New York, destroyed in a terrorist attack in September 2001. That reference did not make the film any less meaningful for them, quite the reverse; however, the name was not Jackson's choice and obviously its recent associations could not have been predicted by him. So, this is a case in which extra-diegetic or contextual factors have added substantially to the text's potential meanings.

One rule to ring them all ...

To explore those meanings, and the strategies by which they are constituted, we come back to the idea of a primer – a guide to the literacy that is shared by many viewers. Such a guide would also explain why authors and designers make certain choices – consulting the literacy of their projected audience(s). As noted earlier, this is inevitably an eclectic mix of concepts since it must be drawn from many different disciplines that have constituted visual literacy studies up to now. It is also not a straitjacket for the designer – a set of rules that must be followed to produce an approved text. Instead, it can open up for the designer or author the possibilities for text production within current literacies by mapping the ways in which users respond to visual materials. It can also suggest ways in which the current boundaries (of visuality) can be pushed in order to produce new texts and new meanings. Which the user will then incorporate as part of standard literacy – so the designer both caters to and also develops the literacy of the user.

Some of these elements are related to the visual strategies used within the text – to tell its story and make its meanings. These are intrinsic or diegetic visual elements such as colour, line, layout, and specific images. Others are the contextual (extra-diegetic) meanings that arise from its contemporary social and cultural context – as discussed above in relation to *The Two Towers* – or which arise from the text's relationship with other texts. These include the relationship between a particular genre of text and others in the same genre (how a film relates to other films, or a web site to other web sites), or how intrinsic textual elements relate the specific text to other genres and their meanings.

The following section explores some of the concepts we can use to understand the meanings – or potential meanings – of visual text, particularly by situating it in relation to other texts.

Reading the visual

Discourse is a useful term to employ with the visual as it gives us a way of discussing its meaning-making power. Discourse is conventionally related to the verbal, and sometimes is used to mean conversational exchange. However, the essence of the exchange is the communication of meaning – and that, too, is the function of the visual. We can use the meaning of discourse derived from Foucault – a set of statements that articulate a particular way of thinking, feeling and being in the world. Visual text can be very effective in communicating such statements, either through direct representation or via the kinds of intertextual references discussed above. One example would be the use of German Fraktur type (discussed in the previous chapter) in race hate or white supremacist newspapers, journals and web sites. Its value in those contexts is that it evokes the beliefs, values and feelings now associated by those groups with the Nazi party, with which they align themselves. So a simple font choice evokes a discourse – Aryan supremacy.

In the work of H.R. Giger, discussed earlier in this chapter, we might locate other discourses, one of which is Gothic. As noted in that discussion, Gothic is more than a style; it is a set of statements or meanings about the world, all of which are fundamentally interrogative. Gothic questions the meaning of 'normality' by being provocatively engaging – either erotically, sensually, sexually, or intellectually. We might, therefore, locate in Giger's work a Gothic discourse that signifies his work's engagement with what constitutes normality or conventionality. We can also locate in his work the Freudian discourse that is typical of much surrealist art, where it again questions our constructions of normality and conventionality. In this Freudian discourse the boundaries of the normal and the conventional are located by the eruptions of the repressed, whether that be repressed sexuality or the repressed birth trauma that is a particular interest in Giger's work.[7]

So discourse is a term that can be used with the visual, not only the verbal, to discuss the kinds of meanings a text can make available to users/viewers. And, as I suggest in later chapters, the term is equally useful with other modalities such as sound. In other words, discourse is a term that can be used to describe meaning-making across a range of modalities and so is particularly useful in the study of multi-modal texts. It enables us to discuss the meanings generated by a specific modality but also by the interaction of modalities (verbal with visual with sound, and so on). Another cross-platform term is genre.

The term 'genre' was used in the previous chapter to refer to different kinds of written text, such as email, chat-room, listserv, (we)blog. However, it can be used with any set of texts using similar strategies to make meanings. And again note that this is a use of genre that is not rule-driven. It is not a way of prescribing how texts should be composed, but rather of describing how texts are read. In other words, we are not interested in the notion of genre because it tells us how a text *should* be composed and read, but because it enables us to understand the kinds of meanings users *do* generate from them. Knowing the kinds of responses users are likely to have to a particular strategy enables the author or designer to utilise that strategy – or not – in the production of a text.

Web sites, for example, are a relatively new genre and the ways they are composed and read are constantly modifying or evolving. In order to understand this as more than a technical phenomenon (though it is also that) we can begin by noting the basic function of the web site – which is to communicate with users. Using the Bakhtinian understanding of genre means coordinating the (potential) meanings generated by the site for users and the context of their production (broadly, their social and cultural context; more immediately, the producer they represent). Our knowledge of the meaning-making, textual strategies used at the site enables us to generate this analysis.

Overall, though, the concept of the web site as a genre enables us to situate this particular type of text within the vast textual network that constitutes our cultural environment. It is like some other types of text, but also unlike them. For example, it is like newspapers and magazines in that it uses a mix of modalities (verbal and visual), and its multi-modality also recalls film and television (in the combination of visuals and movement). But it is also unlike them in that it uses a small screen, like television, but unlike film, magazines or newspapers. And it is interactive in a way that none of those other media are, offering the user the possibility of self-directed activity.

Because of its specific characteristics the web site can be conceptualised as a distinct genre. It has its own meaning-making practices – verbal, visual, acoustic, kinetic – and combinations of these. It has its own social and cultural function – as an information source, as a form of identity for its producer, as an articulation of contemporary values, beliefs, feelings and ideas. And it has its own way of addressing users – via those meaning-making practices and in relation to the networks of meaning-making and distribution in which it is embedded. Accordingly, it can be assessed, explored and enhanced in those terms, all of which focus around its fundamental purpose – which is to communicate with users. So understanding the generic practice of a web site is central to analysing its usability.

Visually, this means understanding the visual strategies on the site as integrally related to the meanings generated by the text – about information, about identity, and about contemporary values, beliefs, feelings and ideas. This means understanding that every visual choice is significant – meaningful and meaning-filled – even the choices that do not work effectively. For example, a designer may have used a flash animation annoyingly on a site in a way that seems to the user not to enhance the purpose of the site but merely to demonstrate that the designer knows a new technological tool. This is meaningful. It tells us how alluring technology can be, that it can obscure the designer's focus on the primary purpose of the site – which is communication. Or, we may encounter a site that looks very impressive but is impossible to navigate – where a designer has been so involved with making a site look impressive that, again, she or he has overlooked its primary function – to communicate. Further, the designer has ignored another of the primary characteristics of the web site – that users need to feel self-directed; frustrating their ability to navigate can only produce irritation. So, visually, the notion of genre enables us to analyse a particular web site – or other multi-modal, multimedia text – by situating it in relation to other texts in the same genre, which share both its function as communication and the strategies by which this function is realised.

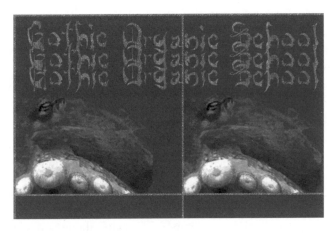

FIGURE 3.4 Gothic Organic Style: Viewed at www.ccs.mq.edu.au/bodmod, 08/04/2005, designer Aree Cohen.

Intertextuality enables us to understand how the web site relates to other visual genres – not simply formally, but also in terms of (potential) meanings. For example, designer Curt Cloninger discusses Gothic Organic web site design (see Figure 3.4) in his book, *Fresh Styles for Web Designers*:

> The Gothic Organic Style is 'organic' in that it uses human forms, plant forms, and other organic shapes and textures as its building blocks. ...

> The Gothic Organic Style is 'gothic' for two reasons. First, like the Gothic architecture that birthed the early cathedrals, gothic organicism is intricate, billowing, overblown, and all-encompassing. ...

> The second reason for the 'gothic' name is slightly less scholastic. The pioneering practitioner of gothic organicism, Aurelia Harvey, owes a debt to the contemporary underground 'gothic' scene – death rock, black clothing, self-mutilating performance art, and the like. (2002: 12–13)

Having explained the style Cloninger goes on to specify its possible uses:

> Because the Gothic Organic Style is ultimately sense-engaging, it is most applicable for branding or product-enhancement sites. Have you been hired to do the promotional site for a new album or film? Are your clients looking to create an experience that leads fans to explore the themes and ideas beneath the product's surface? Then gothic organic design is a logical approach. ...

> Other possible commercial applications for this style include sports sites, trekking/tour sites, cruise ship sites, and any site that seeks to create a 'you are here' immersive environment. ... (2002: 13)

Cloninger situated the style (or genre) of Gothic Organic in relation to other examples of Gothic: from early Gothic cathedrals to the contemporary Goth scene. Using that style meant that some of the meanings of Gothic accrue to the site – particularly, the notion of intense sensory engagement. And it is not difficult to imagine how a designer with an inter-textual understanding of the meanings of Gothic for contemporary users is able to utilise the meanings in design. So a site for singer, Marilyn Manson might stress the associations of Gothic with explorations of embodiment and of how we classify what is 'normal' or socially acceptable. Using the style on an extreme sports site, however, as Cloninger suggests, would mean drawing rather on Gothic's intense sensuous engagement with the world.

Using intertextuality as a reference term for understanding the visuals, therefore, engages us with the cultural history of the visual in western society. That seems an overwhelming task, and it does require an intense engagement with the visual. However, the object of study is contemporary visual culture deployed now and its (potential) meanings for users, which is a slightly less overwhelming task. For example, it means knowing about Gothic because the genre has great resonance now – for artists like H.R. Giger and Marilyn Manson as well as for adolescents testing the boundaries of 'normality' as they explore identity, gender, and sexuality. And arguably, the more subtle an author or designer's understanding of the genre is, the more effective her or his use of it can be – as she or he, intertextually, activates meanings that have been obscured by time, but are nevertheless within current visual understanding.

Reading the web site

To exemplify the use of these concepts we might consider some different kinds of web sites. All of the texts considered below are web sites in that they have the same overall purpose, function and strategic operation: they are communicative practices, that utilise the potential of a particular set of technological practices, and are mobilised by users in a particular way (via a specific set of literacies). However, they are also members of a specific sub-genre of web site – again determined by the function and purpose of the site. Those different functions and purposes mean that they address users differently, employ different textual strategies, work to construct specific identities in accordance with their function. So web sites might be grouped into categories such as shown in Table 3.1 – and this is not meant as an exhaustive list.

This way of categorising web sites identifies them in terms of their func-tions, on which is dependent their deployment of the textual strategies used to construct web sites (for example, uses of verbal, visual, acoustic text, kinesics, spatiality). The value of this form of identification is that it enables us to locate the potentials of a site, rather than prescriptively determining how it should be composed. Furthermore, it enables us to make the kind of dis-cursive analysis of the site that is one aim of this study of multimedia. This is best illustrated with an example.

TABLE 3.1 Types or sub-genres of web site

Some types or sub-genres of web site	Characteristics
Government/Institutional	• serving the public, by giving access to information • creating an identity for that government instrumentality • supporting the instrumentality by buying products
Commercial	• selling a product or service • creating an identity attractive to consumers • identifying the provider with the product/service
Fan	• providing a creative outlet for the fan • publishing views and/or information about the fan subject • creating a community of fans to share their interest • identifying that fan as a supporter of the fan subject
Portal	• providing access to a range of sites offering products and/or services • creating an authoritative identity, so users will return • selling products and/or services
Family	• communicating with family and friends • reinforcing the extended family • generating a particular family identity
Educational	• serving the clients by making educational services available • creating an environment for self-directed learning • selling the service • constructing an authoritative identity

HistoryWired: an example of analysis

The *HistoryWired* web site (see Figure 3.5), developed by the National Museum of American History at the Smithsonian in Washington, D.C. (historywired. si.edu) is a government or institutional web site. As a site located at a national institution *HistoryWired* has a number of purposes dictated by its function as representative of the US state: to communicate effectively with users; to represent to them the nature or identity of the democratic state of which it is an instrument; to articulate to/for them the meaning of citizenship. There are also functions related to its function as a museum: to educate users; to allow them access to the collections it houses; to demonstrate for them the values of the society it represents. So how does *HistoryWired* visually realise these functions?

Generically *HistoryWired* locates itself within the genre of web site by its use of what has become a standard layout (though this may change as visual literacy changes). For example, a banner identifies the site ('HistoryWired – A Few of our Favorite Things') at Left, and provides links ('About the Program', 'Help', 'Comments', 'Smithsonian Institution') at Lower Right. Above the links and within the banner is a field of stars, which become increasingly blurred as we move right. At the bottom of the page is information about the program

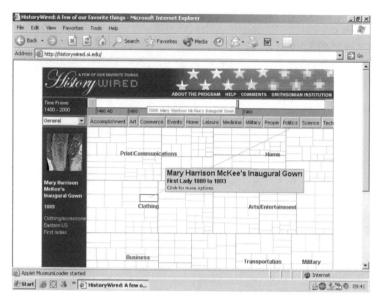

FIGURE 3.5 *HistoryWired* front page, viewed at historywired.si.edi

makers ('Smartmoney.com') and another list of links (horizontal) including those at top and some others: 'Technical Requirements', 'Text Only Version', 'Online Shopping'. Occupying the rest of the page is a mosaic over which the user moves the cursor to reveal items from the museum's collections. This mosaic is also headed by banners – one giving a 'Time Line', the other a series of categories ('Accomplishment', 'Art', 'Commerce', 'Events', 'Home', and so on). A frame to the left of the mosiac surface is activated by cursor movement across the mosaic, when it provides a graphic and some basic information about items verbally identified on the mosaic surface. This layout, with basic identifiers at top and bottom, and links given and reiterated at top and bottom, is a recognisable web site design.

Furthermore, *HistoryWired* locates itself as a specific kind of web site – an institutional site that is a museum site – through the combination of service provided (information about specific items kept at a museum, about the nature of US democracy, about US history), through the address to the user (as learner, as citizen), and through visuals (of museum objects and, as we shall explore, of the process of learning). So we might think of this web site as falling within a taxonomy such as that shown in Table 3.2.

TABLE 3.2   Types of institutional web site

Genre	Sub-genre	Text/Site
Web site	Institutional web site	Museum/gallery Public utility (water, electricity) Library Government department (tax office etc) Public service (police, firefighters, etc)

The address to the user is also a combination of factors and features, relating to its basic identity as a web site, and its more specific role as institutional and museum site. As a web site it provides the user with a multimedia experience; it provides links to other sites that enable the user to expand the experience as desired; and it gives the user an experience of self-directed activity. As an institutional site it constructs for the user a narrative about the society and culture(s) it represents and articulates – and this is necessarily a narrative that is acceptable to current authorities. It also constructs for the user the position of citizen of a democracy. This means that the user is not locked into a particular narrative in order to understand and use the site. In fact, the concept and visual design (particularly the mosaic) visually present both the freedom and limitation of the democratic citizen: the freedom to create a narrative pathway, but its containment within a particular set of authoritative (authorised) narratives. In other words, the citizen of a democracy is free to construct any narrative she or he chooses about the history and culture(s) of the state, but should not expect that each chosen narrative is equally valued or respected. This locates the major debate within most contemporary Western democracies – about which narratives should be valued and respected and which rejected, and on what grounds. The mosaic is not a melting pot, reducing all cultures to a bland version of the mainstream, but it is also not unbounded.

HW is also a museum site and so (in accordance with contemporary museological principles) situates the user as an active learner. This role is created by the guided navigation that is a feature of this site – information presented within a particular framework (realised by the kinds of graphics used, the information verbally presented, and the links provided). Visually this role is constituted by the user's interaction with the mosaic. When the user stops the cursor on a mosaic shape, a verbal description of an object is revealed – and that description is linked by vectors to the time-line banner and to one or more of the categories listed in the second banner.

At the same time, in the frame at left an image of the object is shown along with basic descriptors that situate the object. For example, the object 'John Quincy Adams's Ivory Cane' is linked to the time line at 1844, and to the category banner at People and Politics, and the material in the left-hand frame includes an image of the top part of the cane, an identifying label, and then the descriptors – '1840s', 'Clothing Accessories', 'Eastern US', 'Presidents', 'Slavery'. The visual presentation of the descriptors indicates that they are also hypertext links, and that additional information pertaining to the object can be found at a site identified via that descriptor.

So the cane is interesting because it creates a web of meanings that incorporates a time (the 1840s), a specific mode of dress (Clothing Accessories), a place (Eastern USA), a prominent social role (Presidents), and a social and cultural practice that has shaped the USA as a nation (Slavery). In other words, the page situates the object historically and conceptually. Further, those specific descriptors are situated in relation to two specific parameters – a time-line and a set of conceptual categories (including 'Art', 'Science', 'Home',

FIGURE 3.6   *HistoryWired* header, viewed at historywired.si.edu/index.html

'Leisure', 'Politics') drawn from social history – that effectively demonstrates to the user how the significance of the object is constituted institutionally (by the museum). All of this is visually realised, both as a series of connecting vectors and via an attractive image that effectively creates a series of vectors from the user's eye to the vectors on the page. Visually, then, the page constitutes information and learning in a particular way – as the placement of a particular object in relation to a historical period, social history and disciplinary formations. In other words, the site does not just instruct the user; it visually demonstrates to the user how to learn.

The other role of both institutional and museum sites is to construct an identity for the site's producer – which is both the US government (institutionally) and the Smithsonian (museum). Many of the strategies discussed above – especially the production of a particular narrative or set of narratives about US history and culture – are part of this construction of identity. However, other intrinsic textual strategies are also employed to create an identity for the site. For example, the colours used in the header (see Figure 3.6), along with its simple graphics, carry multiple meanings.

The ground colour of the header is blue – solid at left, horizontally striated at right. On this right-hand side, the blue is studded with two parallel rows of stars, as if this segment were a section of the US flag. The stars are white, and running along the bottom edge of the banner is a line of red – so that the iconographic colours (red, white and blue) all appear on the banner. The combination of colours and iconography immediately locates the site as from the US. The use of blue is also significant in itself. Blue is conventionally associated with the mind, with contemplation, intellectual pursuits, and intellectual authority – compared with the hotter colours such as red and orange that are associated with immediacy, passion, and the body. So the site is constituted in the header as devoted to serious pursuits, to the intellect, with the implication that this is an authoritative site – particularly when backed with the authority of the US government (signified by the iconography).

The header also constructs other meanings: for example, about the relationship between the institution and technology. In the header the word, 'History' is written in an Old English manuscript style. One association is, again, authority. This type of font is used on many official documents where it imitates the handwritten manuscripts of the past. This association is apparently the reason many L.A. street gangs use a similar font for their gang names and logos. However, that font may also suggest that both traditional history, and perhaps the museums that construct that traditional history, belong to an earlier time. The techno-font used for the word 'Wired' constructs a visual transition to a different culture – the culture of the late twentieth- and early twenty-first century, which is transforming the society and its institutions. This transition is echoed at right where the stars of the (implied) US flag are increasingly blurred, pixilated. This visual deconstruction of the image spells out for the user not only the move to the digital in museum culture, but also the ways in which this move has prompted a deconstruction of earlier museum practice – which is not to say that users are necessarily drawn into debates about museology. Users may simply be alerted to something new – and that newness is threaded through the museum's address to the user as well as its conception of the role of the museum in contemporary life.

Visually, the image of the mosaic reinforces the user's appreciation of a new approach to museology at the *HW* site. This site engages users visually with an immediacy and responsiveness not possible in a bricks-and-mortar museum. Further, it offers a visual snapshot of US history and culture that eschews the monocultural 'grand narrative' of the past. The mosaic visually confronts the progressive time-lines that dominated much museum practice in the past. Instead of a one-dimensional explanation of how the USA got to be what it is today, the mosaic constitutes both history and culture as a patchwork of events and objects, each of which contributes to the assemblages that we call history and culture – or histories and cultures. And while, again, we might critically acknowledge boundaries to this mosaic – by what objects are chosen, what stories are told – we can nevertheless acknowledge its power as a socially- and culturally-inclusive formulation of society, culture and history.

Interestingly, the *HW* site omits the Smithsonian logo, which appears on most other Smithsonian sites. This is not necessarily an important point for many users whose focus is on the site content. However, it might cause some conjecture about the relationship between this site and the Smithsonian proper. Does this omission suggest internal political debates at the museum? Did *HW* find it important to its aims and to the view of history it presents not to reinforce its connection with the Smithsonian? Perhaps the omission of the logo was an aesthetic choice – but then are aesthetic choices ever devoid of cultural, social and political meaning? The reason that this question arose was not because there is any reason that this site should visually acknowledge its parent site; after all, it does verbally provide a link back to the Smithsonian. It is simply that, at present, it is a convention with many institutional sites to provide a visual link back to the parent site, where a convenient logo is available. This reinforces the point that reading is generic and conventional; not to follow a convention creates questions.

So the visuals at the *HW* site perform a series of crucial functions in relation to the identity of the site – as an institution representative of government and as a museum representative of a society and its cultures. The visuals constitute the meanings of that institutional identity for users via a particular interpretation of democracy and citizenship, and they constitute the museum as not only a display cabinet, but also a place of learning. They constitute users as contemporary democratic subjects and citizens, living within a complex multicultural society, with particular freedoms and also particular limitations. It also constitutes them as learners, providing a framework for information retrieval that encourages them to situate that information within a society and history familiar to them, and so to transform that information into knowledge about their society and themselves.

The *HW* site operates not only as a social history site, informing US (primarily) citizens about their own history (and how to construct that/a history); it also operates as a government institution, and so acts as a representative of the US state. And it is a museum site, with a mandate to inform and educate visitors/users. The material on the site had to be presented in a way that balanced all those different demands: in other words, the strategies that enabled the site to fulfil these complex social and cultural demands were both extrinsic and intrinsic – to do with the design and presentation of the site and its content.

Reading visual conventions: *HistoryWired*

This section introduces some of the concepts that we might use to understand and analyse the visual presentation of the multi-modal, multimedia text. As noted in the analysis of verbal text we are dealing with a set of (multimedia) texts that is in a state of evolution – so that aspects of the visuality will change with changes in their role and function, as well as in the development of software. Again, it is important to note that this is not a set of rigid rules for the construction of a web site but instead is a mapping of some of the visual strategies currently in use. The analysis of *HW* has already identified many of these strategies.

The use of a *mix of modalities* is a defining characteristic of multimedia. *HW* uses verbal and visual text together – an image of an object is linked to verbal categories and descriptors – to present objects from its collection within a social and historical context; to address/position users as democratic citizens and as active learners; and to represent the museum and the site as a government instrumentality.

Another crucial visual element is *layout* – how the different textual elements are arranged in relation to one another. The central mosaic of the *HW* site enabled specific objects to be presented within a network of relationships that represented a way of understanding history. It also focused audience attention on that feature of the site – access to objects, rather than on questions about the selection of objects and the kind of history that selection then constructs. In other words, layout has both an epistemological and ideological function in *HistoryWired*.

Gunther Kress and Theo van Leeuwen present a way of analysing layout in their book, *Reading Images* (1996), which is based on detailed analysis of a range of Western visual material (for example, painting, photographs, advertisements) in a variety of media (for example, newspapers, magazines, books, films), and through talking to professional designers and artists engaged in these fields. They developed a layout diagram that encapsulated their findings (see Figure 3.7).

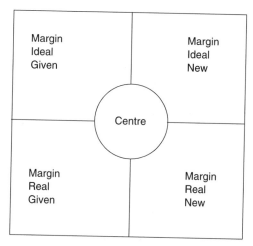

FIGURE 3.7 Based on Gunther Kress and Theo van Leeuwen, *Reading Images* (1996)

In this diagram Kress and van Leeuwen assign meanings to the four quarters of the grid, as well as to the central position. The Centre is identified as a point of focus for the composition, while elements at the Margin are generally less prominent. The other terms used, Ideal and Real as a horizontal division of the space (Ideal at top, Real below) and Given and New as a vertical division (Given at left, New at right), require more explanation:

> For something to be ideal means that it is presented as the idealized or generalized essence of the information, hence also as its, ostensibly, most salient part. The Real is then opposed to this in that it presents more specific information (for example, details), more 'down-to-earth' information (e.g., photographs as documentary evidence, or maps or charts), or more practical information (e.g., practical consequences, directions for action). This is of course no less ideological. (Kress and van Leeuwen, 1996: 193–4)

The terms, 'Given' and 'New' are glossed as follows:

> For something to be Given means that it is something the viewer already knows, as a familiar and agreed-upon point of departure for the message. For something to be New means that it is presented as something which is not yet known, or perhaps not yet agreed upon by the viewer, hence as something to which the viewer must pay special attention. … The structure is ideological in the sense that it may not correspond to what is the case either for the producer or for the consumer of the image or layout: the important point is that the information is presented as *though* it had that status or value for the reader, and that readers have to read it within that structure, even if that valuation may then be rejected by a particular reader. (Kress and van Leeuwen, 1996: 187)

Again, this is not a rigid map to be followed but a provocative set of ideas about layout that a designer or analyst might consider, based as it is on a cultural history of Western design.

Applied to *HW*, Kress and van Leeuwen's diagram locates the centred mosaic as the focus of the site. The banner head and social history descriptors at the top of the page are 'Ideal', giving the essence of the information at the site, while the more prosaic detail about the site construction is situated below in the 'Real' position. In the left-hand or 'Given' position we find basic information, positioned as non-controversial, about the images located through the mosaic. As Kress and van Leeuwen note, however, all of these choices are ideological in that they position users to accept particular versions or views of the information at the site – as discussed above in the analysis of the web site.

Another common visual element is the *use of images*. *HW* presents many different images (objects in the collection) but the central image is the mosaic, which operates as an image for the diverse cultures and histories that constitute the collection and the museum. As suggested earlier, the mosaic can be viewed in many different ways, from idealism to cynicism, so – even if it was originally an artefact of the software – it serves an important function for this particular site.

Another visual strategy is the use of different *fonts* to evoke particular meanings and ideas. This has been discussed in both this and the previous chapter. The move from tradition to innovation, from conventional history to social history, from old to new museology, from bricks-and-mortar to on-line museum, is encapsulated in the move from an Old English script typeface to techno-style typeface in the site name, *History Wired*.

Use of *colour* in a multimedia text is often a key to its function, either extrinsic or intrinsic, or both. The use of colour in John Huston's film of Herman Melville's *Moby Dick* (1956), for example, shows this complexity. White is used to signify death and corruption, as described by Melville. The ship features the white whalebone struts and supports described in the book; Ahab's (white) whalebone false leg is given visual prominence in the film, including an introductory close-up; and we see the white whale itself a number of times. But the filmmakers also used colour in another way – to locate the text historically. The film is coloured in sepia tones, which are associated in photography with nineteenth-century pictures. So colour has both a diegetic, narrative role in the film (as in Melville's book), and a contextual function of locating the film historically. On the *HW* site the red, white and blue of the US flag established the site as a government or institutional site, one function of which is to represent the state. From this identification we can trace the logic behind many of the meanings at the site, such as its focus on citizenship and on notions of democracy. And it also leads the critical user/audience to an examination of the principles that underlie its practice – what it doesn't acknowledge about the nature of its democracy, or the ways it defines citizenship.

Visual *trajectories* can also generate meanings within the multimedia text. On *HW* the construction of vectors models a way of learning for users, so that the trajectories at the site are crucial to its function. The discursive analysis of the site addresses not only the elements connected by the trajectory (how are objects, events, ideas and categories connected in particular ways? what is omitted in this set of connections?), but also the act of connection that produced the trajectory (what kind of history is being taught? how does this position the user?).

As noted above, these are just some of the concepts that can be used to understand, and to analyse, the meanings offered by the visuals at the site. The purpose of this analysis is to demonstrate both some of the strategies available to designers in the construction of a site and the kinds of meanings that are associated with those strategic choices. Further, the analysis demonstrates that the choice of intrinsic textual strategies is also determined to some extent generically, by the kind of site or text with which the designer is engaged.

If the text is a web site, then the designer needs to be aware of the exigencies of the particular kind of web site with which she or he is engaged. If the text is another kind of multi-modal, multimedia text – a magazine, newspaper or film – then the generic demands of that text-type will need to be considered, and strategic choices about visuals made on that basis. For example, layout choices for a magazine are complicated by the fact that the reader views both a single page and a two page spread; therefore, choices about layout on each page need to account for the visuals on each page and on the double-page spread, as both will construct meanings for the reader. And governing all these choices is the social and cultural role and function of the magazine – what kind of magazine it is, what its objectives are, what kind of reader address it employs, and so on. In other words, the relationship between textual strategies, generic choices and social and cultural practice of the text needs to be understood. That alignment of textual practices and meanings is the basis of the analysis of *HistoryWired*, enabling us to understand the practice of the text, the kinds of meanings it makes, and the role it offers to users.

In conclusion ...

This chapter has not attempted an exhaustive listing and analysis of every visual strategy that a designer or author might use with a multi-modal multimedia text. Instead, the purpose has been to demonstrate that visual strategies are not simply chosen for aesthetic effect; or, rather, that their aesthetics is inseparable from their politics. They not only attract viewers, but also construct abstract ideas or concepts, and position users to receive those ideas and concepts in particular ways. In order to analyse these texts, then, we need to develop a vocabulary or set of concepts that we can use to explore that meaning-making practice – as both a set of textual strategies and a corresponding set of cultural and social meanings. This vocabulary can enable us both to explore the texts that users encounter and to inform the design and development of those texts.

The cross-disciplinary terms, genre, intertextuality and discourse were used to both locate the texts analysed and to discuss their (potential) meanings. More or less implicit in these analyses also is the notion of the viewer/user as a social subject, negotiating subjectivity through her or his viewing of these texts. Equally, the role of the visuals in evoking, constructing and deconstructing issues of identity is also a common feature of the discussions of visuality.

The other concepts used specifically with the visuals – layout, colour, image, font – are not intended as an exhaustive list of possible visual strategies, but merely as a sample of the ways in which the meanings of visuality in texts can be explored. In each case the significance of particular choices was explored not only for its aesthetic appeal (how it made the multimedia text 'look good'), but also for how it contributed to the meanings it offered. And here again the concepts of discourse, subjectivity, identity, viewer/user/reader become important – as ways of communicating non-specialist understandings about the meanings of the text.

The study of visuality has recently become a major disciplinary field, correlating with the development of multimedia technologies. There is now a range of texts (for example, Kress and van Leeuwen, 1996; Mirzoeff, 1998, 1999; Sturken and Cartwright, 2001) that introduce the reader to many of the principles discussed above and to the analysis of the visual meanings of multimedia for a range of different audiences.

The next chapter explores another meaning-system that has also, only recently, begun to develop its own non-specialist vocabulary and field of study – sound. Again, our concern is how this meaning system operates in our everyday lives, how we organise it in ways that make it meaningful, and so how it is used in multimedia texts to create meanings for listeners/users.

Notes

1   This has never really changed. Charting the dress and roles of women in all *Star Trek* series, including the most recent *Enterprise*, shows the apparently insurmountable difficulty experienced by the entertainment industry in representing women as professional people. In the most conservative sense, women have to be experienced first as female bodies – and then accepted for their professional skills. So Captain Janeway is a *female* starship captain; Captains Kirk, Picard, Sisko and Archer are just starship captains, their masculinity implicit in the role/profession itself. In other words, the professions are already coded as masculine; the presence of women in those professions is often mediated by the wearing of skin-tight clothing (T'Pol, Seven of Nine) or by feminine stereotyping (the nurturing Troi, waspish Belana Torres, tomboyish …). Still, they are there and the writers often use their presence to expose the stereotyping that is implicit in their construction – as when Seven of Nine as a newly-liberated Borg drone explored male reactions to her embodiment in the episode 'Revulsion'.

2   This essay can be found at: www.redsun.com/type/abriefhistoryoftype/

3   See examples of Nguyen's work at www.myfonts.com: Voila, Blink and Droplet.

4   This distrust of technology in Jackson's film is based on Tolkien's pastoral theme throughout *The Lord of the Rings*.

5   *We of the Never-Never* (1908) is the name of a famous Australian book by a nineteenth-century female writer, Mrs Aeneas Gunn. It describes her life in an outback station or farmstead, where she lived isolated from white settler society and among indigenous people who worked on the station.

6   Though many traditional grammars were quite inflexible – were written as sets of rules like a catechism – that did not stop speakers, writers, readers and scholars from challenging them, and eventually changing them.

7   This interest is evident not only in the *Alien* films, but also in many of Giger's artworks such as the *Passage* and *Birth Machine* series.

FOUR

SOUND

'Ssshhhwiff'

When an exhibition of *Star Trek* memorabilia was shown at Sydney's Powerhouse Museum several years ago, attendants reported that a favourite exhibit with visitors was a recording of *Star Trek* sound effects. The exhibit comprised a panel on which each sound had a separate button that visitors could press. When I visited the exhibition, there was a queue to use the exhibit – and also cheerful onlookers joining in with the person taking a turn. According to one of the museum attendants, the visitors' favourite sound by far was the swish of the automatic doors on the *Enterprise*; in fact, it was so popular that the button repeatedly broke from over-use. Yet, as *Star Trek* viewers know, the doors on the original set never were automatic; the technology to enable that did not exist at the time. Instead, stagehands stood behind the doors and manually moved them each time a sequence was filmed.

The 'ssshhhwiff' sound of the *Enterprise* doors can be read as multiply significant. On the one hand, it represents the series itself. At the time of its original broadcast *Star Trek* was the most technologically sophisticated drama on television, as comparison with contemporaries, *Lost in Space* and *Doctor Who* illustrates. The automatic doors signify that sophistication as they demonstrate the incorporation of advanced technology into everyday life; that is, the technology is not shown as a 'marvel' but simply as a feature of everyday living. So the 'ssshhhwiff' (remarkably like the cut and paste function sound made by my Mac!) signifies both the television series and its diegetic world of advanced technology – both of which have nostalgic appeal for viewers. But, on the other hand, there is also the insider knowledge about those doors – that they weren't real at all, any more than the transporter beam that teleports people and things over space-time. For knowing viewers (and many choosing to visit the exhibition could be reasonably supposed to be in this category) the 'ssshhhwiff' has another, metatextual function. It identified *Star Trek* as a vastly entertaining narrative in which loyal viewers were involved – and with which they played games, remaking the characters and plots to construct their own *Star Trek* worlds. They knew the doors didn't actually work as shown, but chose not to know that (to suspend disbelief) for the sake of the programme's *mise-en-scène*. That knowing suspension of disbelief, like (but also unlike) their suspension of disbelief about the transporter, represented their engagement with the programme and its world.

Where it differs from the transporter is that it is, as noted above, so domestic – a signifier of advanced technology operating in everyday life – rather than a scientific marvel (like the transporter). So the reason for the surprising (to the attendants) popularity of that sound is likely to be that it articulated multiple meanings for visitors – about the programme, its future world, the role of technology in everyday life, the narrative play engendered by the programme, and viewers' pleasure in all of these meanings. And all of this was captured by one evocative sound.

This chapter addresses the role of sound in our lives as a means of exploring its uses in multimedia. Sound is a less developed strategy in IT-based multimedia because of the current restrictions on bandwidth. However, with the spread of broadband and the increased availability of bandwidth for the reception and production of multi-modal genres, sound is likely to play an increasing role. At this point the use of sound on web sites is minimal and on e-mail virtually non-existent. And interestingly, the mobile phone – which is rapidly becoming part of the IT network – is as much a written as a spoken phenomenon. So sound is at an interesting point in its development as a semiotic system.

This chapter explores the role of sound by reference to a series of scenarios, most of them drawn from everyday life. For each scenario, the implications of this everyday experience are explored in some detail, by reference to recent (and some less recent) theoretical writing about sound. In particular, my concern is with the relationship between sound, meaning and embodiment – and how the individual subject experiences sound as a meaning-making, not just aesthetic, practice.

Sound scenarios: engaging the listener

Scenario 1   I walk into a gallery of the new National Museum of Australia. One of the most striking features is that the sombre, silent museum of the past has gone. Not only does this new museum have interactive exhibits that speak to you, and fixed exhibits with a sound and voice track on a repeat loop, it has overlapping sounds. At certain points the visitor can hear more than one soundtrack – different voices, voice and music, voice and sound. It is an invigorating experience that speaks (literally) to the purpose and function of this museum, which is to interrogate the nature of identity – not to represent an unproblematic and unproblematised monocultural view of the state and of individual identity and citizenship.

Scenario 2   I take a young child to the opening of *Star Wars I: The Phantom Menace* (2000). Young children have sensitive hearing, not yet dulled by the environmental noise adults have experienced. The Dolby Sound System kicks in with John Williams's famous *Star Wars* theme and the child writhes in pain, clamping his hands and my hands over his ears. The decibel level of the soundtrack makes the experience of the film an embodied one – but for the child the embodiment is a painful one.

Scenario 3 I am watching *Star Trek III: The Search for Spock* (1984). The *Enterprise*'s Chief Engineer, Montgomery Scott, enters a turbolift in the newly commissioned (rival) starship, *Excelsior*. Shortly afterwards the lift announces that Scotty has reached the floor he had previously requested and adds, 'Have a nice day!' Scotty sourly responds, 'Up your shaft!'

Scenario 4 In Peter Jackson's film, *The Lord of the Rings: The Fellowship of the Ring* (2001), Frodo (Elijah Wood) realises that Gandalf (Ian McKellen) cannot escape with them from Moria – and screams in agony, 'Gandalf!'

Scenario 5 Students completing a degree in architecture are given an assignment: to map the soundscape of a length of coastline and then use that map in the design of a building suitable for that location.

Scenario 6 The cafés around town are occupied by business people, students, academics and others who are writing reports, assignments, project outlines, policy documents.

Scenario 7 A twelve-year-old child responds to exhortations to do his homework by observing that he is just burning a music disk for a friend – and he will start any minute.

Scenarios: sounds and meanings

Each of these scenarios is about sound – environmental sound, natural sound, music, voice, and how those sounds affect the people and communities that live with them. They are about how those sounds create meaning for listeners, as well as how those meanings are incorporated – again, literally – into listeners' lives. The sounds we hear – voices, music, noises – carry meanings that go beyond the directly representational. The sound of a door slamming is not simply the noise of wood on wood or wood on metal; it also raises a range of connotative possibilities – an argument has occurred and the confrontation ended with a slamming door; someone is late for work and has run from a house slamming the door in haste behind them; a child has exuberantly run from a room to meet a friend; a door blows shut in a breeze. So the slam of the door may signify heightened emotion (anger, anxiety, joy) or it may simply indicate the materiality of our world. The point is that the sound has the potential to mean – just as the words and visuals we discussed in the two previous chapters have the potential to mean. And the listener sifts these potentials in relation to context in order to interpret a particular sound at a particular time and place.

In each of the following explorations one of the scenarios above is explored for its meanings as individual, embodied experience, and the theories and studies that enable this analysis are also explored. Again, the purpose is to enable us to not only understand the role of sound in the life of the user, but also to begin to predict the creative ways in which sound may become part of the multimedia environment.

1   Soundscape and meaning

The first (museum) scenario locates in the soundscape of the museum the complexity of sound and voice in the everyday life of the citizen – a complexity that is not only physical, but also conceptual. At times, or in particular spaces, the visitor hears overlapping voices. These may be the overlapping acoustic/ auditory shadows of specific exhibits, or the communication system of the museum interrupting the soundtrack of an exhibit, or it may be the voices of other visitors interrupting the soundtrack of an exhibition.

The overlay of soundtracks (acoustic shadows) can be distracting, but it also demonstrates the multivocality of the museum – the fact that the museum tells not just one story about the history of Australia, but many stories, some of which overlap, some of which are in conflict. As the visitor moves to focus on one particular voice and its story, she or he moves from the other voice, silencing it. And then repeats the process in order to listen to the other voice. The museum could have forestalled this process by separating the voices, yet it did not. Effectively, it positions the visitor to make a choice, and to recognise that choice – that she or he has had to silence one voice in order to listen to another.

In the same way, the voices of other visitors enter the multivocality of the museum soundscape. In passing comments on the exhibits visitors enter the process of argument and opinion formation that is the conceptual arena of the museum. This interplay could be minimised by the use of sound within the museum – at worst, by the kind of moozak that Murray Schafer identifies as stifling thought and making judgment impossible (Schafer, 1994: 96–8). Instead, the sound density of the museum encourages talking and discussion, as well as (over-)hearing. In other words, the museum reinforces one of its fundamental conceptual arguments, about the nature of identity and the development of notions of history not only in the acoustics of the exhibits but also in the arrangement of the museum's acoustic space. So this soundscape makes a powerful contribution to the museum as a place of social and cultural interrogation.

This analysis makes a simple point about sound, that it is discursively meaningful – just as are verbal and visual text. Decisions about the soundscape of the museum may not have been consciously expressed in the terms above, yet would have been made in relation to both the overall purpose or function of the museum and the demands of specific exhibits. Given the direction of contemporary museological principles (that position visitors as active learners), it is not surprising that the soundscape should take the form described above.

At this point it is worth noting the value of the term, *soundscape*, in discussions of the sound at a given site or production. This term is most closely associated with the work of Murray Schafer who describes it in this way:

The soundscape is any acoustic field of study. We may speak of a musical composition as a soundscape, or a radio program as a soundscape or an acoustic environment as a soundscape. We can isolate an acoustic environment as a field of study just as we can study the characteristics of a given landscape. ... A soundscape consists of events *heard* not objects *seen*. (1977: 7–8, italics in original)

Schafer's work and its contribution to contemporary studies of sound is discussed further below.

2 *Lucas and surround sound: embodiment*

Scenario 2 addresses a different function and power of sound – to touch the individual physically as well as emotionally. Schafer makes this point in his book, *The Soundscape*: 'Hearing and touch meet where the lower frequencies of available sound pass over to tactile vibrations (at about 20 herz). Hearing is a way of touching at a distance ...' (1994: 11). And in a later chapter Schafer notes that people hear 'from zero decibels to approximately 130 decibels (where sound sensation is converted to pain)' (1994: 115). The producer of the *Star Wars* films, George Lucas, is known for his concern about the sound systems available for viewing his films, as well as for the specific use he makes of sound in his films. Viewers of the *Star Wars* films are familiar not only with John Williams's famous music score but also for the deep rumble that signifies movement through space for the large star cruisers and for the high-pitched whine of the small star-fighters. Yet, space is a vacuum; there is no sound (as we know it) in space. Nevertheless, Lucas has made that sound synonymous with space travel for generations of viewers. And he also uses its pitch and intensity of sound to create this experience as embodied for his viewers. As Schafer notes, at certain frequencies sound vibrations become tactile sensations: Lucas's star-cruisers rumble not just through space but through the viewer's senses. The viewer is engaged not only visually and aurally by Lucas's film but also tactilely: she or he sees, hears and feels the film.

The significance of this use of sound is that it interpolates the viewer into the narrative of the film even more powerfully than the visual and verbal text – or, at least, it potentially does so. Schafer writes about this phenomenon in relation to popular music, where he discusses it in terms of immersion versus concentration. For him immersion implies a society seeking 'unification and integrity' (Schafer, 1994: 118). In the case of film we might postulate that the use of loud, low frequency sound may be used to situate the audience within a unified and integrated narrative; that is, that the sound may position the audience to experience the narrative as unified and integrated. Many film composers have discussed the role of the soundtrack as stitching the film together, creating an emotional environment or response in viewers and at times disguising problems in the film's structure. This is not quite the point being made here. In the case of Lucas's low frequency rumble we are refering to a more encompassing quality of the sound, to literally touch the viewer and draw that viewer into the world of the narrative. For these viewers the narrative makes sense because it is their world; they are in that soundscape – or, perhaps more correctly, it is in them.

So sound can be touching in more than a metaphorical sense. It is a semiotic that is experienced bodily, as more than a bundle of sense impressions to interpret. Sound can bodily move us, and we embody ourselves in (response to) sound.

This leads to another aspect of sound that Schafer and others (notably Attali (1985)) discuss – sound as an expression of power. Schafer notes that the authority to generate loud sounds signifies power (1994: 74). Once the generation of loud sound was the prerogative of the Church, which held ultimate authority in Western societies. As the West became more secular, so too did the institutions and practices with a mandate to generate this level of sound – the sound that moves people. For Schafer, the industrial revolution was a decisive period in the development of the secular world and it is marked acoustically by the proliferation of sound; loud machine sounds that transformed the high fidelity world of the pre-industrial world to the low fidelity world now characteristic of Western societies:

> During the Industrial Revolution, sacred Noise sprang across to the profane world. Now the industrialists held power and they were granted dispensation to make Noise by means of the steam engine and the blast furnace, just as previously the monks had been free to make Noise on the church bell or J.S. Bach to open out his preludes on the full organ.
>
> The association of noise and power has never really been broken in the human imagination. It descends from God, to the priest, to the industrialist, and more recently to the broadcaster and the aviator. The important thing to realize is this: to have the Sacred Noise is not merely to make the biggest noise; rather it is a matter of having the authority to make it without censure. (Schafer, 1994: 76)

In the cinema George Lucas's Dolby Sound System is granted the authority to generate sound at a level Schafer identifies with Sacred Noise – the sound that affects embodiment and so enters bodily into the experience of everyday life. So sound can reveal the lineaments of power and authority in a society. In contemporary Western society it is perhaps not surprising to find that the film industry, as represented by Lucas, is powerful and so able (authorised) to generate noise at a level that even its target audience may find disturbing and even painful. Further, Schafer regards sound as imperialistic when it is sufficiently powerful to create a large acoustic profile (1994: 77). And the *Star Wars* soundtracks, as projected in the cinema (according to Lucas's specifications), have a large acoustic profile. So what kind of imperialism are we dealing with here? Schafer refers to the imperialism of industrial machinery, which signified the ascendance of a particular world-view – one which Heidegger would identify as fundamentally technological: in Schafer's terms, 'Industry must grow; therefore its sounds must grow with it' (1994: 77). In subjecting the child viewer to thundering bass sounds Lucas not only literally incorporates the child into the world of his narrative, but also reveals that narrative to be not simply the story of a boy from Tattooine. Instead, the narrative drive of *Star Wars* is revealed as the interpellation of the child into an industry conglomerate with one major mission: to subject(ify) that child as a consumer. Hence, the need to break the child's defences, to overwhelm the senses with a spectacle that makes critical discernment difficult. This is a spectacle of enforced bodily engagement that works to dazzle the child into a sensory engagement that can be manipulated into consumer desire. Of course, it may have quite the opposite effect, leading the child to reject the source of such discomfort. Yet, as Schafer notes, the tendency to identify sound with power may actually work to engage the listener.

Sound can operate imperialistically to control the space occupied by an individual listener, by saturating the space acoustically. Unlike the museum soundscape, that of a theatre thundering the *Star Wars* theme is not a space of interpersonal debate and negotiation; it is an imperialist space governed by the authority that generated that sound – whether we figure that authority as George Lucas, the Hollywood studio system, or global capitalism. This draws attention to the role of sound in the negotiation of subjectivity.

Just as individual subjects constantly renegotiate their subjectivity in relation to the written and visual text around them, so they are influenced by sound in their formation of subjectivity. Sound may be used to interpellate the viewer into a narrative – and hence its ideology – in an almost Althusserian sense, as James Leahy notes:

> Though it is obviously possible to reject Westerns, or even Hollywood films in general, on ideological grounds, as many people do, once one has opened up to the force and complexity of emotional experience the best can offer, it is difficult to avoid being swept away by the rich interaction of the many discursive strands that constitute the film's narrative, themes and dramaturgy. The viewer's awareness is being engaged by so many different channels of visual and aural information that habitual political and moral judgement may be suspended. (2003: 64)

Leahy describes the rich combination of visuals and sound – not sound alone – as having the power to distract viewers from political and moral judgment. Yet, I would argue that it is the physical apprehension of sound that is particularly important in creating this power. Visuals alone can be powerful, yet are perceptually distant. Sound, however, takes that visual perception into the body of the viewer – creating a perceptual complex that is difficult to resist.

In processing this audio-visual experience the viewer/listener is positioned within the diegetic world of the text, physically as well as emotionally and intellectually. And that also means that the viewer is positioned to accept the values and beliefs that motivate that world – which is not to say that all viewers walk away from a film accepting its values and beliefs. However, the ability of a film to enter the perceptual world of the viewer will powerfully influence that negotiation – and the physicality of sound needs to be acknowledged as a powerful factor in this negotiation (though arguably it could work just as much against the film as for it).

Later in this chapter I return to the subject of sound in film, noting the ways in which this use of sound contributes to our understanding of it as a semiotic system – and multimedia strategy.

3 The automated voice: against the grain

In *Star Trek III: The Search for Spock* (1984) Montgomery Scott verbally insulted the turbolift of a twenty-third-century spacecraft – and audiences laughed uproariously. One evening recently I received a phone call from a marketing company – either selling a product or attempting to perform a market survey. The voice identified itself as automated – and my response was shamefully close to Commander Scott's: I immediately hung up. Why these responses in these specific situations? Scott was aboard a vessel that was meant to supersede his own beloved *Enterprise*; so his feelings are already hostile. Furthermore, he is about to sabotage the ship's engineering. When the lift addresses him, Scotty regards the communication as impertinent and reacts with hostility; he is not amused. The audience's laughter at this scene seems to be prompted not only by the scatological response ('Up your shaft'), but by the perceived victory of the human (Scotty, the less advanced *Enterprise*) over the technological (*Excelsior*) – and particularly by the refusal of the human to be situated (pandered to, positioned) by the technology. In doing so the film articulates a human fear of (the power of) technology that is found in many contemporary texts (notably *The Matrix* (1999)).

In the telemarketing example, I was simply not prepared to listen while an automated device intruded into the private space of my home, and tried to sell me something. Furthermore, I was affronted that the intrusion was perpetrated by a company that was not even prepared to pay human agents to speak to me; instead they took the cheap option of using a computer voice (I sometimes wonder if this was an experiment to gauge how quickly respondents would hang up the receiver). By contrast, I have no problem with telephone banking, which also uses automated voice, because in this case the user has a sense that the transaction is in her or his control – the voice prompts acting only to facilitate the transaction, not to interact on a peer-exchange level. The sales transaction, whether in the form of direct marketing or market research, for me requires a human interlocutor, someone who will engage in an exchange of information on a peer basis. This means that if I want clarification on an individual basis, I can ask for it – not find myself constructed as part of a certain category who may require further information about part (c) of the question or issue at hand. This also raised my concerns about how this exchange was categorising me for the purposes of the exchange. So, again, the reaction to the automated voice reveals the same fundamental distrust or unease with technology as did Scotty's actions in *The Search for Spock*. Further, it uncovers one of the reasons for that distrust, which is our awareness that automated exchanges are programmed through the categorisation of individual users – a process to which we have no conscious input and over which we have no control. As well, there is concern about the ways in which we are shaped by the technology we use in the process of these exchanges. In other words, that we are becoming our technology – with all its limitations, as Heidegger and others have argued.

This same concern was expressed in an episode of the television programme, *Frasier*. At one point Frasier needed to find out a telephone number so he phoned an information line. He then began to speak in a totally affectless, robotic voice that amazed and amused the others present, who looked at him as if he had lost his senses (literally!). But then Frasier shrugs, the others nod, and the laugh track signifies the general audience acknowledgment that this technology is so pervasive and so powerful that it forces us to act like it (affectless, robotic) in order to interact with it. This also raises questions about the implicit values and beliefs we are coerced into accepting in order to use the technology – which is James Leahy's point about film in a different guise/mode.

By contrast we might consider the response of Mac users to the absurd programming that leads the Mac to excuse its inability to perform certain tasks by saying, in the affectless tones of a robot: 'It is not my fault ... ' The ridiculous feature of the message is the presumption that the user would attribute 'fault' to the machine. However, it may be that this is not the intent of the message. Instead, this might be read as a knowing, self-satirising response, inviting users not to blame the machine, but to join the designers in acknowledging that there are some things the Mac cannot do and that to demand any more is simply ridiculous – as ridiculous as attributing 'fault' to a machine. So in this instance the combination of flattened affect (and in the Australian context, the alien(ating) North American-accented English) with the plaintive, affect-laden disclaimer combines to generate a message from designer to user, through the medium of the machine that serves both. The message to users is that they are in control; they are not fallible like these machines, but creative and powerful like the designers. This identification between users and designers offers the user a perception of control over the technology that is a feature of what Ben Shneiderman called 'the really pleased user' (Shneiderman, 1987: 180).

The affective qualities of the human voice, not utilised (and skilfully displaced) in the Mac example, are most clearly shown in the importance of non-verbal sounds in the communication of meaning. Of course, there are non-human characters that have managed to communicate very effectively by such means. The most famous is probably George Lucas's character, R2D2 – the small 'droid who is so popular with fans that he, or it, appears in all the *Star Wars* films, despite the on-going problems with his, or its, movement.[1] I ascribed a gender to R2D2, because it is somehow clear that 'he' is male, despite the fact that the character looks like a cross between a dalek[2] and a pepper-pot, unlike his companion, C3PO who is humanoid in shape. R2D2 communicates through a series of high-pitched squeals and lower-frequency sounds that are deeply affecting.[3] His sounds are then translated by C3PO, the protocol 'droid, for the benefit of the audience and/or other characters. R2D2's squeals and groans are like the excited verbal responses of a young child – the long sentences and paragraphs that have all the sound contours of spoken language, but none of the verbal content – the meanings of which have to be interpreted to others by a loving parent or companion; in this case,

C3PO. So the sound of R2D2 identifies him/it as childlike in his emotional appeal: for adults he has the appeal of a child; for children he is the imaginary companion they long for. In other words, R2D2's sounds operate for the viewer and listener as pure affect, the interpersonal aspect of a voice stripped of its verbiage.[4]

The affect-flattened and/or unengaged, non-corporeal voice of information technology is a sound that has a particular significance for us, as contemporary social subjects. It signifies our concerns about the power of that technology in our lives. And our responses to it also show the power of the real/non-synthetic human voice to signify qualities that we associate specifically with human be-ing. Yet, this does not preclude the use of synthetic voices in appropriate contexts – those that require no interaction (such as telephone banking), ironic uses that position listeners as the designers intend (the Mac voice), empathetic uses that reproduce particular human voice qualities in order to elicit a positive response from listeners (R2D2's reproduction of the proto-language sounds of young children). Like the visuality of verbal text, the sound quality of the human voice is a characteristic that has often been overlooked because of our fetishisation of the word. Thus, this scenario begins to explore some of the complex meanings associated with that embodied sound – and this study is continued in the next scenario.

4 Frodo's scream: acoustic ontology

The scream scenario evokes a number of situations in which the human voice creates meaning less by its verbal content than by the nature of its sound – its tonal quality, pitch, timbre and so on. When Frodo (Elijah Wood) screams out Gandalf's name in Peter Jackson's first *Lord of the Rings* film, the sound of his voice carries the grief and terror of loss felt by not just that character, but by all the characters and, through identification, by the audience. Frodo's scream follows Gandalf into the depths of Moria, creating the vast depths into which Gandalf falls with the Balrog. Yet, it also envelops those who stay above, the rest of the fellowship, who flee from Moria into the surrounding hills and from there to Lothlorien. This is achieved by the complexity of Elijah Wood's voice as he screams. It is a voice shredded by fear and grief to which all his companions – and the audience – respond; not a controlled, contained voice that distances all responses. The rawness of the scream creates an embodied response, rubbing against the ends of nerves already jangling from the violence of the battles in Moria.

Michael Chion writes of the scream in cinema that:

> ... it's not so much the sound quality of the scream that's important, but its placement. And this place could be occupied by nothing, a blank, an absence. The screaming point is a point of the unthinkable inside the thought, of the indeterminate inside the spoken, of unrepresentability inside representation. It occupies a point in time, but has no duration within. It suspends the time of its possible duration; it's a rip in the fabric of time. The scream embodies a fantasy of the auditory absolute, it is seen to saturate the soundtrack and deafen the listener. (1999: 77)

Chion goes on to identify the scream with the female voice. The male voice, he holds, can project a shout, but not a scream. And the male shout is fundamentally different in that it 'is a shout of power, exercising a will, marking a territory, a structuring shout, *anticipated*'. The woman's shout, or cry, is, by contrast, 'the shout of a human subject of language facing death: What it embodies, rather, is an absolute, outside of language, time, and the conscious subject' (Chion, 1999: 78, italics in original).

Chion's description of the (female) scream applies equally well to Frodo's anguished call to Gandalf. Frodo's cry is repeated at the beginning of the second *Lord of the Rings* film, *The Two Towers* (2002), in which, as before, it momentarily mutes all other sound. Like the 'screaming point' theorised by Chion, it is 'where speech is suddenly extinct, a black hole, the exit of being' (Chion, 1999: 79). Gandalf's fall is the end of a mode of being for Gandalf himself, and for those who have relied on him. When Gandalf returns in *The Two Towers*, metonymically summoned by Frodo's cry, he is no longer Gandalf the Grey but Gandalf the White, a more powerful being – Christ-like in his Fall into Hell, his wrestling with a devil and his resurrection. The screaming point is not so much a point at which being exits, so much as a point where everyday life ceases; infinity is embraced (as we see in Gandalf's eye in the movie); and a new mode of being emerges. The pathos of Frodo's scream generates the emotional energy required for this transformation. Into it is packed all the grief and longing and need and love that re-form Gandalf into a mighty wizard and leader.

Studying the voice (and the scream) is like the brief study of typography in Chapter 2, in that we are concerned as much with the non-verbal elements of the communication, as with the meanings of the words. The meaning of the communication, we noted then, was not just the meanings of the words, but a complex interaction of the lexis, the typography, and the context. With the scream we are studying the interaction of lexis (if there is any), voice quality (the 'grain of the voice') and the context. What the study shows is that the sound of the human voice, in and of itself, carries meanings that are crucial to the communication.

Theo van Leeuwen attempts to capture these qualities in his discussion of voice timbre and quality in his *Speech, Music, Sound* (1999). He locates the following '[k]ey sound quality features': '(i) *tension*; (ii) *roughness*; (iii) *breathiness*; (iv) *loudness*; (v) *pitch register*; (vi) *vibrato* and (vii) *nasality*' (van Leeuwen, 1999: 140, italics in original). In each case van Leeuwen describes the physiological or bodily comportment that produces sounds that are characterised by these adjectives, as well as the kinds of feelings that these sounds often evoke. For example, with vibrato the 'vibrating sound literally and figuratively *trembles*. What makes us tremble? Emotions' (van Leeuwen, 1999: 134, italics in original). He also notes that vibrato has another side – the vibrations of the natural world or of machinery – which may evoke quite different meanings. As a quality of the human voice, however, vibrato is most often associated with intense emotion (like Frodo's scream), and its meaning captures the embodied state that generates it and that it produces in the listener. And van Leeuwen notes that sound is always multidimensional; it is not represented as one of these qualities but as a combination that is appropriate to the situation. So the human voice in any particular situation has a range of potential meanings available in the choices made of voice quality and timbre – whether to be tense or lax, rough or smooth, breathy or not, soft or loud, high or low, vibrato or plain, nasal or not. The embodied tensions involved in generating some of these choices – for example, tenseness, roughness, loudness, vibrato – communicate that tension to listeners, and may be more or less appropriate to a particular situation. For example, when that combination (tenseness, roughness, loudness, vibrato) is used in Springsteen's 'Born in the USA', it conveys the disillusion and grief of a young man forced to face the realities of his own country's social and ethical dysfunctionality and propaganda. If a sentimental love ballad were sung using the same combination, listeners would most likely hear the song as a spoof – that is, the words would convey one set of feelings (sickly sentimentality) but the vocal delivery (tense, rough, loud, vibrato) another; the resulting clash a satiric take on the sentiment of the song. This same strategy was used by *The Sex Pistols* in their performance of 'God Save the Queen', which thereby changed the song from a patriotic hymn (the literal meaning of the words) to a critical commentary on contemporary Britain.

Van Leeuwen notes that Barthes writes of 'the grain of the voice' – ' "the materiality of the body speaking its mother tongue", "something which is directly brought to your ears in one and the same movement from deep down in the cavities, the muscles, the membranes, the cartilages"' (1999: 128) – as escaping the semiotic and the social and providing pleasure. I would argue that the embodied experiences of generating and of hearing sound do not have to escape the semiotic and/or the social to be pleasurable. In fact, their pleasure may depend on their reference to the social – as with Springsteen's song. Springsteen is arguing directly that the embodied experience of the social can lead the individual to a more complex understanding of the world. Furthermore, the embodied experience of his song – particularly evident in the scream, which cannot be reduced to a set of words (as the lyrics of songs so often are) – communicates that understanding to listeners.

We are only just starting to develop the non-specialist, critical language by which to discuss the acoustic qualities of the voice and their role in meaning-making. Tom Paulin (2003) draws attention to the need for this understanding of voice when he notes how much he dislikes hearing actors read poetry: '… every so often Radio 3 … would wheel out John Gielgud reading Tennyson. I can't do that voice, but what a terrible, terrible verse reading, elocutionary voice that is …' (2003: 46). The same critical understanding can tell us why opera singers sound so terrible singing popular song, when their cultivated, pure, correct diction and voice production destroys the emotional quality of the music. It can also help us understand the power of Springsteen's scream and Bono (of U2)'s wail, the vocal dexterity of rap, the affective power of Elijah Wood. Further, we can then explore how this (vocal) sound is deployed discursively, to generate particular meanings in a text – like Springsteen's evocation of working-class alienation and helplessness.

5 *Discovering the soundscape*

Tom Paulin's identification of the ontological meanings of sound establishes the importance of sound to our understanding of place and being:

> ... sound has all sorts of ontological meanings for us. It is to do with our dwelling in the world, with our being. It's part of that, as it were, ontology of relationship which we have to the entire universe. (Paulin, 2003: 36)

In assigning architecture students the task of mapping the soundscape of a particular location and then using this in the design of a building at the site, their instructor acknowledges how the sound of a site *is* the site – so a construction at a particular site needs to work with that sound (whether harmonically or as counterpoint).

Architecture has traditionally been associated with music, through concepts of rhythm and proportion. The 'Introduction' to *New Organic Architecture* argues:

> Organic architecture is living, rather than frozen, music, performed in the continuous present. With its juxtaposition of harmonies and discords, its diverse rhythms and syncopated movement, and its asymmetrical proportions and structure, it has closer affinities with modern music than with classical compositions. (Pearson, 2001: 24)

And the 'Introduction' goes on to quote Jacques Gillet:

> The building site as it expands
> is like a quartet in four movements.
> The sub-foundation is a powerful allegro moderato.
> The lofty terrace is the adagio cantabile,
> huge movement both quiet and steady.
> The whole orchestration is to come.
> Capitals, vaults, frames and stained-glass constitute
> the scherzo,
> moving from sestenuto to prestissimo.
> The superstructure is the rondo finale apassionato. (quoted in Pearson, 2001: 24)

In this set of musical metaphors the common element between music and architecture is structure. Whether structured like contemporary music, as is modern architecture, or like more classical compositions, architectural design, it is argued, encompasses and defines space as does music. It is useful to repeat this metaphor here because it leads us not simply from music to sound and its relation to architecture, but also to the analysis of the role of music in constructing – or perhaps colonising – the acoustic space in which we live.

The relationship between sound and space was raised earlier in the discussion of Lucas's Dolby Sound System – though the focus there was on acoustic space and its effect on embodiment. The relationship between music and sound – or music and noise – is also an area of debate for theorists such as Schafer and Attali. Schafer and Attali use the terms, sound, music and noise, whereas I use the term 'sound' to include all acoustic elements – organised, orchestrated, natural, artificial. Reference to noise is more typical of those with an interest in and familiarity with traditional musicology, where noise is often contrasted with music. Sean Cubitt, in *Digital Aesthetics* (1998), discusses the controversies engendered by John Cage's *4'33"* – in which a pianist sits at a piano silently for four minutes and thirty-three seconds. The debates about the piece focus on whether its silence – and consequent revelation of ambient sound – is deconstructive of music as a discourse and a practice. Cubitt quotes Douglas Kahn's response:

> The main avant-garde strategy in music from Russolo to Cage quite evidently relied upon notions of noise and worldly sound as 'extra-musical'; what was outside musical materiality was then progressively brought back into the fold in order to rejuvenate musical practice. ... But for a sound to be 'musicalized' in this strategy, it had to conform materially to ideas of sonicity, that is, ideas of sound stripped of its associative attributes, a minimally coded sound existing in close proximity to 'pure' perception and distant from the contaminating effects of the world. (quoted in Cubitt, 1998: 96)

Cage's own programme notes are also quoted: '... we have mastered or subjugated noise. We become triumphant over it' (quoted in Cubitt, 1998: 97), as is William Carlos Williams's note on an earlier Cage piece:

> I felt that noise, the unrelated noise of life, such as this in the subway ... had actually been mastered, subjugated. The composer has taken this hated thing, life, and rigged himself into power over it by his music. (quoted in Cubitt, 1998: 97)

Cubitt's own judgment of *4'33"* is that it 'simultaneously colonises and erases the world under the semiotic system of music, even in the act of remaking the musical apparatus so that it can so colonise' (1998: 97). For Cubitt, then, Cage's composition reveals the role and the power of music as a semiotic system to colonise noise – where that noise is the sound of everyday life, with all its meanings, complexity and contradiction.

Murray Schafer acknowledges this contemporary rethinking of the meaning of music in his teaching manual, *The New Soundscape* (1969). In his opening chapter, 'Yes, but is it Music?', Schafer notes that his class argued for two days about a definition of music. He wrote to John Cage and received the following response: '*Music is sounds, sounds around us whether we're in or out of concert halls: cf. Thoreau*' (italics in original) (Schafer, 1969: 1). Schafer glosses the Thoreau reference as 'where the author experiences in the sounds and sights of nature an inexhaustible entertainment' (1969: 1). He concludes:

> Today all sounds belong to a continuous field of possibilities lying *within the comprehensive dominion of music*. Behold the new orchestra: the sonic universe!
> And the new musicians: anyone and anything that sounds! (Schafer, 1969: 2)

This might be read in a number of ways. It may be interpreted in the way that Kahn reads Cage, as bringing the sounds of the world into the domain of music – which thereby acts as a colonising discourse. Or it may be, as Schafer himself suggests, a way of moving beyond the dichotomy of music/not-music to an engagement with all sound, which Schafer constitutes as a study of the soundscape. There may be a parallel here with the move from specific forms of text study such as Literary Studies and Film Studies to the interdisciplinary field of Cultural Studies. Cultural Studies includes the study of literary and film texts but does not employ the same analytical criteria as the older forms of study. For example, it does not employ a canon of great works, against which specific texts are rated. Instead, it explores the context in which the specific text was produced and the meanings it had for its readers or viewers then, as well as the meanings the text has for readers and viewers now – in order to understand how the text operates as a cultural practice. The study of the soundscape is similarly inclusive and interdisciplinary, situating sounds in terms of their meaning and function as cultural practices. And one of the materialities of sound that soundscape studies recognises is the role of technology in both the production of sound (as noted earlier) and in what we recognise as music. Schafer notes, for example, the influence on composition of tape recording, which enables environmental sounds to be inserted into a performed piece (1969: 2; 1994: 111). Soundscape studies, therefore, is not prescriptive, but descriptive; not judgmental, but analytical; inclusive, rather than exclusive. Its role in relation to the analysis of multi-modal, multimedia texts lies in its recognition of the embodied and pervasive role of sound in the user's interaction with the text.

Attali, too, traces a genealogy of music that situates its role socially and culturally. In his book, *Noise: The Political Economy of Music* (1985), Attali maps the function of music via a series of tropes: Sacrifice, Representation, Repetition, Composition. His analysis is even less confined by the concepts of traditional musicology than that of Schafer. For Attali, music is a way of channelling violence and noise – the disruptive elements that threaten social order as well as the powers that maintain social order: '*Noise is a weapon and music, primordially, is the formation, domestication, and ritualization of that weapon as a simulacrum of ritual murder*' (Attali, 1985: 24, italics in original). By ritualising violence music enables the dominant social order to be established and maintained with the tacit approval of its subjects:

Music is inscribed between noise and silence, in the space of the social codification it reveals. Every code of music is rooted in the ideologies and technologies of its age, and at the same time produces them. (Attali, 1985: 19)

Attali maps the four networks in which he sees music as implicated, starting from the earliest order-producing role in Sacrifice where music confirms the possibility of society, whilst encoding (in the noise it channels) the possibility of its subversion or collapse. With the rise of the bourgeoisie Attali locates another role for music as carrier of information, its performance at specific sites patronised by the aristocracy and the wealthy bourgeois. For the first time music actually becomes 'music', commodified for its exchange-value: its political function is to enact that process of exchange via representation:

Music demonstrates that exchange is inseparable from the spectacle and theatrical enactment, from the process of *making people believe*: the utility of music is not to create order, but to make people believe in its existence and universal value, in its impossibility outside of exchange. (Attali, 1985: 57, italics in original)

The harmonies of eighteenth-century musical composition are seen as the ideological tool that established the concepts of representation, harmony and balance as the fundamental tenets of rational thought: '... the bourgeoisie of Europe finessed one of its most ingenious ideological productions: creating an aesthetic and theoretical base for its necessary order, *making people believe by shaping what they hear*' (Attali, 1985: 61, italics in original).

The dominance of Representation, in Attali's schema, is broken with the advent of recording. Through mechanical reproduction the musical performance is severed from its context; the consumer is no longer an audience-member or listener. Like Adorno, Attali sees mass production as a form of death, a path to quietude and passivity. The relationship of the consumer to the recorded musical performance is predetermined, trapped in the paradigms that constructed that performance. Innovation is not possible.

For Attali, the pleasure of the consumer is in a sense that of belonging, which is enacted through Repetititon. It is a very pessimistic vision: '*in a society in which power is so abstract that it can no longer be seized, in which the worst threat people feel is solitude and not alienation, conformity to the norm becomes the pleasure of belonging, and the acceptance of powerlessness takes root in the comfort of repetititon*' (italics in original) (1985: 125). This is a form of Foucauldian (self-)discipline that discounts the disruptive forces that Attali allows are constantly threatening to disrupt the musical harmonies. And yet Attali acknowledges that all of these networks are co-present, that music has not passed simply from one stage to another but that all phases coexist in our complex interactions with music. So music is both ideological tool of the bourgeoisie and the sign of its transitoriness; it enacts representation, even as representation itself is subject to repetition; and it enacts the socially formative act of sacrifice even as it is implicated in networks of abstraction that signify the alienation of social subjects from the means of production.

Attali also offers a fourth phase, which is ultimately redemptive. In this phase, Composition, the individual enters fully into the creative process, unconstrained by the paradigms that have governed earlier forms of musical production. Production is individual and yet fully engaged socially and interpersonally. It embraces noise, in Attali's terms, and forges from this noise new conventions by which to communicate with others: 'It makes [communication] a collective creation, rather than an exchange of coded messages' (Attali, 1985: 143).[5] As an embodied practice music will become an embodied exchange, a mutual experience of the pleasure in communication.

Attali's analysis situates music as symptomatic of the nature of contemporary social relations and political practice. He glosses this in terms of the relationship between knowledge and music:

Everywhere present, lurking behind a form, knowledge molds itself to the network within which it is inscribed: in representation, it is a model, a schema, the value of which depends on its empirical suitability to the measurement of facts; it is the study of partitions (*partitions*, also 'scores'). In repetition, it is genealogy, the study of replication. In composition, it is cartography, local knowledge, the insertion of culture into production and a general availability of new tools and instruments. (Attali, 1985: 147)

We might note the similarity here between composition and contemporary notions of regionalism and localization. Replacing the abstract study that characterised earlier formations is an engaged practice that emphasises shared meanings and inclusive narratives. Knowledge is understood as contextual, as a cultural practice not an objective reality. And again our study leads back to a fully contextualised and acculturated understanding of the role of sound in the multimedia text.

Sound is not only an acoustic or sonic materiality; it is a way of thinking and interacting.

6 The acoustic environment

Creating a soundscape The hypothesis above might explain the actions of those who choose to work in a crowded café or streetscape. People have a variety of different accommodations to sound when they work, or even when they are performing different kinds of work. Some listen to music; others to voices. Some listen to music while performing certain kinds of work; voices with different kinds of work; and require silence with yet another aspect of their work. In each case we might argue the individual worker constructs a soundscape within which to perform the specific operations.

The scenario raised earlier was the person working in a café. Since much conventional thought about work has stressed the need for isolation and quiet – witness the design of the traditional office, the home study, the library carrel – how might we understand the choice to work in a noisy public environment? Michael Bull's study, *Sounding Out the City: Personal Stereos and the Management of Everyday Life* (2000), offers some possible explanations. Bull is particularly concerned with personal stereos such as the Walkman, his thesis being that individuals use them to manage everyday life. Bull argues that people use this technology to generate an acoustic environment that effectively marks out a personal time/space location for them. It is their own place, within the public space. It can therefore operate as a site of (personal) resistance against hegemonising forces operating within society.

Bull's thesis is interesting not only for his proposed reconstrual of the role of the personal stereo, but also because it acknowledges the role of sound in constructing the social. Bull quotes William Welsch's work on the visual and auditory as contrasting modes: whereas the visible 'persists in time, the audible ... vanished in time'. The visible is concerned with 'constant, enduring being, audition on the other hand, with the fleeting, the transient, *event like*' (Welsch, quoted in Bull 2000: 117). And Bull goes on to comment on Welsch's observation:

Whereas vision is a distancing sense, hearing is one of alliance ... hearing ... does not keep the world at a distance, but admits it. 'Tone penetrates, without distance.' Such penetration, vulnerability and exposure are characteristic of hearing. We have eyelids, but not earlids. In hearing we are unprotected. Hearing is a sense of extreme passivity, and we cannot escape from acoustic congestion. That is why we are especially in need of protection acoustically. (Bull, 2000: 118)

At first glance it might seem that Welsch's observations are contradictory. If the visible is enduring in time/space but the audible is transient, fleeting, why is the audible so disturbing? Surely it can be shrugged off as simply part of the white noise against which we conduct much of our lives. Opposing this is Welsch's observation about earlids. We can choose not to view many of the cultural practices that constitute everyday life – newspapers, magazines, television programmes, films, web sites, books, letters. It is harder to choose not to hear the cacophony of sounds within which we live. Though we can and do block our recognition of much of what we hear, categorising it and choosing not to engage with it, we do hear it. In other words, as described above, we hear sounds that may have many different meanings. If we engaged actively with all of these meanings, we would live in a permanent state of auditory wonder and conceptual confusion. Instead, we automate many of our responses, though Welsch's point remains: we have no earlids.

For this reason Welsch is led to a conclusion about hearing that has only relatively recently been discussed among critical theorists, which is that we are most vulnerable acoustically. Where the visible enacts critical distance, the audible enacts connection. Like the editing in many films, or the crafted soundtrack, it works to suture us seamlessly into the everyday life of our society. However, it is also the semiotic system that has been least studied for its social and cultural meanings – as Theo van Leeuwen noted many years ago. At the banal level sound locks us into the life of a community *because* it enables us to perform everyday tasks such as navigating the streets. We are thereby constructed as contemporary urban subjects, our traversal of time/space determined by systems of traffic flow that are adjudged optimal for our society at a particular time/space. We are *subjected* to the bureaucratic control of our social space, and of us as individual subjects operating in that space. Implicit in this banal control of our time/space, however, is our complicity with particular political and ideological ideas and values. For van Leeuwen and many others the sounds of our society have long operated to suture us into ideological positions of which we are barely conscious. This may well occur via the functional sounds of traffic lights, warning sirens, aircraft overhead, cars in the street, people at play, televisions chattering. Or, it may be a function of the manipulation of musical sounds, with their acculturated meanings, in relation to specific set of ideas and values. In his book, *Speech, Music, Sound* (1999), for example, van Leeuwen examines the revision of the News theme of a publicly-funded national broadcaster, the Australian Broadcasting Corporation. In the acoustic changes to the theme, he locates a move away from (colonial) imperialism with its strong sense of hierarchical authority towards a sense of community, as well as an engagement with a discourse about the media that locates it as an important cultural and social agent within both domestic and public spheres (van Leeuwen 1999: 60–4). He concludes that these changes are reflected not only in the presentation of the news but in the broadcaster itself as it moved towards styles of programming and broadcasting more typical of commercial television and radio. The ideological and political motivations behind, and ramifications of, such a change are complex and far-reaching.

So, for many commentators at least since Adorno, sound has performed a crucial task in our construction as social subjects.

Murray Schafer made a similar point about moozak. By masking the everyday soundscape of that environment, Schafer argues, moozak constructs an acoustic environment that effectively deafens the customer or client. She or he is prevented from assessing that space by an acoustic environment that fictionalises it – inserting it within narratives of other times and places, evoking memory and myth to situate the individual within an acoustic/ conceptual environment that masks the purpose of that space and its activities (which is, usually, to sell things). The fact that moozak was installed widely with so little opposition indicates, for Schafer, our complacency about sound; we do not appreciate its potential to shape our lives.

On the other hand, Bull's argument about sound is that the individual stereo user is actively constructing a personal acoustic space under her or his control, within which the user can make decisions about her or his life. Tia DeNora makes a related point about some of her respondents' uses of music:

> Respondents described how they used music that they associated with the production of concentration and circumstances in which mental activity and focus were predominant. In short, music was used here to reproduce an aesthetic environment of 'working' and to circumscribe within that environment 'where the mind can go'. One literally stays tuned, through such practices, to a mode of concentrated focus, to the mental task at hand. (2000: 60)

For some workers, it seems, the random noise of a busy soundscape performs a similar function. The streetscape sounds somehow enable that worker to screen out all sound distractions – sounds she or he might otherwise have to listen to and engage with. However, we might suggest another function as well – which is that the acoustic experience of the streetscape weaves the worker into the fabric of everyday life. Bull likens this experience to Adorno's description of the function of the 'hit' song for the listener. In remembering the song, Adorno argues, the listener 'turns into the song's ideal subject' and, at the same time, identifies with all those others who have also identified themselves as the subjects of this song – the other fans. This eases the listener's feeling of isolation: 'In whistling such a song he bows to a ritual of socialisation, although beyond this unarticulated subjective stirring of the moment his isolation continues unchanged' (Adorno quoted in Bull, 2000: 131). There is a critical element in Adorno's description of this experience that we might question. If the acoustic experience situates the listener within a social, rather than an individual(ist), framework, this might be a way for the individual to create, through the soundscape in which she or he chooses to work, a sense of social connectedness that is appropriate to that work – or, more specifically, to the conceptual framework and individual consciousness she or he chooses to mobilise in relation to that work.

The space of sound   This scenario and the one on architecture and sound raise another issue that has yet to be considered, which is the 'space' of sound. The individual soundscapes of the previous scenario can be conceptualised as a space around the listener, whether it is the street-sound that engulfs the café worker, or the soundscape of the personal stereo user. Bull reports these responses of personal stereo users:

> [It fills] the space whilst you're walking ... It also changes the atmosphere as well ... (Sara: interview number 50) (Bull, 2000: 33)
>
> It's like looking through a one-way mirror. I'm looking at them but they can't see me. (Julie: interview number 12) (Bull, 2000: 77)
>
> Because I haven't got the external sort of noises around me I feel I'm in a bit of a world of my own because I can't really hear so much of what is going on around me. (Mandy: interview number 43) (Bull, 2000: 32)
>
> If I'm in a difficult situation or in new surroundings then I think nothing can affect you, you know. It's your space. (Paul: interview number 45) (Bull, 2000: 34)
>
> It fills the space whilst you're walking. (Rebecca: interview number 49) (Bull, 2000: 35)

There is a slippage in these formulations between space as a physical property and space as conceptual, which effectively deconstructs our understanding of space. Instead of space being seen as a natural property, waiting to be claimed or mapped, it is understood as created by the ways in which we constitute our world. We create space in order to map it, colonise it, own it. A most striking example of this occurred in Australia, when the country was colonised by the English. The English did not recognise the prior occupancy of the country by indigenous peoples and so they did not recognise this as an already occupied, socially- and culturally-shaped space. They constructed what later became 'Australia' as a geographic entity in the process of their occupancy, which they saw as colonisation. For indigenous peoples of Australia, on the other hand, for whom the country was not *terra nullius* but a rich and complex social, cultural, spiritual entity, the arrival of the English was an invasion. This invasion began the violent seizure of their land and the fundamental denial of indigenous rights and cultures. Indigenous 'space' was effectively nullified by the English and renamed English territory.

In other words, space is never simply material or geographic; it is always a social, cultural, political and spiritual construction.

In creating a personal soundscape for their work, then, café workers and personal stereo users are also creating space. This is a space that effectively maps for them a place within which they can operate. Here I am using the space/place distinction referred to by de Certeau and others; where 'space' refers to the institutionally created and sanctioned environments within a society. Alternatively, 'place' refers to the local, and sometimes individual, environments within those spaces that can operate as sites of resistance or of tactical evasion or withdrawal. Effectively, the individual expands or contracts the borders of their personal space – or 'place' – in order to create an environment within which they can live effectively. For many personal stereo users it means creating a place in which they feel protected from social surveillance, as described by respondent, Julie, in the quote above from Bull (2000).[6] In Julie's description the role of acoustic space in the management of her life is clear; it is, for her, a place of resistance against socialising forces, particularly the gaze of others. The significance of Julie's description for this argument is that she is not, actually, free of the gaze of others; they are looking at her just as much, or as little, as they have always done. However, within her own acoustic environment (place), Julie feels free of any need to constitute herself in response to those gazes. The change is in Julie, and it is generated by her constitution of a place for herself that she perceives as outside the social constraints generated by the (gendered, sexed, classed, ethnicised) gaze. Julie's place (acoustic space, her soundscape) is like all other space in that it is social, cultural, political, and spiritual. However, unlike social/ institutional space the personal space/place created by her use of the personal stereo is also under her control.

Sound deconstructs the nature of space by revealing it to be a conceptual construct used to colonize areas of the natural environment in the name of particular cultural, social, political and spiritual beliefs. Individuals may generate personal places within those mapped spaces, which are the sites of resistance against those beliefs. Sound is one means by which such sites are created.

7   Making music

This same individual negotiation of space/place can be seen in the production of soundscapes by people using the resources of contemporary information technology. For the young boy of my scenario, and for many others as well (as the success of Knapster attested) one of the joys of the technology is the access it provides to music on-line or via CDs played through their computer's CD drive. The huge success of the Apple iPod is further testament to the appeal of this technology. The iPod combines the use of a computer (to download music from a CD or DVD) with an external portable device (the iPod itself) that enables the users to store a vast sound library (equivalent up to 30,000 songs, depending on the model) that s/he is able to organize and play on demand (and note that recent iPods also store and display colour photographs). With freely available software young people are able to compile and burn CDs of their favourite songs, in the same way that their parents compiled party tapes. Yet, there is an added pleasure for these young users in their control of a sophisticated technology that is so inextricably networked into their lives. When their parents compiled tapes at the same age, they were manipulating a technology that functioned in their lives as an entertainment medium. When today's teens use their own personal computers to create their own compilation, they are using a technology that they also use for a variety of other purposes: watch films, do research for school projects, write their homework, chat on-line with friends, send e-mails, keep a weblog, find out film-times, check out their favourite films, songs, performers, sports, and so on. In responding to the convergence of uses offered by this technology, then, the young user enters into that technological space as an active and creative consumer. In other words, she or he is not simply positioned as a passive recipient of products offered via the technology, but as a creative user of that technology.

It might be argued that the young user is, nevertheless, only able to use the technology in already programmed ways. Yet, here it is possible to invoke again Michael Bull's extensive study of personal stereo use, *Sounding Out the City* (2000), and Tia DeNora's study, *Music in Everyday Life* (2000), to argue that the youthful disk burner is doing more than enacting a role generated by the technology. Instead, the user actively explores and constructs her or his own subjectivity, performs an identity, generates a personally-rewarding and comfortable acoustic space, networks her- or himself into a peer-group environment, and incidentally learns to use the technology in ways and for purposes for which it may not have been intended – and so effectively changes the (meanings of the) technology.

At least, this is the most positive reading of this activity; it can also be read as interpellating the user into the technological environment very effectively, by appealing to her or his sense of autonomy – an autonomy dependent on the technology itself. This is perhaps where this user needs not only the skill to design a product, place or environment, but also the ability to situate that creation – and her- or himself – in relation to contemporary society and cultures.

Sound ... signifying ...

As this set of everyday scenarios and their analysis demonstrates, sound plays a critical part in our everyday lives. It is one of the ways that we situate ourselves in the world; one of the ways we are. Accordingly we can analyse our construction of acoustic space, as well as the acoustics of our construction of space, in order to understand the discourses that operate in those spaces.

One of our major models for sound in multimedia is cinema, since this is the medium in which most of us experience the integration of sound with other semiotic systems, particularly the verbal and visual. And much of the most interesting thinking about sound has come from those involved in film, either as makers or critics.

Sound (design) for film

> 'Sound is 50 per cent of a film, at least. In some scenes it's almost 100 per cent. ... Sound is a great pull into a different world. And it has to work with the picture – but without it you've lost half the film. (David Lynch)[7]

Walter Murch described his vision of the role of sound designer for film as he discussed his work on the film, *Apocalypse Now*:

… that's where the use of the term 'sound designer' came from: I had worked out a conceptual and technical design for the sound of *Apocalypse* that involved graphs indicating all six channels,[8] and then three and then one, for both the sound effects and the music throughout the whole film, and how sound would evolve and change through the three-dimensional space of the theatre. … So there was a comprehensive design made in advance, thinking about what sound space might be right for each moment in the film. (2003: 97–8)

Murch describes a role for the sound designer that includes not just specific elements of the sound (music, sound effects, ambient sound, dialogue), but a comprehensive understanding of how these different elements might be integrated in an overall design for the film. And this design includes also an appreciation of changes in the acoustic space of the theatre, which means that the sound is different for audience members at different locations. As Randy Thom notes: 'Sound travels about 40 feet each millisecond, which roughly corresponds to a frame of 35mm film time. That means that in a typical movie theatre the sound is two frames later in the back of the room than it is in the front' (2003: 136). Murch's use of the multi-modal term 'sound space' signifies the comprehensiveness of the sound design process in which sound is not simply an illustration of the visuals or a way of creating mood or emotion, but a critical feature of the film's meaning-making. In his formulation the 'space' of the film includes the 'sound space'.

Randy Thom notes that Murch's vision is not generally realised in Hollywood where the sound designer is:

… a kind of hired gun who is brought in because he or she knows how to operate samplers and synthesizers and create rocket ship sounds and space alien vocalizations and that sort of thing, which the more conventional sound editors might not know how to do or might not have the tools to do. It certainly doesn't conform to what Walter imagined a sound designer could be when he invented the term. To him a sound designer was somebody who would guide the overall treatment of sound in the film, and that concept is pretty much unheard of in Hollywood. (2003: 122)

Thom records here the conventional practice of sound design, whereby various sound elements are allocated to different professionals – composer, foley artist, sound editor, sound designer – without any overall concept of how these different components will combine. As Murch notes: ' … there's a perennial cat-and-dog fight between the music and sound effects departments on almost every film' (2003: 86). Murch goes on to say that every film has moments where both music and sound effects believe they should dominate, but that the argument is usually resolved in favour of the music 'for various artistic, political and economic reasons' (2003: 86) Murch's set of reasons identifies the fundamental relationships that mobilise any textual practice. Sound is one of the meaning systems that operates within this network of constraints and possibilities.

The meanings of (film) sound

For our purposes it is important to locate the kinds of meanings (artistic and political) that sound brings to a text in order to understand how these meanings are enabled or silenced by the economic and political contexts within which the (film) text operates.

When we examined the way that visuals operated in a text, we located practices that were extrinsic and intrinsic – the former relating the text to its textual, social and cultural environment and the latter operating within the text as part of its meaning-making, both diegetic and extra-diegetic. We can do the same for sound. With film as our case study we can locate the ways in which the sound operates extrinsically – generically and intertextually to generate particular ideas, beliefs and feelings. And we can examine some of the intrinsic sound practices and how they also generate meanings that are part of the meanings of this text.

Contextual meanings and sound

The terms, generic and intertextual are again useful in locating the meanings of film sound. Anahid Kassabian notes in *Hearing Film* (2001) that classic Hollywood film music is 'a semiotic code' (2001: 36). Another way of understanding this is to say that classic Hollywood film music is a specific genre of music. As Kassabian argues for film music and we might argue for all film sound (as well as every other textual strategy), audiences learn the meanings of this genre by experience. There will still be individual differences in the interpretation of these meanings; however, the meanings of the particular strategies are, to some extent, predictable – just as a writer knows that particular language strategies are likely to be read in a particular way, or a visual artist knows that particular visual strategies are likely to make particular meanings for viewers. Randy Thom acknowledges this generic function of sound when he notes:

> ... in order to be a sound designer, you have to start thinking about sound as raw material. You have to forget about the way things really sound, or at least be able to forget about it for a while, and think about how this sound makes you feel. (2003: 126)

Thom's concern here is with the meanings of particular sounds and how they can work within a film. In generic terms, however, he describes the conventional function of film sound, which is not necessarily anything like 'real' sound. Audiences have a learned understanding of all film sound, which includes film music. When the *Star Trek* viewers of my opening paragraphs hear that 'ssshhhwiff' when watching the show, they know that somewhere on the starship, *Enterprise*, a door has opened – even as they also know that the doors on the sets did not automatically open at all. That 'ssshhhwiff' is not 'real' but a convention used to identify the diegetic world of the text as twenty-third century, and to locate the text within the genre of science fiction – specifically, through its focus on technology. In fact, the meaning of 'ssshhhwiff' is not 'door opening' so much as it is 'high technology' – and discursively this constitutes the text within a progressive episteme for which scientific development was both exciting and enlightening (in all senses of the term).

The 'ssshhhwiff' of *Star Trek* was one of the sounds that located the series within the genre of television science fiction. In the same way, other conventional sounds – or soundscapes – locate films within specific genres. For example, a layered, orchestral music score situates a film within the genre of Hollywood studio film. As soon as the audience hears the opening bars of John Williams's *Star Wars* score, they know they are watching a Hollywood studio film – whatever its (sub-)genre. That generic location enables them to predict the textual strategies and meanings they are likely to encounter: for example, the film is likely to have a happy ending or, at least, a satisfying resolution, since this is characteristic of the studio film. And the politics that enable those conventions are also familiar: for example, simplistic characterisations that identify heroes as 'good' and their opponents as 'evil', a conventional narrative structure that leads to the resolution of an initial problem encountered by the hero.

Kassabian contributes further to the analysis of film sound by identifying two different strategies in the scoring of the Hollywood film – which we can apply to a range of multimedia texts. She describes these in terms of audience response or identification as assimilating identifications and affiliating identifications. The assimilating identification is associated with the composed score – like Shore's score for *The Lord of the Rings*. Such scores 'draw perceivers into socially and historically unfamiliar positions, as do larger scale processes of assimilation' (Kassabian, 2001: 2). And she adds that these scores 'try to maintain fairly rigid control over such processes [of identification], even as – or because – they encourage unlikely identifications' (Kassabian, 2001: 2). The problem with such scoring is that of the suture: it can draw audience members so deeply into the diegetic world of the film that they lose their ability to assess critically the kinds of meanings being made – the film's politics or ethics. Though Kassabian focuses on music, it seems that her principle would extend here to all aspects of the sound – the sound effects that argue the (conditional) reality of an action or event, the vocal qualities that align us with particular characters and against others, the soundscape of a community that makes one society attractive and another repugnant. We might argue with the implied passivity of the audience, even whilst acknowledging that the film-makers have made sound choices in order to position their audiences in particular ways in relation to the characters and events in a film.

Kassabian also discusses affiliating identification, which she associates with compiled scores. She argues: 'These ties depend on histories forged outside the film scene, and they allow for a fair bit of mobility within it'. And she adds: 'If offers of assimilating identifications try to narrow the psychic field, then offers of affiliating identifications open it wide' (Kassabian, 2001: 3). In other words, by using music that audience members associate with other events or situations, the score foregrounds the intertextual practice, encouraging viewers to bring other (individual) associations to the film. So, for example, Kassabian discusses the role of popular music in *Thelma and Louise* as 'ground[ing] the entire narrative in the everyday' (2001: 81), rather than locating it as some sort of feminist fantasy. Audience members may be drawn into the narrative by their appreciation of a song yet, even as the song musically informs a particular event or character, the familiarity of the audience with the song in other contexts means that it cannot be contained by that event or character. For these reasons, Kassabian argues, 'affiliating identifications open outward' (2001: 141). So, for example, the use of Motown songs in the scoring of *The Big Chill* (1983) locates the time-frame within which the characters first met and formed their friendships. But those songs will mean different things to a range of audience members: they will recall a utopian period of social prosperity and political activism for many white 'baby boomers', but a time of intense political struggle for many black 'boomers', while many contemporary teen audiences would understand them in terms of nostalgia.

Kassabian argues that the compiled score is more likely to create a critical distance in audience members because it encourages their own input into the meanings of the music. However, we need to consider all aspects of the sound before deciding that this scoring is necessarily 'open'. For example, if the music reference is located within a soundscape that reinforces particular meanings, then it seems likely that members of the audience are more likely to hear those meanings as appropriate to their interpretation of the film rather than to import their own memories. Kassabian discusses the use of the Temptations' song, 'The Way You Do the Things You Do', in *Thelma and Louise*. This song is heard from the car radio as Thelma and Louise drive along the highway and the women sing along exuberantly, using the song to express their freedom, joy and friendship. Kassabian notes, however, that 'they cannot contain the meanings of the songs' (2001: 82). Thelma and Louise cannot, but perhaps the composer or sound designer can. In situating that song within a soundscape that includes the sounds of the car, of wide open spaces and of the women's voices, as well as the threatening sounds of the detective's search, then the meaning of the song is effectively narrowed for the audience. The song's erotic connotations are redirected by the soundscape (voices, car, wind, desert sounds) into an expression of their perceived freedom – of release from masculine authority and from the constraints of conventional heteronormative gendering and relationships. At the same time the soundscape also places that perception of freedom within the domain of an intrusive state authority that (despite the sympathetic response of the detective working their case) is working to re-contain them. When the sound design is considered, rather than the music alone, then the score seems less 'open' than Kassabian suggests. This does not deny the power of the musical reference to engage the audience with the text; it simply suggests that this reference text also performs a narrative function not so different from that of the composed score.

In her conclusion Kassabian notes that her argument suggests that affiliating identifications, which she associates with compiled scores, are 'more politically progressive or aesthetically innovative' (2001: 144). However, she also allows that the score is only one meaning-making element and may be working quite differently from other aspects of the film. As just one sound element, the score must be read in relation to other acoustic elements – just as images in a visual text must be read in relation to the layout or *mise-en-scène*. So, for example, the hobbit leitmotif is charming when played during the Hobbiton sequences in Jackson's *The Lord of the Rings* – and makes meanings about community, but striking when played during Frodo and Sam's final climb up Mount Doom – where it makes meanings about courage and fellowship. In some ways the purpose-driven nature of the score does not allow the plethora of possible associations of a compiled score. Yet, as already noted, some of the complaints about the *Lord of the Rings* films is that they used sound to situate the characters ethnically or racially – the hobbits as Irish or Celtic, the orcs as 'savages', non-Whites – which argues that even the composed score is read intertextually.

As Kassabian notes specifically of the score:

> Any score and its film can only play a probability game: in creating a set of conditions, some engagements are made more likely than others. But no matter what direction the score takes, toward assimilating or affiliating identifications, the process will not engage all perceivers. The score's offer will sometimes fail to be taken up. (2001: 143)

In locating the generic and intertextual associations of sound – including score, sound effects, voice – we map the probabilities the sound makes available to audiences. Further, we can identify in the use of sound the evocation of particular discourses that are part of the film's meanings and may either reinforce or contradict discourses generated by other textual elements such as the visuals. This study differs from Kassabian only in situating the score within the soundscape of the film in order to locate its meanings whilst acknowledging, as does she, that the score itself generates meanings.

Diegetic or intrinsic meanings: analytical terms

Having discussed the ways in which generic positioning and intertextual references of sound generate meanings about a text, it is useful to explore some of the specific features for what they may bring to a multimedia text.

In the scenarios with which I began this chapter I have already discussed at some length the possibilities created by vocal quality. Mike Figgis describes how he uses the 'pulse and musicality' of actors' voices to create the meanings of a scene (Figgis, 2003: 11–12), while Theo van Leeuwen gives us detailed commentary on how vocal qualities generate meanings (van Leeuwen, 1999). The relationship between voice and embodiment is another issue raised in the scenarios above – both by the role of actors such as Elijah Wood and by the automated voices discussed in other scenarios. Kaja Silverman discusses the role of the voice as a signifier of presence – and hence guarantor of meaning – in her book, *The Acoustic Mirror: The Female Voice in Psychoanalysis and Cinema* (1988). She quotes Charles Affron:

> Sound ... guarantees immediacy and presence in the system of absence that is cinema. Images that constantly remind us of the distance in time and space between their making and their viewing are charged, through voice, with the presence both that uttered words require for their transmission and that they lend to the viewing of the art. (Silverman, 1988: 43)

Silverman concludes: 'When the voice is identified in this way with presence, it is given the imaginary power to place not only sounds but meaning in the here and now. In other words, it is understood as closing the gap between signifier and signified' (1988: 43). So the voice of cinema exemplifies the logocentrism, with its metaphysics of presence, that Derrida has so eloquently deconstructed. Our acceptance of the authenticity of the speech act sutures us into the narrative constructed by the speaking subject; film instantiates that episteme by constituting its narrative through the speech of individual characters. Silverman notes: 'This emphasis upon diegetic speech acts helps to suture the viewer/listener into what Heath calls the "safe place of the story", and so to conceal the site of cinematic production. It is the sound analogue of the shot/reverse shot formation' (1988: 45).

This is particularly apparent in those texts that disrupt this identification of character and voice. Silverman discusses the exploration of 'talking pictures' in the film, *Singin' in the Rain* (1952), one plot line of which concerns a silent star, Lina (Jean Hagen) whose raucous voice is totally unsuited to her screen image. The film features a sequence in which different voices are dubbed onto her screen performance – destroying the verisimilitude of the character, and the actress's career. Silverman notes, however, that this deconstruction of the voice does not affect the rest of the film: 'the larger diegesis of *Singin' in the Rain* is at no point challenged, nor does its representational system falter for a moment. In effect, a "false" narrative structure gives way to the "true" one; the voice is returned to its rightful "owner" ... ' (Silverman, 1988: 47). By contrast, the John Sayles video of Bruce Springsteen's 'Born in the USA' disavows this conventional lip sync practice, drawing the viewer/listener's attention to the performance and to the words of his song.

Voice is a meaning system that utilises its aesthetic qualities in the generation of meaning in texts. And a critical part of its appeal in multimedia texts occurs when it occupies the same 'space' as a human actor. The effect of this on audiences is to suture them into the narrative in such a way that critical analysis or distance becomes very difficult. Yet, this can be deconstructed, as in the Springsteen/Sayles text.

Other sound strategies work in a similar way, aligning audiences with the narrative or distancing them from it. That identification is not necessarily naturalistic. For example, Michael Chion describes Tarkovsky's use of the sounds of breaking glass in a scene from *Solaris* (1972) in which the hero's 'wife' (the planet construct) swallows liquid oxygen. As he notes: 'We do not hear them as "wrong" or inappropriate sounds. Instead, they suggest that she is constituted of shards of ice; in a troubling, even terrifying way, they render both the creature's fragility and artificiality, and a sense of the precariousness of bodies' (Chion, 1994: 39). In this way, a sound that is diegetic, but not naturalistic, conveys a feeling – and a set of meanings – that are consistent with the narrative and the discourses it mobilises.

On many other occasions, of course, the aim is to be naturalistic – at least, in terms of cinematic realism. So we noted earlier, Randy Thom's description of the generic or conventional nature of film sound; that the sound designer works not (or not only) with the material properties of sound, but with the feelings aroused by particular sounds, which have been identified with particular situations and emotions by, among other things, their repeated use in cinema or other media. The film 'punch' sound is familiar to all viewers of Hollywood films, even if it bears little resemblance to the sound of a real life punch. Hearing that sound confirms the action we see, just as the actor's dubbed voice confirms the actor's image. Michel Chion refers to this union of sound and image as *synchresis* (Chion, 1994: 63).

One way of classifying sound in film is as diegetic (part of the soundscape of the story or plot) and non-diegetic (constituting the narrative that the story or plot illustrates or is an instance of). For example, if a character in a film throws himself through a window and falls to his death from a building, the sound of breaking glass is diegetic, but the music score that often accompanies the action, reflecting/creating the audience's response to the action, is non-diegetic. The importance of this categorisation is that it enables the audience member to consider how those different kinds of sounds situate him or her in relation to the story and its narrative. So, the breaking glass sound positions the audience to accept this action as 'real' within the story, while the accompanying score can be analysed for how it situates the audience to feel – sympathetic, scared, uncaring, enthralled. Whichever of these emotions is evoked tells us a lot about how this action works within the narrative; for example, whether this is a sympathetic character; whether the film has a caring attitude to humanity or whether some people are expendable; whether its morality is complex or quite simple (bad character = deserves to die).

There are many excellent recent texts that detail some of the different sound strategies used in film, and the ways they work to position audiences: for example, Elisabeth Weis and John Belton's collection *Film Sound: Theory and Practice* (1985), Claudia Gorbman's *Unheard Melodies: Narrative Film Music* (1987), Kaja Silverman's *The Acoustic Mirror* (1988), Kathryn Kalinak's *Settling the Score* (1992), David Schwarz, Anahid Kassabian and Lawrence Siegel's collection *Keeping Score: Music, Disciplinarity, Culture* (1997), Michel Chion's *Audio-Vision: Sound on Screen* (1994) and *The Voice in Cinema* (1999), Anahid Kassabian's *Hearing Film* (2001), and Larry Sider, Diane Freeman and Jerry Sider's collection *Soundscape* (2003). Each discusses some of the terminology – technical or critical – used to describe and discuss film sound. Each attempts to relate the technical features of sound with their discursive practice. They discuss, for example, the ways in which sound can be used to create continuity in a film, which performs the practical role of forwarding the narrative and the discursive task of constructing the philosophical basis on which this vector rests. Rather than try to compress all of these different critical terms and debates into a few pages (even if that could be done), I want to finish this section by restating the point that multimedia sound comprises all of the sound in a particular text – the music, sound effects, vocal quality and voice – and how they interact. The final section of this chapter is an analysis of sound in the opening scenes of a film, *The Day the Earth Stood Still* (1951).

Sound analysis: *The Day the Earth Stood Still*

This analysis, conducted with a colleague, Dr Mary Macken-Horarik, focused on the sound design of the film and how the different sound elements – score by Bernard Hermann, sound effects (including special effects and everyday sounds), and vocal quality – worked together to create the soundscape of the film.

Background and story

The Day the Earth Stood Still (1951) is a science fiction 'classic'. It is an interesting film for the period, not least because its major alien figure, Klaatu (Michael Rennie), is presented not as combative and imperialistic but as peace-making. It is the conflict-ridden Earth that is presented as the potential predator – an unusual story in a Cold War film. *The Day the Earth Stood Still* satirises the paranoia of the McCarthyite USA, yet it employs the paranoia-making threat of massive weaponry (which arguably produced the McCarthyism in the first place) to argue its point.

The sexual politics of the movie is also very interesting. A romance sub-plot is characteristic of science-fiction, but in this film the romance between Klaatu and widow, Mrs Benson (Patricia Neale), is not consummated. Klaatu eventually returns to his own planet, leaving Mrs Benson alone – a remarkably autonomous and courageous woman, particularly for a 1950s film. The sad but loving final glance between Klaatu and Mrs Benson is the space of a desire for a life not confounded by (McCarthyite) paranoia and the violence to which it leads – the violence that led to Klaatu's shooting and that means he must now return to his own planet in order to survive the attack.

Analysis: opening scenes

We analysed a number of sequences of the film, including the opening scenes. To do so, we mapped the interaction of visual and verbal text with the sound (see Appendix). In these scenes we encounter all of the sonic elements that characterise *The Day the Earth Stood Still*:

1   *Score*: Bernard Hermann's score includes the use of the theremin which had been used in film to signify either psychological strangeness or threat (as in *Spellbound* (1945), *The Spiral Staircase* (1946)) or otherworldliness (*It Came from Outer Space* (1953), *Forbidden Planet* (1956), *Rocketship X-M* (1950)).[9] Here it serves both purposes, signifying Klaatu's extra-terrestial origins as well as the threat posed by Gort to Earth – which, metonymically, indicates the threat Earth poses to itself through its disharmony. In the opening scenes the score carries both meanings, with the threat mainly located at the site of the spaceship and embodied by Gort.

2   *Voice*: is used to generate many different meanings in these opening scenes. The flattened affect in the voices of the military and the bureaucrat, Mr Harley, contrasts with the controlled affect of radio announcers, and the excitement of the man in the street calling that 'They've landed'. Klaatu's cultivated, resonant voice contrasts with these, and also with the voices of Bobby and the landlady – so that the landlady identifies him as from New England (that is, cultivated, upper class). Klaatu's voice locates him, contradictorily, as the civilised being compared with the less cultivated voices of everyday folk and the controlled voices of the military and media professionals – which suggest repressed panic.

3   *Sound effects*: the saucer sounds and the 'zip' noise of Gort's laser locate Klaatu, Gort and the spaceship as extra-terrestrial. However, it was notable that the pitch of these sounds verged towards the (higher) limits of human hearing – which is conventionally associated with 'sublime or superhuman events' (Schafer quoted in van Leeuwen, 1999: 109). While this might indicate the need for fear, it might also suggest great good. The exception here is the Gort theme, which utilises the low pitch commonly used to signify threat and also great power.

4   *Everyday, diegetic sound*: the sounds associated with human (US) society are of weaponry and military mobilisation (opening scene), ambient noise (the hospital), media commentary (the Washington street), ambient home noise (the boarding house).

The interrelation of these sound elements generates a set of meanings: human society is warlike and aggressive, extra-terrestrials are cultivated and civil, extra-terrestrials are powerful and threatening, human society is liable to panic and fear, and to irrational responses. The contradictions inherent in this set of meanings (Which is more threatening – extra-terrestrial power or human fear and irrationality? Who is more civilised – the affect-flattened military and bureaucrats and controlled panic of the media or the cultivated (New England accented) extra-terrestrial?) create the basis for the narrative to follow, with its exploration of human paranoia and aggressiveness.

This simple analysis showed that the sound can be considered as a design, not a set of separate elements – illustrating Walter Murch's original conception of the role of the sound designer. So, each element could be considered separately for the meanings it generated – the score and its use of the theremin, vocal qualities of the characters and broadcasts heard by the audience, special effects, and everyday, diegetic sounds – and this was achieved by noting its generic and intertextual significance and meanings. However, their narrative significance in these scenes of *The Day the Earth Stood Still* can only be understood by interrelating them. And even then, as many of the writers discussed above have noted, what results is a set of possibilities, dependent on audience familiarity with the different sound elements and their history and uses. When those generic and intertextual meanings are traced, then the sets of possible meanings generated can be located – and their discursive significance discussed. In this film this analysis identified a discursively complex text that fundamentally contradicted the basic proposition of its time – that Western society is the benchmark of civil behaviour and anything outside (non-Western, extra-terrestrial) is inferior.

The multimedia soundscape

The argument of this chapter is that sound should be understood and analysed discursively for its role in the meaning-making practice of multimedia texts – just as the previous chapter argued for the analysis of visuals. This echoes the argument made by Anahid Kassabian about Hollywood scores in *Hearing Film* (2001) that 'classical Hollywood film music is a semiotic code, and ... it can and should be subjected to various semiotic and cultural studies methods, such as discourse analysis and ideology critique' (Kassabian, 2001: 36). The chapter opened with a series of sound scenarios in order to introduce the notion that sound is not only pervasive in our lives, but also that we engage with it in ways that are not simply random and individual. Instead, sound – including music – is perceived by us in culturally and historically specific ways. In other words, all sound is perceived in terms of semiotic codes that we can mobilise to generate particular meanings – or, at least, the possibility of particular meanings. And accordingly, all sound can be analysed for the discourses it introduces into a particular text and/or soundscape. Sometimes this is a soundscape largely designed by the individual listener – as in the case of the walkman wearer or the worker who chooses to work in a public space; at other times, it is the design of a film-maker who works to engage an audience with a particular story and narrative; or it may be the operator of a web site who wants to sell to, or inform or entertain a user. In each case we can explore this sound discursively for the kinds of meanings it offers the audience/user/listener and for how it (potentially) positions her or him (or how the user positions her- or himself) in relation to particular ideas, attitudes, beliefs and feelings.

The next chapter takes up the complex issue of movement and how it, too, can be read both as intrinsically meaningful (in a particular text) and as discursively meaning-making. And in order to explore these meanings I look at both the historical development of our understanding of movement, its textual construction, and its significance in a range of contexts and practices, including embodiment, web sites and modes of knowledge formation.

Notes

1 The exhibition, *The Art of Star Wars*, held at the Barbican in London (2001) included a very funny sequence of bloopers in which R2D2 fell over, ran into walls, tripped through doorways, along with Lucas's discussion of the ambulatory problems with the character.

2 The cyborg creatures from the early BBC science fiction series, *Doctor Who*. The daleks were a combination of organic and machine – a physically-degenerated humanoid creature housed in a metal shell.

3 A similar example in a different semiotic system (movement) occurs in the science fiction film, *Silent Running*, in which the small 'droids, Huey, Luey and Dewey stump around the spaceship like toddlers taking their first steps. When one has his/its foot caught as a section of the ship is about to be destroyed, the frantic forward and backward movements he/it uses to try to free him/itself are deeply affecting – because they are so like the movements of a distressed child.

4 Michael Chion names *Star Wars* as one of the three most influential films of the 1970s and 1980s in relation to sound. He notes the references in the film to *The Wizard of Oz*: for example, noting C3PO's similarity to the Tin Man – and he characterises R2D2 as Toto, the dog. This seems to me to underestimate R2D2's popularity. Whilst Toto, and their own dog, does fill the role of imaginary friend for many children, R2D2's abilities go far beyond this. He is, in fact, the only character who appears intact through all five *Star Wars* films and he takes a major role in all of them. So he, and his characteristic sound (which I would think has the status of what Murray Schafer calls 'a soundmark') have a role and power in the films that Chion's assessment doesn't capture.

5 This vision is very similar to that proposed by Kress in his article on the growing dominance of the visual (1997). Kress argues that design must replace critique as a dominant mode of thought and production.

6 Bull gives many other examples of this use of the stereo, see particularly Bull, 2000, pp. 73–8. See also Tia DeNora, *Music in Everyday Life* (2000).

7 David Lynch, 'Action and Reaction', a video interview, in *Soundscape: The School of Sound Lectures, 1998–2001*, ed. Larry Sider, Diane Freeman and Jerry Sider (London and New York: Wallflower Press, 2003), pp. 49–53.

8 Murch is referring here to the standard 5.1 sound for films: ' … three channels of sound behind the screen (left, centre, right), two channels behind the audience (left back, right back); and one non-directional track of super low frequencies (15–60hz). That last track is the ".1" of the 5.1 because it contains so little audio information.' (2003: 97)

9 Philip Hayward, 'Danger! Retro-Affectivity! The Cultural Career of the Theremin' in *Convergence: The Journal of Research into New Media Technologies,* Vol. 3, No. 4 (1997), 38.

FIVE

MOVEMENT

' … to boldly go where no man has gone, before … '

While these words were spoken by an unseen narrator, the starship, *Enterprise*, flashed across television screens in the late 1960s. The movement of the starship established the trajectory of the story – beyond, to the stars – before we saw a character or experienced an event. The movement itself was meaningful, and the final vector – left to right, lower to upper screen – established a sense of exuberance, thrust, progress, characteristic of the 'space race' era.

Consider the meanings of this opening sequence if the starship had ended following a different vector – right to left, upper to lower screen. The meaning of the sequence would be quite different; the tone established would be down, in both physical and metaphorical senses. The *Enterprise* would seem to be nose-diving and there would be a sense of closure, if not disaster. Further, the movement would seem to be 'back' to the past, rather than exuberantly forward into the future.

And note, also, that this is a specifically Western reading of the *Enterprise*'s movement. Like the other modes of communication already discussed – written, visual, aural – movement is both meaningful and culturally-located. As students of body language and of kinesics attest, much of the meaning in human communication is conveyed by the movements of speakers and listeners (for example, Axtell, 1991; Neill and Caswell, 1993). Multimedia texts, too, utilise movement in making meaning – and sometimes that includes the movements of those interacting with them. Furthermore, information technology has a particular relationship with movement because of the use of movement metaphors to explain its practice and their implication in our understanding of knowledge formation.

Movement and speed: conceptualising technology

Gilles Deleuze entitled his first book about cinema, *Cinema 1: The Movement-Image* (1986) because the characteristic, and shocking, feature of early cinema was the movement of the image. Early cinema confronted viewers with the movement, the motility, of life in a way that other art-forms could not. English artist, J.M.W. Turner, attempted to do the same thing in his painting, *Rain, Steam, and Speed – The Great Western Railway* (1844), of which Jack Lindsay writes:

> Turner wants above all to catch and define Speed, which means also expressing time as a crucial aspect of a violently changing world. The impetus of the engine is brought out by making the engine darker in tone, sharper in edge, than anything else, so that it rushes out in aerial perspective ahead of its place in linear perspective. He uses the intermingling or superimposition of different moments to define a direction in time as well as a pattern of tensional movements in space. (1985: 150)

As Lindsay notes, Turner's painting captures the critical feature of the Industrial Revolution, its re-definition of time (as a measure of (labour-) power, as linear). Further, it represents the perception of inexorable speed that both excited and frightened the people of the early to mid-nineteenth century.

Over a half-century later, at the beginning of the twentieth century, the Futurists breathlessly recorded their fascination with that perception of speed. Gino Severini in his 'The Plastic Analogies of Dynamism – Futurist Manifesto 1913' wrote:

> Indeed, one of the effects of science, which has transformed our sensibility and which has led to the majority of our Futurist truths, is *speed*.
>
> Speed has given us a new conception of space and time, and consequently of life itself; and so it is perfectly reasonable for our Futurist works to *characterize* the art of our epoch with the *stylization of movement* which is one of the most immediate manifestations of life. (1973: 124–5, italics in original)

Futurist art captures not only the perception of movement but also the way in which that movement is incrementally produced. So Braggaglia's *Young Man Rocking* (1911) represents the rocking motion through the painted image of a head in motion, the motion represented as a series of blurred, superimposed images – like a photograph in which the shutter speed is too slow to capture the motion. Balla's paintings, *Dynamism of a Dog on a Leash* (1912), *Little Girl Running on a Balcony* (1912), and *Violinist's Hands* (1912), all use the same technique.

These Futurist paintings can be seen as painterly responses to the time-lapse photography of the late nineteenth century, produced by photographers such as E.J. Marey and Eadweard Muybridge. These nineteenth-century photographic images made visible what had never before been visible, creating a new understanding of movement. However, this technique also constructed motion in a particular way, as a series of incremental movements. This was an artefact of the technology available; yet it became our understanding of movement. It was different from Turner's image of the train, rushing like a demon through the darkness. In the later nineteenth-century photography and in many of the early twentieth-century Futurist paintings movement has been tamed: reconstituted as scientific observation or controlled aesthetic form.

In the late twentieth and early twenty-first century we are once again dealing with new technology, or technologies. The industrial revolution of the early nineteenth century was based on steam power. The power of the steam engine – whether a train or a factory machine – radically altered Western society, consolidating the power of the bourgeoisie and changing communal structures that had been in operation for centuries. People became *mobile* for the first time – leaving their traditional communities to find work; *moving* from one class to another as their work practice and wealth changed; sometimes leaving one country for another in order to live in this new industrial society. Movement was not simply a matter of embodied motion; it informed our understanding of social life as class allegiance, nationality, community and cultural identities all became *mobile*.

In the late twentieth century the dimensions of identity (such as class, ethnicity, gender, sexuality) became mobile – to such an extent, in fact, that the notion of identity itself came under erasure. Identity was seen as implying stability – a lack of movement, or mobility – that was no longer credible. Many of the metaphors used throughout the twentieth century for the individual subject – from the *flâneur* of the early twentieth century to the nomad of the late twentieth century – were based on the concept of movement. The *flâneur* traversed the early modern city, experiencing life as an individual citizen of an industrial society, located within a nation-state that was constantly re-defining its identity within the world community. The nomad of the late twentieth century, on the other hand, experienced life as a series of encounters with individuals, communities, cultures, institutions and corporations. This ongoing process of negotiation, and of re-formation, constitutes theindividual subject(ivity). This is a subject in the constant process of becoming, and that becoming is conceptualised not only in movement but also *as* movement.

In the early twenty-first century speed and movement have the same conceptual and erotic charge that they had for Severini and the Futurists. Information and communication technologies are rated by their speed of product delivery – the speed of a modem, of uploads, of web site loading and function. When Paul Virilio writes of the popular press's conception that '*speed is information itself*' (1995: 140, italics in original), he records the late twentieth and early twenty-first century fascination with both speed and information. Quoting Philippe Breton, Virilio recalls 'the relative definition of speed: "*Speed is not a phenomenon, it is the relationship between phenomena*" so that "*the reality of information is entirely contained in the speed of its dissemination*". And so INFORMATION (matter's third dimension) is only ever "*the designation of the state a phenomenon assumes at a given moment*"' (Virilio, 1995: 140, italics in original). The fluidity of this model recalls Turner's demon-engine rather than the incremental vision of the Futurists or the factory-clock of Fritz Lang's *Metropolis* (1926) (see Figure 5.1).

As Virilio suggests, information is a moment in the history of a phenomenon, frozen in space-time for the user's/researcher's study, transfixed in the web of associations that constitute the phenomenon at that particular moment. And speed is the means by which that moment is accessed, whereby it might be argued that speed itself constitutes information. Virilio's conception of information as movement is given imaginative form in the onanistic rhetoric

FIGURE 5.1   Fritz Lang (dir.) *Metropolis* (1926), viewed at http://www.
celtoslavica.de/chiaroscuro/films/metropolis/metro.html

of William Gibson's *Neuromancer* (1986). In that book Case, the main character, describes his journeys through cyberspace in terms of movement and speed – metaphors that have shaped the popular understanding of information technology.

Case creates a new perception of embodiment, the individual subject in union with technology, given access to the power of the machine. From the Futurists to Case, the dream of cyborg union with the machine has involved the perception of movement – through real or virtual space. The individual melded with the machine in an impossible, transgressive, wildly erotic coupling. For Marinetti, the union is with the car: 'We went up to the three snorting beasts to lay amorous hands on their torrid breasts' (Marinetti, 1973: 20). For Case, it means being physically jacked into the console of a computer. And in both cases the physical union of human with machine results in the sensory, and sensual, perception of movement – through geographical or cyber space.

Information technology is embedded in and saturated with metaphors of movement. This chapter traces the role of these metaphors, as well as the related notion of speed, in our use of this technology. Further, it considers how movement functions – as an on-screen presence, as a metaphor for access to successive units of information, and as a habit of the body of the user.

Speed and power

For many involved in the contemporary information and communication industries, speed has taken on the character of a fetish, often controlling the way a function or service is conceptualised – without reference to the users or clients for whom the function or service is intended. To give an everyday example: an on-line transport directory for bus travel in New South Wales provides users with journey information. The user must log in the street addresses of departure and destination and the destination time required; a route is provided, including directions to the nearest bus stop. However, no provision is made for the user who wishes simply to browse the timetable. Without knowing the background to the web site design, it seems that the designer has been entranced by a technology that enables the kind of mapping the site performs. Whilst this may be very useful in some situations, the low tech option of perusing a timetable, which is arguably more useful to regular travellers, is not available on the site. The point here is that the operational speed of the technology – which enables the more complex mapping function – has enthralled the designer, to the extent that she or he has ignored the needs of users/clients.

A colleague who works in the IT industry provided another example. He is enrolled in a Master of Business in Technology course and related the following anecdote. The major topic for his seminar group one week was the role of new technologies in enabling businesses to cater to users/clients. His fellow students were very impressed by the technical capabilities of the technology and talked enthusiastically about the fact that they could design cars that were tailored to the needs of individual clients. So, rather than simply having production lines of similar vehicles, production lines could be set up to customise the car to the client. They envisaged this as cars that incorporated specific features from a range of current vehicles – perhaps the engine of a BMW with the body of a Mercedes and the inside cabinetry of a Jaguar. But, my friend argued, you need to ask why clients want a particular car in the first place. Most BMW or Jaguar or Mercedes owners do not buy their cars primarily for the engineering. They buy those cars because of the status associated with them – because of the other people who also drive them. By driving those cars they become *de facto* members of that privileged and successful group. A car that is a hybrid of many different cars, with the distinguishing features of none, would not enable this kind of identification and so might have no attraction for buyers. Yet, my friend could not get his points across to this seminar group – that cars are not technical but cultural artefacts and that their meanings for most drivers are cultural, not technical. For my friend, this refusal to discuss the cultural meanings of products was indicative of many of the attitudes he has encountered in the IT industry, which he hears expressed as the 'stupid user' phenomenon. This is an industry term for the user who cannot understand how to use a web site or other multimedia text. It has not occurred to many to consider that the fault may be with the design of the site or product. In attempting to understand this attitude my friend was led to the conclusion that it is an expression of an ideology of power; that the power of the technology in terms of its speed of information processing and the options that speed makes possible in a range of exchanges (goods, services, information) may blind its designers/operators to the actual wishes and needs of the users with whom they engage.

In terms of the above argument, what he encountered was the erotics of speed represented first by Turner and later by the Futurists. He described it as an ideology because of its function in obscuring the user's real (that is, cultural) interaction with the technology and the possibilities it makes available.

A recent film about the power of technology and its potential problems, *Minority Report* (2002) dramatises many of these issues. In the story the hero, Detective John Anderton (Tom Cruise), needs to move incognito through the city. He is thwarted in this by the fact that every time he passes a department store, the store's computer recognises him by his iris print and publicly addresses him – telling him about recent products he may wish to purchase (presumably based on his pattern of purchasing). As a plot element this creates enormous tension as the character is constantly afraid of being recognised and/or traced; in the story the incident demonstrates the way that IT has pervaded the lives of citizens so that they have no privacy. For contemporary audiences this incident provokes both humour and concern. Audiences exhibit the wry humour discussed in the previous chapter that is also a concern about the use of technology (the issue discussed in the story). However, it can also be read as dramatising contemporary concerns that our use of information technology is prompted by this ideology of power (the fascination with speed, its erotics as well as its actual capabilities) rather than by an understanding of how this technology is situated in the everyday lives of citizens and of the community – that is, that there is a failure of vision about how technology is and can be incorporated into individual and community life as part of its cultural matrix. Instead, there is a fascination with power, speed and, ultimately, information that leads to such disastrous events as the development of nuclear weaponry; Oppenheimer's quotation 'I am become Death; the destroyer of worlds' rings out anew.

Movement and knowledge

We commonly talk about 'being moved' by something or someone. This usually indicates a combination of emotional response ('I was so moved, I cried') and grounded analysis. It is an embodied response, involving conceptual thought, the relationship of ideas to the individual subject's own life experience, and a subsequent corporeal response with an empathic element. And it is often these moving experiences that individuals credit with changing their lives; Saul's fall from his horse – the moment of epiphany. The experience is said to shift one's perspective on life (another movement metaphor) and, in the process, to create new knowledge.

So can we associate physical movement with the creation of knowledge? The notion of 'being moved' focuses our attention on the embodied nature of the apprehension of ideas; that is, on the fact that the conceptual thinking does not occur in some kind of disembodied state. Instead, the focus is on the notion of 'being' where that being is physical or corporeal and so is situated in space-time as an acculturated social subject. This makes the point that ideas are not experienced in some sort of decontextualised, ahistorical, asocial realm, but that ideas or information are processed into knowledge by the individual in a particular context, at a specific location, with particular socio-cultural characteristics. So movement is a physical correlate of, as well as metaphor for, the transformation from the old to the new state of being that incorporates this knowledge: 'I (the old me) was moved (to a new me) by witnessing that event or hearing that story'.

In terms of subjectivity, this perception of movement translates as: an embodied subject with a specific sociocultural positioning, incorporating particular ideas, beliefs, values and ways of acting, being, thinking and knowing has become a different embodied subject with virtually the same sociocultural positioning, but incorporating different ideas, beliefs, values and ways of acting, being, thinking and knowing.

In relation to multimedia, we might consider how this understanding of movement and its role in our understanding of subjectivity features on the desktop or other multimedia text. One starting point is movement at and around the interface: movement on the interface that is a feature of either the particular text itself or of the processing of the text by the user; movement between screens that is a particular feature of the technology; movements of the user – bodily and conceptual.

Moving parts

The only visible moving part to most personal computers is the cursor – and it is not a mechanical part but a representation of the possibility of interaction with the user. Still it moves. Blinking on and off the cursor invites the user to interact with the technology. Yet, even that basic movement needs to be understood to be meaningful. I was given my first computer by the Head of Department when I started my first full-time university position. 'Here,' he said, 'you might as well have this. Every time I try to use it, this little blinking thing comes on and no matter what I try, I can't get rid of it.' To my eternal shame I said nothing and gratefully accepted my first computer. I think that, at the time, I could not quite believe he was saying what he was saying – which was that he really was trying to turn off the cursor. Yet, without a reason for that insistent movement, there is no value in that 'little blinking thing'. Essentially the cursor is just movement; it has no other textual content. It indicates on/off, engaged/disengaged – which is its purpose. If the user does not understand that meaning, however, its purpose is unclear and it can appear simply a distraction or worse; it might read as a blinking warning light, telling the user something is wrong – or needs to be done. My long-suffering Head of Department was reading it that way.

The term, cursor, was familiar to some people from the slide-rule. It was the transparent slide with the thin line that revealed your answer after you had performed various bizarre manipulations of the rule. In that apparatus, the cursor was the point of interface between the user and the (calculating) machine. The blinking line on the contemporary computer screen fulfils the same symbolic function. It informs the user where she or he is on the page – that is, in the process of the interaction – and it serves always to express the potential for the user to interact. The slide-rule cursor did not move under its own accord, of course; it was moved up and down the slide-rule by the user as part of the calculation. This mechanical movement on the part of the user was an essential part of the calculation process, and functioned as a kind of *synecdoche* for the calculation itself.

The computer-screen cursor can be manipulated by the user, too, in that she or he can use a mouse, touch-pad or directional buttons to change its position. However, when not directly addressed by the user, the cursor continues to 'mean' by moving. And, of course, it is not literally moving. Like so much IT-related movement, there is no motion; the movement is metaphorical. The cursor is a line that appears and disappears, according to installed software. Visually, this logic of presence/absence, on/off, appearance/disappearance both attracts attention and conveys movement. Its on/off dis/appearance disrupts the continuity of the screen space for users and so attracts the user's attention. Simultaneously, both through the eye movement it attracts from users and the implied movement of presence/absence (a kind of digital *fort/da*) the cursor is, at base, an exertion (or not) of energy – which is also the essence of action. So the perceived movement of the cursor, which may be mechanically altered by the user's own movements, invites corresponding movement or exertion in the user. For the uninformed user, who interprets it via other technologies, the action invited is eradication; do something to turn it off permanently. For the informed user, the action that is invited is engagement with the technology.

Moving text

Unlike other technologies such as film, most computer-generated texts such as web sites are relatively static. This may be an artefact of the state of development of this technology – like silent movies before audio technology was sufficiently sophisticated to enable movies to 'talk'. There have been some attempts to develop software that enabled movement, 'Flash' being the most obvious. The use of 'Flash' is an example of the fascination with the technology discussed above. After its initial release many designers were enthralled by Flash and virtually all new web sites featured Flash components – which users mostly hated. The reason users responded badly included basic issues such as: many users didn't have Flash and so had to download it before being able to access the site; because of its size the download took a long time for many computers and was inappropriate for many machines – which made the site inaccessible or relatively useless for many users; the movement it enabled added nothing of any meaning to the site for users. The result was that many users reported simply skipping sites that used Flash.

Designers obviously took on board the criticism from users, so that movement on most contemporary sites is minimal. And when movement is used, there seems to be an attempt to give it a function, from the perspective of the user. For example, some advertising uses animation, but it tends to be minimal and related conceptually either to the product or to the medium. So, for example, on a web site for Thomas Cook Clothing (Australia), the page that features wet-weather gear has a small green frog hop across the page (as a sound effect of thunder and rain plays). This is a fairly obvious and literal use of graphics and movement, but it has interesting cultural connotations because of the role of the green tree frog in mapping environmental degradation. Because the disappearance of the frog has been used to monitor pollution levels in the environment (often from spraying of pesticides), the frog took on the role of 'green' signifier; a bit of a hero for the environment movement. When it hops across the screen, therefore, the frog carries with it, virtually subliminally, accrued cultural meanings that add positive value to the page content. Its hopping motion, which is cartoon-like rather than realistic, draws attention to it and activates its feel-good associations. At the same time its appearance does not seem openly tokenistic as there is a real-life context for it – our association of thunder, rain, water and puddles with frogs. So the movement here is associated with the product advertised: we need wet weather gear to go out in the rain that is a natural environment for frogs.

In his essay, 'Gestures in TypeSpace', Bob Aufuldish writes about his typography course, TypeSpace, that explores the typographer's use of gesture: 'By "gesture", we mean the movement of the letter(s) or words in space and time in the pursuit of transferring meaning' (2001: 49). Aufuldish explains the aims of the course: 'We encourage the students to physically act out the gestures they want their letterforms to have and then try transferring those gestures to animation' (2001: 49). And he gives as a beautiful example one student's animation of the name, Ahab from Melville's *Moby Dick*: '... the "Aha" moved forward smoothly, and the "b" trailed behind, complete with scraping sound, to express how Ahab's wooden leg – severed by Moby Dick – had permanently altered Ahab's gait ...' (Aufuldish, 2001: 49). Aufuldish's critical association of movement with meaning is the key to this enterprise. The student's animation of Ahab not only captures the physical reality of walking with an artificial limb (in fact, Ahab's false leg is not made of wood, but carved from whalebone!), but also expresses Ahab's loss of (mental) balance that leads to his obsessive pursuit of the white whale. So the meaning the student transferred with this animation was not simply a literal transcription of Ahab's physical disability, but refers to the characterisation of Ahab himself – and to the analysis of obsession that is central to Melville's book. This is a more profound example of the use of movement than the simple frog animation described above, but both have a place in the creation of a multimedia text.

At other times, the movement is associated generically with advertising. Movement may be used to attract the user's attention to an advertisement even when there is little association between the product or service and the movement shown. As contemporary consumers, users are used to processing such attention-grabbing movement, which seems problematic only when it interferes with the user's scan of the page (as with early Flash designs). When movement is contained within a frame that does not obscure the main content of the page, users seem tolerant of the application. And some users may enjoy the liveliness (animation!) it brings to a page that might otherwise be visually boring – as many portal sites are.

As noted earlier, web sites currently feature minimal textual movement, for reasons that may be primarily technical. Other multimedia texts, that do not have the same technical constraints, employ movement more fully. Museum exhibitions and art installations, for example, employ movement as a central element in their meaning-making. At the National Museum of Australia in Canberra a very different kind of textual movement takes place in one of the first exhibits that the visitor encounters inside the building. The National Museum of Australia takes the initiative on the matter of visitor positioning via the installation, *circa*. This installation consists of a revolving platform of seats that turns the visitor to face sets of screens showing images of Australia, while listening to a highly affective discourse about Australian identity. At the end of this journey of identity formation, the visitor is deposited at the entrance to the Exhibition halls – primed to experience the different exhibits as examples of Australia in the making.

The images in the *circa* installation are affecting and beautiful. They show the beauty and power of the land itself and the diversity of the Australian community, combined as a unique historical and geopolitical entity. The accompanying voice-over constructs the viewer within an Australia at its highest potential – with the power and possibility to achieve a genuinely diverse and cooperative community. It does not, unsurprisingly, discuss the bloody history of Australian White settlement, the ongoing issues of inequity for indigenous Australians, or other endemic problems of injustice related to indigenous Australians or the treatment of refugees. And, it might be argued that it would be unrealistic to expect any national museum to begin by spelling out a society's problems and differences (though interestingly the Garden of Australian Dreams, which occupies the forecourt and that some visitors do visit before they enter the Museum, does just that).[1]

The technology of the installation is interesting. While the use of video screens and soundtracks is contemporary and very familiar (given the use of such large screens in shopping malls, train stations, etc., as well as the everyday experience of television), the experience of being shunted around on a moving platform is almost quaint. It recalls two earlier visual technologies: the eighteenth-century panorama which used life-size painted scenes to give the viewer a sense of being in a particular place and time, and the nineteenth-century diorama where the visitor was seated in darkness and shown a series of illuminated watercolours. And there is a sense of the fairground about it as well – the merry-go-round or mystery ride – which intensifies the old-fashioned feel of the experience. At the same time, the layering of sound and the intensity of the visual imagery makes this an experience of the video age, engaging aural and visual senses. This sensory engagement is accompanied by movement, the kind of involuntary movement of the fairground ride (though not as fast as most!). Perhaps the critical notion here is that the movement is essentially involuntary; the visitor is moved as and when the moving platform dictates and not at her or his own volition. And the movement is not only physical, but also emotional and conceptual. The sensuous beauty of the images and the affective narrative that accompanies them are designed to 'move' the visitor in every sense of the term. So, in occupying the movable platform, the *circa* visitor has ceded some control to the museum, which then orients the visitor – metaphorically as well as literally – to the exhibits.

The visitor is multiply engaged by the experience of *circa* to consider the role of the exhibits as part of the composition of Australian nationhood; that is, as part of the fantasy that is contemporary nationhood. The patent fabrication of the experience – the old-fashioned ride, the audio-visual commercial for nationhood – is simultaneously affecting and deconstructive. In the most literal sense it demonstrates the imaginary community of contemporary Australia – robust, happy, working together to make a community. At the same time it demonstrates the myth-making process in action: a series of beautiful images, cleverly composed, accompanied by an interpersonally-loaded soundtrack. Nationhood and community are constructed using contemporary technologies. The visitor is ushered through a doorway into the museum proper to engage further with the process of constructing a nation – and for some visitors *circa*, with its multiple movement(s), prepares them to be critical viewers.

Directed movement

Another kind of textual movement involves vectors that are built into the site, to guide users in either accessing or processing the site. These vectors may be either confined to a particular page, or move the user between pages. In this set of movements the relation between movement as physical and as conceptual is evident. In directing the user from one point to another – from the representation of one phenomenon to another – the site effectively constitutes what Virilio called 'information': '*the designation of the state a phenomenon assumes at a given moment*' (Virilio, 1995: 140, italics in original).

This process is demonstrated on the *HistoryWired* site discussed in Chapter 3. When the user logs onto the site, an 'Instructions' window opens that explains the practice of the site: '*HistoryWired: A few of our favorite things* is an experimental program through which you can take a virtual tour of selected objects from the vast collections of the National Museum of American

History.' The following paragraph begins the instruction on how to use the site:

> Begin your tour by visiting the main object map. The map is divided into regions, which represent broad object categories. The smaller 'squares' represent individual items from the museum's collections. Move the mouse over an object square to see the name of the object. More information and a thumbnail image will also appear on the blue panel to the left. Yellow lines point to relevant themes, and the timeline at the top will indicate the date of the object. (http://historywired.si.edu/index.html)

This practice constitutes basic historical research – locating an object in relation to a series of parameters that signify its role in social history. So, for example, the object identified as Nineteenth-Century Quilt is located by a vector as relating to Events and to Home – two of the 'themes' identified in the horizontal axis at top as comprising American social history/life. Another vector identifies its temporal location as mid-1800s. In the panel at left a reproduction of one of the quilt motifs appears along with a series of links: Midwestern US, Quilts, Textiles, Westward Expansion. A typical page layout looks something like that shown in Figure 5.2.

The movement on the site is constituted in several ways: the user moves the cursor over the mosaic, causing successive linked objects to be identified in small text panels. If the cursor stops on one of these panels, the vectors immediately appear, locating the object identified in the text panel both temporally (the time-line) and thematically (in relation to those themes chosen to typify American social history). Simultaneously, the graphic and links appear at left.

The appearance of graphic and verbal text in the left-side panel constitutes movement through the interplay of absence and presence that characterises movement on screen. Its simultaneous appearance with the object's appearance in the mosaic signifies identification – though it is interesting to place this practice in relation to Roland Barthes's analysis of the operation of narrative in which, he noted, the consecutiveness of events is often equated with consequence (Barthes, 1977); that is, because one event follows another, we tend to believe that the former event caused the latter. In accepting this on-screen logic we adopt a similar narrative logic: these text-objects appear at the same time, so therefore they are related. This simple identification is a successful (movement) strategy – and yet it is also a narrative strategy that we can usefully deconstruct, not an objective mode of classification. So we might, for example, question whether there should be a separate link to Women's role in social history – given that quilts are usually identified as a female activity; or whether the quilt should be associated with particular ethnic groups or communities, with a specific link indicating this. This kind of question locates what named links might be there, but are not, and how those omissions constitute a particular version of American social history by their absence. So a movement that, in this case, is an invoked simultaneity leads us from the notion of identification to absence – and thereby to an analysis of the narrative trajectory in which the object is embedded. The analysis of that trajectory

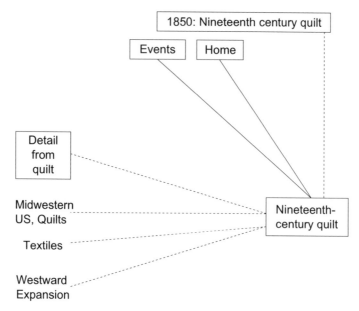

FIGURE 5.2   Modelling the vectors seen on the *HistoryWired* web site

constitutes a deconstruction of the version of American social history constituted at the site.

The vectors on the site are also examples of invoked simultaneity; however, their linearity and the connection they graphically present can be read as a linear analogue of movement. They represent connection, and connection is fundamentally a process of binding – one thing to another, one thought to another (from the Latin, nectere, to bind). As the eye, following the vector, moves (physically) from the object in the mosaic to its descriptors (Events, Home, mid 1800s), a conceptual movement is made simultaneously: this object is connected to the categories of Events and Home and as a phenomenon of the mid-1800s; its connections to those categories constitute its significance. This practice of locating the object in relation to, connecting it with, significant categories is also a mode of historical understanding. So the implied physical movement at the site, the vectors that are the linear analogue of movement, guide the user through a set of conceptual movements that constitute a mode of historical research and understanding. Movement constitutes not just information, but a mode of knowing/knowledge.

Because they constitute that knowledge through a *particular* set of connections, however, the vectors also reveal the premises that structure this version of social history. So, for example, the quilt cited in the example above is connected to the time-line, Events and Home. However, it is not connected to other categories at the site, which include Accomplishment, Art, Commerce, Leisure, Medicine, Military, People, Politics, Science or

Technology. Yet, it is conceivable that a mid-nineteenth-century quilt could appear in all of those categories: as an Accomplishment, it represents a form of domestic artistic practice that is still recognised as characteristic of nineteenth-century American society. Some viewers also recognize the quilt as an Art, rather than placing it in the lower-status category of Craft – and would challenge the use of an Art/Craft dichotomy. The quilt may not have had direct Commerce links at the time, but it doubtless had commercial significance, if only because it was a way of utilising domestic resources. As a Leisure activity the quilt might be seen as a way of consolidating family and community, as quilt makers work together on the one quilt (quilting companionably) or share patterns and pieces. And so on. The quilt might even be seen as an example of domestic Technology, through its provision of warmth and beauty to the home. This, in turn, might have led to an interrogation of the meanings and uses of the term, Technology. In other words, each category might have been connected to the quilt.

However, a selection was made and the quilt was related to the two categories shown, Events and Home. The quilt is thereby situated as a primarily domestic phenomenon – and as not related to the public and/or professional realms represented by the other descriptors; and so indicates that the site reproduces the Art/Craft dichotomy of High Modernist aesthetics – and its associated politics. An alternative social history might deconstruct that dichotomy, particularly in the light of its significance for gendered cultural production. In other words, for some critics of conservative aesthetics, the Art/Craft dichotomy engenders cultural production in that cultural practices that have been accessible primarily to men and that conventionally address a male viewer have been categorised as Art, while those practices that have been accessible primarily to women and address a female viewer have been categorised as Craft. Furthermore, Art is given a high cultural value; Craft a much lower cultural value. This example demonstrates the theoretical and cultural specificity of the social history that is enacted at this site, as does the set of categories chosen to map a social history of the USA.

A whole other set of categories might have been developed for selected objects to be connected with. In which case we might have a very different social history of the USA being demonstrated for users. For example, this social history might have included Children as a category. In this case not only might different objects have been chosen for display, but many different connections might have been made with the objects on the site. More fundamentally, its inclusion, alongside the more traditional categories such as Military, Commerce and Science would signify a different history – and effectively a different society. It is possible to think of other categories that would change the site and its history in the same way, such as Slavery, Indigenous Peoples. So, tracing the vectors at the site, enables us to understand and deconstruct the site's historical practice, which the site is also demonstrating for, and essentially teaching to, users. It also enables us to locate the discourses operating at the site, such as the colonialism that does not allow for a category such as Slavery, despite the formative significance of that practice on contemporary US society.

So movement at this site *is* the production of a particular kind of knowledge (a version of social history) because of two sets of connections it generates: the connections it makes between phenomena (such as the quilt and the homes and events with which it is associated) and between a specific object/phenomenon and a specific set of categories (for example, between the quilt and the categories of Events, Home, Midwestern US, Quilts, Textiles, Westward Expansion). But, of course, connection is one of the characteristic features of this technology.

Making links

One of the movements most characteristic of this technology is the link – the 'movement' between web pages and web sites that constitutes each user's personal rhizomatic pathway through the web. Calling up a series of web pages is perceived by many users as movement – as the metaphor of the 'Go' button on many browsers attests. Nicholas Burbules identifies the link as the 'key element in this hypertextual structure' (1997: 103) that users know as the web or the internet: 'The link ... is the elemental structure that represents a hypertext as a semic web of meaningful relations' (1997: 105). And Burbules goes on to develop this description of the link:[2]

> ... links do not only express semic relations but also, significantly, establish *pathways* of possible *movement* within the Web *space*; they suggest relations, but also *control access to information* (if there is no link from A to B, for many users the existence of B may never be known – in one sense, the link *creates* B as possibility). (1997: 105, italics in original)

Burbules's explanation of the link employs metaphors of both movement and space that are common to descriptions of the technology. The notion of spatiality is explored further in the next chapter, but here I want to make the same perceptual connection as Burbules, that the link is a movement. It seems no accident that the individual's process of constituting knowledge is often described as a process of 'making a, or the, link' between phenomena or events. In other words, the individual's act of formulating knowledge is experienced as having recognised some relation or connection (causal or metaphoric or metonymic or some other) between one phenomenon and another, or one event and another. And in both cases the connection itself is, as noted above, experienced as a movement.

Judith Lynne Hanna makes similar connections between movement and knowledge in her article, 'The Language of Dance' (2001). Hanna's basic argument is that embodied movement – and particularly, self-conscious bodily movement – is a form of intelligence and a way of both knowing the world and conveying knowledge about the world to others. Hanna's analysis constitutes dance as a mode of communication like language, with its own grammar, tropes, meaning potentials. As self-conscious bodily movement, dance is a way of knowing and of communicating knowledge. So, too, are the basic hand gestures used in teaching: '... researchers found that when elementary school teachers taught math by using gestures that were well-matched to their words (for example, making flat palm gestures under each side of an equation to illustrate that the two sides should be equal), students understood the lesson better than when words and gestures were mis-matched ...' (Hanna, 2001).

Links, too, are perceived as self-conscious movements – though not directly as embodied movements. Yet, as I noted earlier, the (linking) move-ment itself is not, strictly speaking, movement but a perception of move-ment. The crucial element in understanding the practice of links is the basic action of connection as movement. If users perceive links as movement, then might the perceived movement – like the palm gesture under each half of an equation – contribute to the user's engagement in a process of learning and of knowledge formation? The power of the link, therefore, is arguably that it seems (is perceived) to make a significant connection between one phenomenon and another – for example, the information or ideas on one web page with those on another. And since the user her- or himself is phys-ically engaged in 'making the link' by clicking on a button, then this connection is experienced by the user as an embodied practice of meaning-making. This adds a sense of agency to the activity of using links that may or may not be justified intellectually or conceptually. Simply activating links already coded into a web site is no more agential, one might argue, that looking up a footnote in a book. However, it may become more so if the user activates other links, of her or his own choosing, that are not deter-mined by the links built into the original (hyper)text. So the user acts less like the reader of a book than a browser in a library or bookstore, making connections with a range of materials and ideas that the author of the orig-inal text could not have predicted.

The 'browser' metaphor is familiar to users of information technology, where it means the program designed to locate web sites by reference to con-tent key-words supplied by the user. The 'book browser' is a person who moves around a library or bookstore or, more figuratively, the world of books, reading apparently randomly for her or his own pleasure; browser is another movement metaphor. So again we have a kinetic metaphor used to enable the users to have access to the technology – and, more pertinently, to facilitate the process whereby the user retrieves information and, by reference to her or his own existing knowledge and experience, generates new knowledge and new understanding.

It is also worth noting Burbules's point that the speed of the link 'makes the moment of transition too fleeting to merit reflection; the link-event becomes invisible' (Burbules, 1997: 104). But, of course, the transition is invisible – in the sense that there is no move from one site to another;

one site simply replaces another on the monitor. Again, there is a critical relationship between movement and speed in that the speed with which the technology complies with an invocation is read in terms of spatio-temporal displacement or movement, since this is the way that human beings customarily understand speed. At the same time, it is the speed at which the invocation is answered that characterises this technology, transforming it from a super-efficient library system into a qualitatively different medium. Information and communication technologies also enable new kinds of relationships to be developed – between people, and between people and resources – and they are incorporated in new ways into people's everyday lives. Again, returning to Virilio, it is their speed that effectively constitutes information since this is the means by which these relationships are realised. Speed is information; movement – perceptual, conceptual – is knowledge. So, on the one hand, we have the physical act of movement – motility – and its theorised effect on the process of information transmission and knowledge formation. On the other hand, we have a metaphorical account of information retrieval and knowledge formation that is grounded in the perception of movement. Both situations involve embodiment and both are about knowledge formation. In the first case, the physical gestures of the teacher who transmits information or of the child who communicates an embodied knowledge that she or he is unable to transmit verbally. In the second case, the embodied user whose minimal physical action in enabling the link process (point and click) initiates the process of knowledge formation. Both kinds of movement are characteristic of the link.

The role of movement in information transmission and knowledge formation might be considered further in relation to the embodied practices invited or demanded by the use of specific technologies and textual practices.

User incorporated

In a famous essay entitled, 'Techniques of the Body', first published in 1934, French sociologist, Marcel Mauss recorded the changes in the way that French people walked after the arrival of American films in France:

> ... American walking fashions had begun to arrive over here, thanks to the movies. This was an idea I could generalize. The positions of the arms and hands while walking form a social idiosyncrasy – they are not simply the product of some purely individual, almost completely psychic, arrangements and mechanisms. (1992: 458)

Once French viewers started to watch and admire American films and to observe the ways Americans in these films moved, Mauss noted, they began to incorporate some of those moves into their own walking. By focusing on the activity of walking Mauss explored the different ways in which individual bodies are formed through the individual's negotiation of her or his social and cultural environment(s). And he notes differences within, as well as between, societies and cultures. He notes, for example, that he can identify girls who have attended convent schools by the way they hold their hands when walking. Walking, he concludes, is not 'natural'; each society generates a way of walking that is acquired by its citizens. Mauss's research into corporeality led to his understanding of the concept of *habitus*, which he defines as 'the techniques and work of collective and individual practical reason' (1992: 458). This collective and practical reason is realised in '*techniques of the body*'; that is, an individual's embodiment is both idiosyncratic, in that it involves unique physical characteristics and movements, and social, in that aspects of this embodiment are characteristic of a particular society at a particular time. For Mauss the motion of walking was socially, not psychically, idiosyncratic: that is, the movement of an individual body was both generated and given meaning by the social context of that body:

> What emerges very clearly ... is that we are everywhere faced with physio-psych-sociological assemblages of a series of action. These actions are more or less habitual and more or less ancient in the life of the indivdual and the history of the society. (Mauss, 1992: 473)

As individuals negotiate their use of contemporary information and communication technologies, they are embodied in specific ways that impact on their relationship with the material they encounter. In the section above it was noted that individuals have an embodied role in the use of hypertext links; they move the cursor to the link button and click. This minimal physical movement, nonetheless, engages the user physically with the technology; it is as if the user is saying, 'I want to move [moving the cursor] from here to [click] there.' In stating the relationship required – from this representation of a phenomenon (this page, site) to another – the user represents her or his engagement with knowledge formation; she or he will evaluate the relationship between phenomena thus invoked and reach some new understanding (though this may not be the knowledge intended by the link creator).

Yet, the physical act of making/invoking the link also has other meanings. The user's physical engagement with the link process and subsequent navigation of the linked site is part of the process of discovery and evaluation that leads to knowledge formation; it would not otherwise happen. So there is a sense in which that physical movement is essential to the knowledge produced – and also that this movement might, in turn, be seen as incorporating that knowledge into the being of the user. As contemporary sociologist, Pierre Bourdieu notes, what is 'learned by body' is 'what one is' (1990b: 73). Bourdieu refers here to the physical performance of acts that constitute our experience of our world; the embodied practice of using the technology is not substantially different in its significance. The point-and-click link movement incorporates the knowledge formulated by accessing the link into the user's self (however the user mobilises the information obtained via the link). It also constitutes the user as a contemporary embodied subject.

At no other time in history has an individual gained access to information and services by this combination of bodily movements. And these movements are almost always performed while seated, so there is a series of movements involved here that identifies both the technology and its user. In other words, just as the user incorporates knowledge into her or his being by virtue of the physical, as well as conceptual, movements involved in its production, so those movements can be located specifically as the artefact of a specific technology – that thereby interpellates the user. The specificity of this required movement and its demands on the individual can be clearly seen in the problems encountered by those who have a problem with the action: for example, paraplegic users who lack the fine motor control to perform this action easily; blind users who 'read' the hypertext via audio technology and take longer than sighted users to locate an appropriate link.[3] For designers, knowledge of the physical capabilities of users is a crucial element in the development of a site. This may relate to physical limitations of some groups of IT users – or the specific, learned skills of other users, such as the fine motor control of game-players.

Conversely, we might consider the flip-side of the physical engagement with a multimedia text – the embodied pleasure of successfully using the technology. When the user experiences a sense of empowerment or enjoyment at having successfully used technology – interacted with a multimedia exhibit or installation, activated a link within a hypertext document, chosen a web site from a selection offered by a browser, or just typed out a manuscript – this experience is not only intellectual but also physical. The happy, empowered user of human–computer interface design is not a disembodied spirit, but an embodied being, and the physical movements that generated her or his pleasure or achievement are imprinted in the bodily memory of using the technology.

Again this aspect of embodiment might be incorporated in a variety of ways in a successful design: for example, by capitalising on the user's habituated movement to persuade her or him to follow the logic of a particular site. In other words, by rewarding the user's habituated point-and-click movement around a site, the designer can convince the user that this is an effective, efficient and rewarding site to visit. Frustrating that logic might, alternatively, be used by a designer or artist whose intention is to challenge the logic of the web site and its embodiment of the user. In other words, frustrating the logic of the link – because it is the fundamental operation of the hypertext – might be used to challenge the user to consider the practice of this kind of text, as well as to think about the way this process is forming her or his own embodied being. Or, less frustratingly, an artist may utilise the link movement to challenge the technology in other ways. In a recent work Australian artist, Mike Parr, constructed an on-line performance whereby visitors to his web site could use a similar movement to click on his image and thereby activate sensors/receptors that would deliver an electric shock to him. This performance can be read as making a series of points about technology and embodiment. For example, it literally makes the point that technology affects our embodiment. It also demonstrates that people can use this technology to operate on us from a distance and anonymously, which might mean anything from electronic shadowing to 'smart bombs'. And it argues that the technology we use may coerce us to act in ways to which we might otherwise be averse: does the anonymity of the shock delivery tempt us in ways that having to walk up to someone with a cattle-prod does not? In each case the argument depends on a recontextualisation of the familiar movement of click-and-point that we associate with information technology.

Acculturated movement

This final section considers the ways in which conventional movement is incorporated into multimedia text design, and also the extent to which movement metaphors suffuse the language we use to understand ourselves and our world.

So far, the embodied movement we have considered in relation to multi-media has been movement that is generated specifically by the use of partic-ular technology. It is worth considering briefly the ways in which more familiar bodily movements are assumed and mobilised in the production of multimedia texts. In particular, we might note the extent to which these assumptions are culturally specific, which thereby defines their politics. This is another way of approaching Mauss's observation of the cultural specificity of movement; that analysing its derivation (where a particular kind of move-ment originated) can tell you about the cultural assumptions involved in its mobilisation (why it has been used within a text).

Consider, for example, the ways in which the movements of visitors are incorporated into the production of exhibits in the contemporary (multi-media) museum. Many studies have been published to advise curators and designers about how to manage visitor flow around an exhibition space. David Dean summarizes much of this material in his book, *Museum Exhibition: Theory and Practice* (1994). Under the heading 'Behavioral ten-dencies' Dean presents a series of observations as 'natural tendencies' that designers need to account for in designing an exhibition (1994: 51–2). Many of these observations involve movement, such as:

- *Turning to the right*
  Most people tend to favor turning to the right if all other factors are equal. A possible explanation is that this relates to the dominance of right-handedness in humans.

- *Following the right wall*
  Once moving to the right, most people will stay to the right, leaving exhibits on the left less viewed.

  ...

- *Exhibits closest to exits are least viewed*
  The closer people are to an exit, the more they are drawn to it, and the less attention is given to the exhibits. (Dean, 1994: 51)

Immediately above the list in his book is a boxed quote from a study by Ross J. Loomis, *Museum Visitor Evaluation: New Tool for Management* (1987), which is the basis of Dean's first point (as above):

> A long standing observation, at least in the United States, is the marked tendency for people to turn to the right when entering an open or unstructured area. (quoted in Dean, 1994: 51)

The interesting point about Dean's translation of this point is that he has transformed Loomis's cultural location of the observation into a biological or genetic one. Loomis has situated his observation by relating it to studies of visitors in the USA; Dean suggests that the tendency might be located in the 'dominance of right-handedness'.

This transformation by Dean might be seen as an example of a US-centric view of visitor behaviour that uses biological or genetic causality to establish US behaviour as 'human' behaviour. In other words, Loomis's careful cultural location of this practice is lost in the translation. An Australian social history curator, interviewed for another project, evoked the same point, quoted above, about visitors turning right. The curator was discussing the relationship between the Australian curators and the American designers who developed exhibits for the National Museum of Australia. She recalled an occasion when this visitor behaviour was stated as a rule of design by one of the American designers – at which the Australian curators expressed deep scepticism. They insisted on taking the designers to a major Australian museum, the Australian War Memorial, to observe visitor behaviour. What they observed was that the Australian visitors seemed almost wilfully random in their traversal of the site – at least to the American perception. Furthermore, Australian visitors squeezed between text panels where no egress was intended and also boldly walked around or under barriers that clearly identified an area as Staff Only. The curator's point was that the American designer needed to be aware, if only on an anecdotal basis, that rules that might apply very well in the USA might not be (equally) relevant in Australia.

The curator's observation of museum visitor movement was that Australians and US citizens did not move in the same way – in the sense that they did not follow the same trajectories when walking, nor did they respond in the same way to directives. Her concern was that this random and autonomous behaviour of Australian visitors needed to be recognised in order that the exhibit design not be rendered meaningless. For example, if an exhibit was constructed as a narrative that relied on right-hand movement around a wall, then that narrative and the meanings it communicated might be lost on very many visitors who would not walk to the right – even if directed to do so. In other words, for this curator, one of the ways that the cultural difference between Australian and US society was realised was in the patterns of movement adopted by citizens.

For the designer, then, the recognition that movements are culturally specific – either movements of the body (the 'techniques of the body' observed by Mauss) or ways of moving through the world – is essential to developing an information architecture or textual logic that is accessible and attractive to users.

Mapping movement

Whilst acknowledging the cultural specificities of movement, it is also important to note cultural consistencies – like the consistent reading of the left-to-right, lower-to-upper trajectory of the starship, *Enterprise* in the title sequence of the *Star Trek* series. We might map this movement by reference to the layout diagram proposed by Kress and van Leeuwen as typical of Western cultural production (see Figure 5.3). That diagram itself maps the discursive production of information in Western thinking: the Given/New and Real/Ideal dichotomies are characteristic of a progressivist and idealist discourse. The vectors we can draw across that layout diagram capture the meanings of many conventional Western moves.

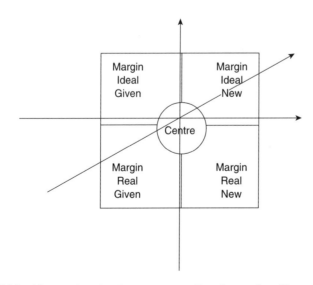

FIGURE 5.3   Movement vectors traverse composition diagram (see Figure 3.7)

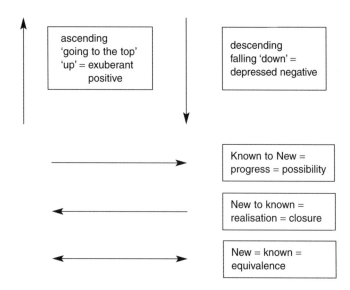

FIGURE 5.4   Vectors that map Given/New trajectories

The move from a Given/Real to New/Ideal position (as seen with the *Enterprise*) signifies progress or opening up, which characterises the conceptual move from specific incident to abstract principle that is characteristic of Western thinking. The less complex vertical and horizontal moves can be read as expressing more specific meanings (see Figure 5.4). The Given–New horizontal movement is characteristically used in explanation, where it expresses equivalence; 'this equals that' – as in the mathematics example discussed earlier. Though it is also likely that the term in the final (New) position will be read as privileged. The Ideal–Real movement, on the other hand, conventionally privileges the term in the higher position – again typifying Western thinking, with its heavenly cosmologies. And the movement from Real to Ideal is characteristically more positive than the reverse movement – as the move from concrete to abstract in a metaphysics that favours abstraction.

We might, therefore, consider the effects on users of positioning them to trace certain movements across a web site. For example, how does this reasoning interpret the typical move to the left to make links on a web site characterise that linkage? As a move from New to Given it implicitly induces the user to read the information at the link as supporting the information on the page – whether that is information on another page of the same site, or on a different site altogether. On the same site it links the user to a page that is consistent with the link page, and provides related information. If the link is to another site altogether, that other site typically is related in some way to the linking site – sharing a philosophy or interest.

The move down the page of a site reads typically as the Ideal/Real structure (see Figure 5.5), with the information lower down the page linking the essence of the site, provided in the top banner, to its everyday application.

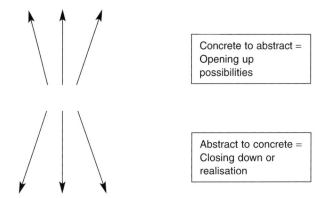

FIGURE 5.5 Vectors that map Ideal/Real trajectories

The *HistoryWired* site can be read in this way, with the categories at the top providing the (Ideal) conceptual positioning of the object, positioned below as Real. Furthermore, the move up to the abstract categories (above) mirrors the ascendant trajectory typical of Western thinking – in which the abstract or Ideal is considered 'higher' than its everyday application or manifestation.

Equally the vertical gesture downwards typically embodies closure – the move from a higher order (conceptual) to the everyday (Real). In conversation these gestures characteristically have these meanings – top-down as closure, bottom-up as an opening up or questioning. Again, with the vertical dimension typical of Western metaphysics as an indicator, these movements mirror the relationship between abstract or ideal and its everyday realisation.

The horizontal gestures can also be read against the history of Western thinking, with the left to right move tracing the trajectory of Western linear narrative; the move from left (the information that is known) to the right (the new information) traces the development of the narrative (see Figure 5.6); So again, a typical opening gesture moves from left to right – whilst a gesture of closure would move in the reverse direction, right to left. This is an interesting

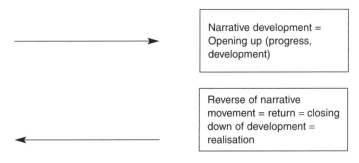

FIGURE 5.6 Vectors mapping narrative

reading in terms of the web link, typically at left, since it suggests that the user who activates a link provided at a site is not opening up information but closing it down. As noted above, this can be read as a consolidation of the information given at the page – that these links support the philosophy of the page, rather than modifying or expanding it. And perhaps in this sense, the link is a closing down, in the same way as a footnote can be – asserting the validity of the known rather than challenging it.

Digital dynamics

There is still a sense in which movement as an embodied practice is read as 'natural' whereas writing, visuals and sound are more clearly identified as cultural practices. Yet, as Mauss and others argued through the twentieth century, embodied movement is a cultural practice – as is our particular understanding of embodiment.

Dance is primarily a movement medium, while contemporary cinema shows the technological transformation of contemporary life through its portrayal of movement. So we might position the movement in contemporary dance and cinema generically and intertextually by reference to earlier genres of dance and cinema – noting, for example, the move away from naturalistic movement and/or editing in many productions. The stylised movement in these texts, which does not invite the same simple identification as naturalistic movement, can signify a fundamental disjunction or alienation from conventional modes of (representing and understanding) movement – and so of understanding ourselves as embodied beings. In recent films such as the *Matrix* trilogy, *Kill Bill*, *Bullet-Proof Monk,* and *Crouching Tiger, Hidden Dragon,* this is evident in generic references to Asian martial arts film. The purpose of the fight sequences in these films can be understood in relation to the kinds of issues addressed in the films, as well as to the film itself as cultural practice or artwork (perhaps particularly significant with *Kill Bill* with its self-reflexivity about film-making as a practice).

Discursively, as noted above, we can locate movement in relation to dominant modes of Western thinking, which can be deployed in very different ways – to tell very different stories or to promote very different attitudes, values and beliefs. So, a narrative that employs naturalistic movement and a conventional narrative structure may be used to tell a story about displaced peoples that conflicts with the official state ideology of the country in which it is performed – which characterises refugees as alien, as other, and does not afford them the same 'human' rights as its citizens. In this narrative, naturalistic movement may be used to demonstrate the non-alien-ness, the everyday reality, of the refugees and to argue that they, like the citizens, deserve human rights.

Within the text, too, intrinsic movement is deployed to tell a story, or to position a user/participant in a particular way. Movements at a web site may locate particular ideas, beliefs and values as significant or important to the user – and these may be the movement of the text or it may be the movement of the user induced by the text. On the other hand, as we have noted repeatedly of information technology, the user is not contained by the text and may make connections – literally, moving the cursor to activate links – not predicted by the site. In this way, the technology demonstrates the active reading practice employed with any text, in which the reader consults an array of intertextual and other references in the process of reading this text. With information technology, the conceptual movement is traced in/by the embodied movement of the user.

The next chapter looks at another textual strategy deployed by multimedia, and this is space. Like movement, space can be used to make specific meanings from the material at the site. More crucially, for multimedia and information technology, space is another metaphor that is widely used to express or describe the operation of the technology itself – to enable users to engage with it: the 'consensual hallucination' of cyberspace (Gibson, 1986).

Notes

1 Interestingly, a recent review of the National Museum of Australia by Australia's current, conservative government recommends the virtual dismantling of the Garden of Australian Dreams and its replacement by a more conventional European-identified forecourt-garden – the complex meanings of the Garden of Australian Dreams apparently too subtle for the reviewers – or perhaps not.
2 Burbules's work on the link will be examined further in Chapter 9, for its contribution to the ethics of IT work. Burbules not only locates a range of different link-types that have different roles in relation to hypertext, but also challenges the claims of some hypertext practitioners that their work is inherently non-hierarchical.
3 The problems encountered by disabled users will be considered further in Chapter 9, along with the issues of technology and embodiment encountered by all users.

SIX

SPACE

Space, the final frontier ...

Although the fictional genre of science fiction developed in the early nineteenth century, with the publication, in 1818, of Mary Shelley's *Frankenstein*, it was not until late in that century, following the success of novels by Jules Verne and H.G. Wells, that science fiction went into space. In the novels of Verne and Wells space was the 'great unknown' – as it still was over a half-century later when the starship *Enterprise* set out on her 'five year mission, to explore new worlds and new civilizations. To boldly go where no man had gone before'.

Science fiction writers used the metaphor of space to explore the cultural and social values of their society. In their work 'space' is a construct of particular attitudes, values, beliefs, behaviours, and relationships that sometimes challenge those of the mainstream, not just reproduce them. In other words, space features not as empty, neutral territory waiting to be given meaning, but is generated as a social, political and ethical construct. It does not exist as a blank slate on which to inscribe a new story, but is a construct of contemporary values, beliefs and ideas, which it either reproduces or interrogates. Henri Lefebvre notes in his study, *The Production of Space* (first published in 1974), that '[a]s Paul Klee put it, artists – painters, sculptors or architects – do not show space, they create it' (Lefebvre, 1998: 178). Makers of science fiction do the same.

In exploring the spatiality of multimedia we need to consider the reconfiguration of space in the early twentieth century, prefigured in science fiction. This re-thinking of space was a critical interest of twentieth-century science; however, it was not confined to the abstract realms of scientific research. It affected the ways that people experienced space in their everyday lives and increasingly served as a deconstructive principle by which to analyse the categories through which everyday life is experienced. Lefebvre characterises the work of architect, Robert Venturi, in this way: 'He sees space not as an empty and neutral milieu occupied by dead objects but rather as a field of force full of tensions and distortions' (Lefebvre, 1998: 184). Those tensions and distortions trace the complex interplays of ideas and ideologies that constitute everyday life.

This chapter begins with a brief overview of the development of contemporary understandings of space/time, before going on to study the spatiality of multimedia – both as conceptual construct (for example, cyberspace) and as textual strategy. The pervasiveness of spatial metaphors in critical writings by Gilles Deleuze and Felix Guattari, which are used often with multimedia, are explored for their contribution to our understanding of multimedia texts. Finally, we consider the spatiality of memory, a crucial concept in relation to digital multimedia.

Space-time: twentieth-century reconfigurations

Lefebvre begins *The Production of Space* (1998) with these claims:

> The fact is that around 1910 a certain space was shattered. It was the space of common sense, of knowledge (*savoir*), of social practice, of political power, a space hitherto enshrined in everyday discourse, just as in abstract thought, as the environment of and channel for communications ... Euclidean and perspectivist space have disappeared as systems of reference, along with other former 'commonplaces' such as the town, history, paternity, the tonal system in music, traditional morality, and so forth. This was truly a crucial moment. (quoted in Hays, 1998: 174, emphasis in original)

We might argue that Lefebvre's analysis is not entirely accurate. Many pre-1910 features have survived, though their significance has altered, if only in that they are no longer the only, or even the natural, ways of thinking, being and acting. For example, tonal music survives – in fact, a host of tonal musics – but tonality no longer occupies the same (dominant and unmarked) position in the musical canon. And, of course, the challenge to tonality was also a challenge to the notion of a canon and to a unifying, homogenising understanding of what constitutes 'music'. Similarly, conventional (Christian) morality exists alongside many other kinds of morality, so that it no longer carries the dominant force it once did. And again, the very fact that it was a dominant force – and that it suppressed other forms of morality – has been challenged. So, even though conventional morality survives, it also is not the unifying, homogenising force it once was. So, strictly speaking, Lefebvre's analysis is correct: these 'commonplaces' no longer exist. Nor does pre-twentieth-century space.

Stanford Kwinter traces the change in our understanding of time to a similar time-frame; for Kwinter, Einstein's 1905 paper, 'On the Electrodynamics of Moving Bodies', in which he presents his Special Theory of Relativity, is a key moment. As Kwinter notes, the crucial feature of this paper was that it changed our understanding of time from a metaphysical one to that of 'just one more dependent (i.e., variable) coordinate in the kinematical transformation equations' (Kwinter, 1998: 590). In other words, time and space were no longer independent variables, 'at least algebraically'; our model of a three-dimensional spatial field moving along a one-dimensional time continuum was no longer sufficient. Instead, space and time were seen as interdependent, and an event or object could only be described fully by reference to all four variables. In other words, the situation of an event or object in time was related to its situation in the three spatial variables and vice-versa; the spatial variables were not constant with respect to time, as had formerly been assumed:

> By making time in this way relative and contingent, space-time and the field were conceived as a new entity, irreducible to their component dimensions, objectively unresolvable with respect to their infinitely varied regions (different speeds = different times), and thickened to consistency by the world-lines that career through them. (Kwinter, 1998: 590)

The 'field' that Kwinter refers to in this formulation replaces older Cartesian understandings of space as existing independently of solid bodies and preceding them. Instead, the field 'expresses the complete immanence of forces and events':

> The field describes a space of propagation, of effects. It contains no matter or material points, rather functions, vectors and speeds. It describes local relations of difference within fields of celerity, transmission or of careering points, in a word, what Minkowski called the *world*. (Kwinter, 1998: 591, emphasis in original)

The 'world-lines' in Kwinter's description (above) of the new understanding of space-time and the field also derive from Minkowski's work. Kwinter glosses them as expressions of a particular set of coordinates for the values of spatiality (dx, dy, dz) at a particular time, dt. This point (dx, dy, dz, dt) constitutes '"an everlasting career" that he [Minkowski] named a world-line' (Kwinter, 1998: 608). And Kwinter quotes from Minkowski's article, 'Space and Time' (first published in 1908): 'The whole universe is seen to resolve itself into similar world-lines, and I would fain anticipate myself by saying that in my opinion physical laws might find their most perfect expression as reciprocal relations between these world-lines' (quoted in Kwinter, 1998: 608). So, no longer is the universe conceived as a huge empty space dotted with objects that are the source of our interest. Instead, it is a vast, interconnected and constantly modifying matrix of space-time vectors or trajectories. These changes in our physical paradigm for understanding the universe are reflected culturally.

Just as the physical universe has been re-defined – from empty space to world-lines – so has our conceptual or metaphysical universe. Russian linguist, Mikhail Bakhtin's concept of heteroglossia is one example of this. According to this notion (introduced into mainstream criticism by French theorist, Julia Kristeva as intertextuality), our cultural universe is a babel of different voices or tongues (heterogolossia). We understand any particular voice among those voices by situating that particular voice among the many; that is, there is no absolute (x, y, z) coordinate for this particular text, but a (dx, dy, dz, dt) world-line that describes the trajectory of that text and the meanings it offers to a range of potential audiences as it intersects with them.

Kwinter makes a similar point by reference to the Futurist artist, Umberto Boccioni. Kwinter quotes Boccioni's contention that:

> Areas between one object and another are not empty spaces but rather *continuing materials of differing intensities,* which we reveal with visible lines which do not correspond to any photographic truth. This is why we do not have in our paintings objects and empty spaces but only *a greater or lesser intensity and solidity of space.* (italics added) (quoted in Kwinter, 1998: 592)

From this perspective the Futurist works discussed early in the previous chapter – Braggaglia's *Young Man Rocking* (1911) and Balla's paintings, *Dynamism of a Dog on a Leash* (1912), *Little Girl Running on a Balcony* (1912) and *Violinist's Hands* (1912) – can be seen as documenting not only the bourgeois construction of time as a series of incremental movements, but also the fluidity of the space-time continuum. In other words, Braggaglia's and Balla's paintings show their figures in motion not as independent of the 'space' in which they are temporally located, but as integrated with that space/time. In other words, the tail of the dog in Balla's painting is not a separate object with coordinates (dx, dy, dz) that occupies time (t1, t2, t3 …) as it performs its up/down wag; instead, it is located by the coordinates (dx, dy, dz, dt) as it moves through the field of intensities that is space/time.

Kwinter notes:

Boccioni's system reveals the dual nature of space: on the one hand, a fixed and extended *milieu* with metrical and dimensional properties and, on the other, a fluid and consistent field of intensities (e.g. forces, speeds, temperatures, color). (1998: 593)

Thus, space can be perceived in two ways. It is dynamism in stasis, like a photograph, an X-ray, or a film still – with properties that can be measured and located, analysed for their significance. And it is also the dynamic field itself, the interplay of intensities, sets of vectors, functions and speeds that generate Minkowski's 'world-lines' – which is another way of understanding Minkowski's definition of the field as 'local relations of difference within fields of celerity, transmission or of careering points' (Kwinter, 1998: 591).

As the work of Bachelard, Lefebvre and Kwinter suggests, the importance of this re-visioning of space is that it impacts on our understanding of both the physical and metaphysical universe. So, no longer is the world perceived as a discrete physical entity rushing through the void of time; instead, in Kwinter's terms, space is incorporated into the body of time. Nor is our metaphysical universe a set of ideas studding a conceptually empty or neutral space. Instead we have, in both cases, a space-time continuum in which physical and metaphysical events form a physical and conceptual heteroglossia, shot through with lines of force. In essence, this is a shift to an ecological or holistic model of social, cultural and individual life in which all events and ideas impact on each other.

The space of multimedia is a late twentieth- and early twenty-first century conception. When considering the space of a multimedia text, then, we are evoking this complex of ideas about space that has so challenged the ways we understand our world – physical and metaphysical. The critical feature of this re-visioning of space-time is this move to a model of interconnectedness or ecology. Our interest here is in how this notion impacts on our understanding of textuality. We might start, for example, by using the kind of dual conception that Kwinter attributes to Boccioni and ask about both the space (-time) inhabited by the text, and the space(-time) within the text.

Cyberspace

One of the most discussed spatial realms of recent years is cyberspace, the imaginary spatial construct that William Gibson coined for his influential early novel about the user experience, *Neuromancer*:

> Cyberspace. A consensual hallucination experienced daily by billions of legitimate operators, in every nation ... A graphic representation of data abstracted from the banks of every computer in the human system. Unthinkable complexity. Lines of light ranged in the non-space of the mind, clusters and constellations of data. Like city lights, receding ... (Gibson, 1986: 67).

As the recent *Matrix* films (1999, 2003, 2003) dramatise, William Gibson's 'cyberspace' metaphor still governs the imaginary engagement with information technology. Chris Chesher writes in his 'Ontology of Digital Domains' (1997) that information technology is fundamentally invocational: that is, it operates only when called into existence by the user. In other words, there is no web page living out there in cyberspace waiting to be accessed by a user; rather, the web page is constituted afresh each time it is invoked by a user. That web page is itself a collection of data organised in a way that is meaningful to the user. Chesher argues here that the technology is not spatial, as the metaphors of cyberspace suggest. Its power, he argues, is speed, or in Virilio's terms, information (Virilio, 1995). The user initiates a process that consists of myriad transactions, millions of incremental steps, carried out at a speed that renders them fluid to human perception. Chesher's rejection of Gibson's metaphor may be technically correct but it does not acknowledge an essential relationship between the movement implicit for users in the technology, and its production of space. Nor does it acknowledge the power of the spatial metaphors used to manipulate the technology: the maps, cartography and grids of cyberspace, the net, the web, site, page.

When the user invokes a web page, there may be no actual spatial movement. Physically, there is no web or net or rhizome with little nodes all along the way that are individual web pages or web sites. Yet, for the user the web or net or rhizome is a common way of visualising – and spatialising – the activity of using information technology. That spatialisation is itself a function of an imaginary set of moves, from one site to another on the web, net, or rhizome. It is that movement that creates the space that is cyberspace. The graphic interface operated by most users is redolent with spatial metaphors – site, page, file, folder, desktop, window, view, page, layout, map, document, format, field. This spatiality may be wholly virtual, but its reality is that it enables the user's manipulation of the interface.

The *Matrix* films bring that spatial imagery to the screen. The 'matrix' of the film has, as its cultural referent, the metaphors and plots of Gibson's cyberspace novels and short stories. As Neo and his companions put on their fashionable suits and dark glasses and travel around their virtual reality, the audience is presented with the spatial metaphor of virtual reality. Our virtuality is a spatial realm. Even if the site is simply a vast computer program, what the viewer sees is a version of three-dimensional, space-time reality. And this equivalence is demonstrated in *The Matrix* when Cypher is shown standing in front of a screen over which is scrolling columns of symbols. Cypher explains that this is more to him than sets of symbols; he 'sees' that virtual world into which Neo, Trinity and Morpheus conduct terrorist raids. Cypher translates the programming language into the spatial construct whereby Neo and his companions experience the (cyberspace of the) matrix. The equivalence between the scrolling program language and the virtual space in which Neo and friends engage the 'machines' is reinforced in the second film, *The Matrix Reloaded* (2003). Even the title of the film stresses that this space is a construct – a program reloaded, to be experienced again, and again. But the experiences of the human team can only be actualised by their virtual reality experiences – in the space that is virtual reality. In the same way, contemporary culture envisions human–computer interactions for the everyday user as movement around and inside a spatial realm. This movement creates a space that is socially and culturally meaningful; this space facilitates or enables the interaction between human and technology to take place.

In his writing about space David Woodhead rejects the commonsense view that 'there exist imagined spaces that are somehow less significant, less *real*, than material, physically bounded space' (1995: 235, emphasis in original). Instead, he argues that 'space does not stand awaiting us to give meanings to it, but the space *becomes*, that space is *constituted*, through meaning' (Woodhead, 1995: 236). In other words, we recognise a particular, limited and bounded, space because of the meanings we give to that space. This is another way – a cultural, geographical or anthropological way – of understanding the re-visioning of space during the twentieth century.

An analogy might also be drawn between the spatiality of information technology and map-making. The courtyard of the National Museum of Australia features an installation known as the Garden of Australian Dreams. It is a complex space, constituted by the placement of objects and the move-ment of visitors in and around those objects. One feature of the Garden is the reproduction, over the concrete walking space, of a section of the map of Australia. A linear drawing of the coastline is painted onto the concrete and the area inside the coastline is traversed by a number of mapping and naming systems: the Mercator grid of conventional map-making; Aboriginal Australian song-lines; fence-lines of cattle stations, indigenous Australian names; names of cattle stations and geographical locations in English. Each of these systems of meanings creates the space differently. The differences between them constitute the history of cultural diversity and cultural antago-nisms in Australia. The Garden of Australian Dreams demonstrates that the geopolitical construct we identify as 'Australia' is the result of a series of dif-ferent dreamings – indigenous, non-indigenous, domestic, scientific, economic, political, social. In other words, the space we identify as 'Australia' is a space created by different, overlapping and contradictory imaginaries.

Cyberspace is also constituted differently by different systems of meaning. The technically-minded might insist that it is not a space and so deny it (that is, cyberspace) meaning, but this is to deny the cultural and social being of the user. An analogy may be the monuments to brutalism that served as public housing in the middle of the twentieth century – rectangular blocks with sufficient space for each family, but no humanity. These housing-blocks not only degraded the people living there (by denying their need for beauty and individuality), they also spelled out the failure of governments and their instrumentalities to understand the basic social and cultural needs of their people and communities. They failed badly; were vandalized; and eventually were torn down – symbols of instrumentalist folly. Web sites are instances of human–computer interaction, with the emphasis on the 'human', not the 'computer'. Understanding that interaction means recognising the cultural practices that enable users to engage with the technology.

In the same way it could be argued that a film screen is not a two-dimensional space on which characters move, but a series of images superimposed rapidly upon one another to create the appearance of movement. There is nothing essentially spatial about films, as Deleuze argues for early film; they are essentially about movement ('the movement-image'). It is this apparent on-screen movement that creates the space that is the *mise-en-scène* of the film. Yet, it would be pointless to argue that viewers should reject the spatiality of the film or the realist movements and interactions of characters. The viewer experience is an engagement with that space, its characters and the narrative in which they (both characters and viewers) are embedded. The technicality of film is an essential feature of its production, and film-makers have a complex technical language to discuss the practice of film-making. However, the same technical language is not appropriate to a discussion of viewing or to an analysis of the viewer experience. Viewers are not concerned with the technical details of camera set-ups or editing – they are simply interested in whether the text works for them: whether the story is credible; the characters believable (in realist or non-realist modes); the issues and ideas articulated are consistent and interesting. The role of the medium in generating the viewer experience is usually only of interest when it is appallingly bad or breath-takingly good. The same might be said of information technology. If a web site is appallingly bad, then usually the technicality of the site is involved – for example, in that it takes too long to upload. Or, it may be strikingly innovative, so that users are impressed by its speed and efficiency. However, in most cases the technicality is the hidden engine of the user's interaction with the text. It stands or falls – is successful or fails – according to whether it engages users. And that engagement is primarily cultural – and that means, perceptually, spatial.

The spatiality of multimedia is the spatiality of the twentieth- and twenty-first century. It is a spatiality created by meaning, as David Woodhead argued. Or, as physicists and metaphysicians might argue, it is a spatiality characterised by interconnectedness, by flow; a four-dimensional spatio-temporal realm in which the flap of a butterfly wing in Tokyo might begin a chain of events that causes an avalanche in Alaska or a cyclone in Fiji. In discussing cyberspace we are grappling with just one of the metaphors used to facilitate a specific technical, social and cultural practice – our use of information technology and the multimedia texts it generates. The metaphor is, itself, culturally-specific. It articulates the experience of using IT for those raised in a particular social and cultural environment – those for whom the notion of data-banks has been created by television and film and who live in, or have visited, big cities. And it is also a metaphor of the 1980s, when the technology was less familiar and users needed a way of incorporating this technology into their lives. Science-fiction film and television and the excitement of the big city provided those key references. It may be that the contemporary technological imaginary is rather different. The spread of mobile phone technology, as well as greater familiarity with the technology, may have changed aspects of that spatial imaginary. Yet, the enormous popularity of the *Matrix* films suggests that the metaphor still resonates for today's users. And what the virtual world of the *Matrix* films tells the audiences over and over again is that the reality we are expected to accept as commonsense is a vast set of interconnected events, world-lines, vectors articulating influences within the field that we locate as our space-time continuum. In the film's terms, it is a vast computer program. That computer program is a linguistic metaphor for the four-dimensional space-time continuum that constitutes the contemporary re-vision of 'space'.

The importance of this spatial imaginary for those working with multimedia texts is that it provides a way of entering the imaginary of the user. This is the imaginary that created the concept of the web, the internet, the rhizome, the matrix – all spatial metaphors for our everyday uses of the technology. The metaphors articulate not only spatiality, but the imbrication of space and time that characterises our contemporary understanding of space – as connectedness. It is this understanding of the user imaginary that also created the graphic interface – allowing users to relate this technology imaginatively to the other spatio-temporal technologies in their lives, such as film, television, arcade games. Further, it enables those users to incorporate the technology socially and culturally into their everyday lives, to recognise both its specificity and its difference, to understand its meanings by reference to all the other meaning-full practices in their lives and to use those meanings in the production of knowledge. The same understanding creates web sites that are spatially meaningful: that is, sites in which the visual and imaginary generation of space contributes effectively to the meaning of the site.

Textual spaces

In exploring the spatiality of the multimedia text we work from the basic principle that the individual text is conceptualised as a continuum, with meanings generated from the relationship between different textual elements, which include what we may perceive as '(empty) space'. We might make this point concretely by noting that an apparently empty space in a painting is not an area devoid of paint. Similarly, space in a film is not an area where there is no film-stock or pigmentation. Instead, this is an area in which the contrast between visual elements – between objects portrayed or between areas of pigmentation – is very high. The area that is less pigmented or less saturated by colour or in which there is no visual image of a person or object may appear to be 'space'. Yet, as noted in the discussions above, none of these spaces is simply emptiness that has not been filled. Rather, it is an area created by the composition of the image or layout in order to generate a particular meaning.

In other media the relationship between elements of a particular text is studied as 'layout' or *mise-en-scène* – the configuration of elements that generates meaning, or, to put it another way, the meaning that generates a particular configuration of elements. The elements referred to here commonly include words, images and other visual symbols, and sound. The elements of an IT text such as a weblog, e-mail or web site usually include words and/or images, occasionally animation, and occasionally sound. The spatiality of the text is constituted by the configuration of these elements, and will include areas that we might commonly refer to as '(empty) space'. Yet those (empty) spaces are generated by lines of a programming language, such as HTML, making the point that this 'space' is not an absence or emptiness, but a crucial (meaning-making) feature of the design.

Poetry is conventionally recognised by the difference between its spatial configuration and that of prose where lines are usually left and right justified. Instead, lines of poetry are usually shorter and are of uneven lengths. Some poetry, such as concrete poetry, plays with the spatiality of the form, adjusting the line lengths so that the poem takes on a particular visual form; which is an explicit way of directing readers to the significance of spatiality in the generation of meaning.

In a similar way we might consider the spatiality of e-mail. Of course, users often have idiosyncratic ways of writing e-mails; however, most e-mail is written as prose – occasionally, with an initial address and signature given separate lines. In explaining the significance of this spatiality, our immediate reference is the letter – a familiar written genre. Just as letters are written communication directed from writer to reader, so is e-mail. However, there are critical differences between e-mail and letters, the most significant being the time of delivery. Whereas letters take days or even weeks to arrive, e-mail often takes only seconds or minutes, with the result that the communication also has something of the immediacy of spoken communication. There have been many studies of the development of e-mail as a genre, but in relation to spatiality one of the major features is the way that the spatiality of e-mail resembles, or differs from, the spatiality of the letter. For example, business e-mails that are addressed to clients often reproduce the layout of the business letter, thereby signifying that they are serious, professional communications. The immediacy of the communication may, in fact, make this layout even more significant. This immediacy can give e-mail a spoken quality that has been responsible for many e-mail problems, particularly through misunderstandings about tone (for example, write an e-mail in caps and consider the tonal effect – it can read as a shout!). Using the conventions of the business letter is, therefore, a way for a business e-mail to tone down the immediacy of the communication which can otherwise leave the client feeling trapped in a one-way spoken communication.

Of course, there are businesses whose communication with clients benefits from the adoption of a more casual, communal or collegial relationship – and many businesses build this relationship with clients over time. In these cases, the formality of the e-mail may be lessened and the client addressed in a more personal way, using conventions that acknowledge the immediacy and 'spoken' quality of e-mail. This is a matter of judgment for the communicator, but it can be guided by an informed understanding of how spatiality is involved in meaning-production.

With more visually-complex texts such as web sites, the situation is similar. Web sites have visual referents in other media that may include magazines, newspaper, film, television, although as the technology becomes a regular feature of everyday life, the main referent will be other web sites. The *HistoryWired* site, for example, makes interesting use of spatiality. We have already discussed this site in some detail, noting how visual features and movement vectors generate meanings at the site – about history, about the site itself, about nationalism, about the museum as an institution. The site uses a mosaic design feature to introduce users to an apparently random selection of objects from the museum collection. Yet, just as every mosaic is constructed from carefully selected units combined into an overall pattern, so too is this mosaic; the pieces chosen for virtual display and the explanations given of them constitute a carefully crafted set of meanings about history, the USA and the museum.

The layout of *HistoryWired* creates the web of meanings that was discussed in the previous chapters, whereby specific objects from the collection are located according to particular categories. This set of connections can be read as an introduction to the practice of history – or a particular form of (social) history. The links at left have another function, which is to locate the site as hypertext – the links demonstrating the way that this technology is able to make information available to the user. These links, along with others on the page, extend the spatiality of the site beyond the physical dimensions of the screen into the data-space of the museum. So the user is invited imaginatively to walk the corridors of the museum, to explore the objects and their meanings in the written descriptions provided. This is a form of virtual museum tour, which spatially invites the user into the museum – or, at least, into the narrative of the museum. The top banner, that identifies the site, locates this complex narrative for the user. This is the site that makes possible this virtual tour, and that subsequently invites the user to participate in a series of narratives about history, democracy, the museum, and so on. In other words, the activities at the site are all spatially located as interconnected. *HistoryWired* constructs a particular kind of history, has particular ideas about the nature of the USA (for example, as a democracy), about democracy, about the role of the museum, and about its relationship with users. The spatiality of the site connects the user into a web of meanings that is the essence of the project that is *HistoryWired*.

Every web site constructs space in the process of making meaning. We can use the ideas about layout discussed in Chapter 3 (Visuals) to understand the specific significance of layout choices – why an image or word is placed at left or right, up or down, on the screen. However, the significance of spatiality per se is that it is a continuum. Elements on screen do not exist in isolation, but are interrelated in ways that are meaningful to users. If these interrelations are obscure, then the meanings of a page may also be obscure for many users. This seems an obvious point, but consider the case of a web site constructed on the principle of a library catalogue. The designer's view was that users would welcome the opportunity to move from link to link, category to category, on the site looking for the information they required – and in the process be given a tour of the activities at the site. This understanding of the site runs counter to most users' expectations of this technology, which is that it enables quick access to information, so that burying information at a site is more likely to frustrate than impress the user. Spatially the library design option has the user wandering a maze, without a sense of control over the process. The second option, that of constructing an information architecture designed to enable users access to information in the most direct way possible, is more like a map, giving users a sense of control over their actions – even if, ultimately, it is the map-maker who determines where they may go within the space.

For designers – the map-makers – effective communication with users means understanding the spatial expectations the user brings to the site. One such expectation is a direct link to information required – which means that the designer needs a detailed understanding of the kinds of information visitors to a site may require, not simply the information that the site-owner wants to convey. Spatially, the meaning of the first option discussed above is a discontinuity – a mismatch between the requirements of the site-owner (to show off activities) and the requirements of users (for information). The resulting spatial discontinuity is likely to result in a literal break in the communication, as the user gives up attempting to find their way through the site. By contrast, a site designed to meet users' needs for information is likely to read spatially as well-planned, clear, efficient.

It is significant that the arrangement of information at a web site is referred to by the spatial metaphor, architecture. The term is used differently by different practitioners, sometimes referring to the visible set of links by which the site operates, at other times to the processes of categorisation that enable those links to be written into the site. In either case the metaphor conveys an understanding of both the complexity of the task, and its combination of art and science. Just as architecture is more than building, so designing a web site is more than translating text into a computer language. Architects create the space that is the living environment of a building by manipulating a range of materials and meanings – building materials, shapes, light, colour, intertextual referents, contextual or locational factors. Web site designers do the same. For both architects and designers the major referent must be the social and cultural expectations of users. If users cannot find their way around a space – worse, if they cannot work out how to connect with that space, to include it in their everyday lives – they will simply avoid it. The building and the web site, like those public housing ghettos, will simply become redundant – and be taken down.

Performing space

For some multimedia texts, spatiality is a key feature of their physical, as well as conceptual, engagement with users. Performance art and installation pieces often engage with the significance of space, physical and conceptual. Bernard Tschumi notes of a performance piece that 'the most interesting part of such performance was the underlying discussion on the "nature of space" in general, as opposed to the shaping and perception of distinct spaces in particular' (Tschumi, 1998: 224). In entering an art installation, one of the first things we often do is to locate ourselves in relation to the objects, images and walls of the space. We attempt to 'read' the space in relation to our understandings of space as a meaning(ful) and meaning-making construct. This new space, a space not of our making and so not confined by our familiar perceptions and beliefs, the meanings we know, can therefore become a space in which new understandings are formulated. And, fundamental to this process, is our participation in this construct as a space generated by meanings that we may come to share; that is, installation art and other artworks often consciously reconfigure our experience of space, part of a project to engage the viewer with new meanings and new ideas.

Yet, multimedia installations may use space in more coercive ways. In the previous chapter I discussed the installation, *circa* at the National Museum of Australia. That discussion focused on the meaning of movement in the installation. We might also consider the meaning of its 'space'. The space of *circa* is constituted by the visitor's movement on a revolving platform in front of a series of screens onto which are projected images of Australia and of Australians. It is a complex physical, visual, kinetic and acoustic space, which seems designed to render the visitor a relatively uncritical consumer of the imaginary construct, 'multicultural Australia'. In a sense, the space of *circa* is the space of the museum; conceptually, it constitutes a map of the museum. It is the map by which to situate the different exhibits and generate their meanings – as aspects of the construct, 'multicultural Australia'. So, the conceptual space of *circa* is not so much deconstructive as cartographic; like the mosaic at *HistoryWired* it offers the visitor a way of reading the objects and ideas that are the concern of the museum.

And *circa* does more than that; it actively positions the visitor in that space. This is not to say that the visitor cannot resist the positioning; however, the combination of embodied and conceptual positioning is very powerful. *Circa* literally, physically, corporeally, enfolds the visitor in a space which is both conceptual and physical – and the visitor has ceded physical control to the exhibit (it would be difficult to get off the rotating platform during the 'show'). As discussed earlier, the visitor has yielded control, authority and power to the institution by agreeing to take part in this exhibition (to sit in a seat, strapped in place, as the platform rotates). The visitor enters the physical and conceptual space of the institution and is constrained by it, at least physically. This exhibit can be read as the obverse of the performance or installation art. Instead of demonstrating that meaning is a function of our positioning, through the interrogation of our assumptions about place (our space-time positioning), *circa* simply orients us specifically within the meaning-making field, without drawing attention to the field. It gives us the narrative key (or key narrative) and sends us off to place the other exhibits within that narrative. *Circa* performs institutional space, not to make the visitor aware of the premises of judgment, but to substitute for judgment.

A critical feature of this *circa* experience, which gives it the conceptual power it has, is its bodily engagement. *Circa* is not only the creation of space, and a movement through space; it is an embodied, affective creation of space – which then mobilises this spatiality in particular ways in relation to the museum. As such, *circa* exemplifies the theorisation of space in recent architectural writing: 'Space ... is directly coupled to the movement and experience of bodies, and is thus divorced from any fixed spatial form that, to the extent that it does still exist, comes to function as the trigger for an affective bodily experience' (Hansen, 2002: 330). In his article, 'Wearable Space', Mark Hansen explores recent architectural writing on spatiality and its relationship to the body, a relationship that he believes has been exposed by the development of digital technologies:

> No amount of freedom from formal constraint can undo architecture's constitutive correlation with embodiment, even if it can shift the locus of embodiment from the pregiven materiality of architecture to the embodied experience of habitation triggered by built form. Indeed ... the more digitally deterritorialized the architectural frame, the more central the body becomes as the framer of spatial information – which is to say, as the source for architecture's constitutive constraint. (2002: 323)

Hansen's article exposes the vital connections between embodiment, space and meaning that are given direct expression in the experience of *circa*. If space is constituted by bodies, or by embodied experience (of which affectivity is an index), then it is not surprising, conversely, that spatial metaphors are used so often to enable our (bodily) engagement with the technologies that shape our lives.

Spatiality: the metaphors

Both separately and together, the work of Gilles Deleuze and Félix Guattari has inspired hosts of readers in the late twentieth and early twenty-first century. They conceived the notion of the rhizome that has inspired many theorists, particularly in the fields of multimedia and cyberculture. In their work the rhizome is the antithesis to arborescence: the random spread of the grasslike rhizome differs markedly from the iterative nature of the tree-root structure, in which a central trunk is the basis or foundation of secondary structures (branches, roots) that spread outwards but also refer back to the trunk. The internet, including the world wide web, has been conceived of as a rhizome, growing haphazardly, reached via various different (browser) pathways. More crucially, our meaning-making is rhizomatic. As we attempt to make sense of a situation, event, encounter, text, our mind shoots off in many different directions – consulting the voices of previous situations, events, encounters, texts, likening and differing, drawing inferences and gathering meanings, formulating opinions and judgments. Deleuze and Guattari argue: 'Many people have a tree planted in their heads, but the brain itself is more like a grass' (1983a: 34); that is, the brain tends to work like a rhizome even though, for many people, easy answers, predigested ideologies (a tree) has replaced the interrogative, rhizomatic process.

Multimedia texts tend to be arborescent rather than rhizomatic. They have a central core of ideas, values and beliefs motivating them, which are conveyed to users and viewers through their textual choices and their references to other texts or events. However, users and viewers tend to work rhizomatically, incorporating those texts within a meaning-making practice that refers them through a series of other texts and meanings as they gather information and work to produce knowledge. For example, a rhizome erupts every time a user logs on to the Internet, tracking her or his way through an idiosyncratic set of sites, situating the meanings of those sites by reference to yet other meaning-making practices (other texts – in other media) known to the user. The 'Go' or 'History' function of a browser shows us a (bit of a) rhizome.

The spatial metaphor of the rhizome captures the interconnectedness of the conceptual space(-time) in which we operate, and its unevenness – forming nodes here and there, shooting off apparently randomly in this direction, now this. It is like watching a film or browsing a web site; generating meanings from our knowledge of other films or web sites, as well as our understandings of this use of language, or this colour, this kind of movement, that sound, in other media, other texts.

Deleuze and Guattari also use the (spatial) metaphors of smooth and striated space, which we can relate to some of our previous discussion. Striated space is space that has been marked out in a particular way, by grid lines, rules and regulations, systems of meaning. The striations confine the meaning potential of the space(-time) within the parameters that characterise the particular set of striations. The space of *circa* is striated by the narrative trajectories that generate 'multicultural, postcolonial Australia'. And the Garden of Australian Dreams demonstrates the striated nature of 'Australia' as a geopolitical space. So the mercator grid drawn on the outline of Australian landscape signifies the incorporation of the Australian land mass within a European system of identifying/creating space. The Aboriginal song-lines do not identify/create the same space or the same meanings. By contrast, smooth space is space that is marked by discontinuities, that is heterogeneous, not yet marked out by particular practices/meanings. It is, therefore, a space of struggle for meaning – or a space created by a struggle over meaning:

... smooth spaces are not in themselves liberatory. But the struggle is changed or displaced in them, and life reconstitutes its stakes, confronts new obstacles, invents new paces, switches adversaries. (Deleuze and Guattari, 1987: 500)

The apparatus of the state works constantly to striate space, to establish its control over those areas – physical and conceptual – in which meaning, and therefore control, is contested.

Space and place

The other metaphors used to describe the practice of meaning-making and its impact on individual experience are space and place. Here 'space' is the institutionalised location within which the individual is located by regulatory social and cultural practices – like the mercator grid or shire boundaries or demographic descriptions. 'Place' is the individual's negotiation of individual being, which is achieved in negotiation with those social and cultural forces. Carter's *agoraios* is the subject in the process of negotiation, constructing a place to lean – but moving on when that place is colonised by regulatory social and cultural practices.

The work of Michel de Certau also relates to this understanding of individual negotiation of space. In his work the strategic practices of the state create the space in which individuals are located, but individuals may tactically resist that positioning to create their own place – which social and cultural practices will attempt strategically to incorporate back into the space of the state. And so a complex interplay of strategy and tactics is generated, which is similar to Deleuze and Guattari's processes of de- and reterritorialisation; the individual works to construct her or his own place within the (regulatory) space in which she or he is socially and culturally located. This metaphor of negotiation and/or resistance is useful in articulating the dynamic practice of subjectivity formation; however it is also important to acknowledge the extent to which the texts and technologies that are part of this negotiation are rule-governed, striated spaces.

Lumpy space

Elizabeth Grosz, writing about space in *Architecture from the Outside* (2001), makes the point that the space or space-time of contemporary thought is not homogeneous, but lumpy, uneven. Bakhtin's heteroglossia, the world of different voices that give a particular text its meaning, is not a smooth, quiet, measured environment, but a mad cacophony – joyous and sad, dark and bright, thin and thick, eddying, clotted in places with concatenations of voices, texts, traditions, and thin in others where the voices are fading, lost. This is not unlike the wagging tale of the dynamist dog – thickening the intensity at a point in the physical field as it momentarily occupies it (at dx, dy, dz, dt) and then vacating it to reduce the intensity to that of the air that was there a moment before.

Similarly, the interrelation of smooth and striated space, and of space and place, is not a homogeneous environment but a site of constant negotiation, of intensities that wax and wane, 'places' that wink in and out of existence. It is important to note the dynamic nature of the space that we metaphorically evoke in our attempts to understand meaning-making and being in the world.

Netspace and user nomads

It is too easy to claim with some net utopians that the Internet is the key to world wide democracy; to configure the Internet as a smooth space – or a place – not yet governed by any single authority, not striated. There is some truth in this claim, as there was in the notion of the 'global village' or as we saw with the blogs of Salam Pax, but it is partial – like Pax's individual negotiation of his cyber-place. After all, the textual genres through which we engage with the Internet exert their own rules of engagement, as does the use of the technology itself. Deleuze and Guattari acknowledge this when they note that smooth space is not, in itself, liberatory – and again in other spatial metaphors, such as the nomad, deterritorialisation, and reterritorialisation.

These metaphors are interrelated. The nomad, for example, 'distributes himself in a smooth space; he occupies, inhabits, holds that space; that is his territorial principle' (Deleuze and Guattari, 1987: 381). The nomad works to create meanings, and knowledges, that are her or his own, and the state works constantly to occupy those meanings and knowledges – to appropriate them and render them no longer a challenge. In other words, the state works to striate the smooth space experienced by the nomad. The nomad, on the other hand, attempts to liberate the striated space of the state through a process of deterritorialisation; to make that space no longer a specific 'territory', whether physical or conceptual. The state then works to restore that space to striation through the process of reterritorialisation; that is, to striate the smooth space so that it is now, once again, a specific territory. The concept underlying these metaphors is that of colonisation, a social, political and economic practice that has had devastating effects on nomadic peoples.

The concept of colonisation articulates the power and influence involved in this struggle for meaning/space. Colonisers subjugate a territory not only by brute force, but also by changing its meaning; situating that territory within its own realm, and reconstituting its indigenous meanings within the coloniser's own parameters. So, in 1770, the land mass of Australia, a multicultural space, became a monocultural construct of the British Empire. It became British territory, administered and understood in British terms. But, as Deleuze and

Guattari point out, the processes of territorialisation are in a constant state of struggle. Indigenous cultures did not accept this territorialisation and so reter-ritorialised the space (conceptual and physical) in their own terms. However, the state apparatus that supported the colonisation and its current manifesta-tion is far more powerful in many arenas (for example, military, economic, legal, and political) than the indigenous resistances. Though it might be argued that in other arenas (for example, what might be called in British terms, ecological or environmental, spiritual, and cultural) indigenous cultures are far stronger. The result has been over 200 years of unequal struggle between different cultures and meaning systems.

In relation to contemporary multimedia the same processes of de- and reterritorialisation are always in process, whether we look at an individual text or the technology as a whole. In examining a specific web site, for exam-ple, we are looking at a striated space, defined by the assumptions of the designer and owner, which include its response to the generic implications of the web site as text. In attempting to communicate with the user, the site operates as a territorialising apparatus, implicating the user within its own narrative, its own meaning-system. The user, on the other hand, may resist that territorialising impulse and reconstitute the meanings of the site within her or his own 'smooth' space – in a contest of/for meanings and knowledges. As our earlier discussions suggest, the *HistoryWired* site might be seen as engaged in this territorialising practice – demonstrating its version of history while at the same time incorporating the user/visitor within its narratives of democracy, US history, the role of the museum. So the interaction with the user constitutes a territory, striated by the assumptions written into the web site. The user may resist those assumptions, by challenging them (Whose history is not being told? What other kinds of democracy are there? Is democracy necessarily the only 'good' kind of government?), and so work to deterritori-alise that space – to constitute it as a smooth space of conjecture about museums, nationhood, history, democracy, web sites, technology, or any other of the many connections the user may make with or through the site. Nevertheless, the site continues to work on the user, incorporating her or him back into its narrative and so reterritorialising the space of the site. This dialogue between site and user constitutes the meanings of that site for that user. The meanings may be complex and contradictory for the user who works against the terri-torialising strategy of the site, working to construct a smooth space outside institutional control. Or, for the user who complies with the narrative occu-pying the striated space of the site, the meanings may be straightforward and relatively unproblematic – as directed by the site.

In the first instance we might characterise the user as nomad, occupying a smooth space of her or his own construction, though noting that society and its institutions work constantly to repossess, reterritorialise, that space – and, effectively, the user/nomad. It may be useful, then, to think of this nomad figure as the *agoraios* discussed by Paul Carter in *Repressed Spaces: The Poetics of Agoraphobia* (2002: 125).

Agoraios, the drifter

The *agoraios* is 'the person who hangs around the marketplace':

> He was a kind of *attached flâneur*. Even if he didn't actively take part in the business of buying and selling, he felt himself to be part of the urban scene. He was a drifter down well-established driftlanes. He could easily change mask and become a shopkeeper. He was like the pedlar and the North African street seller. He was the occupant of the café, and the one who leant against the post. An indication of the communal (non-alienated) nature of his presence is suggested by the fact that a particular part of the day (the forenoon) was set aside for frequenting the agora. (Carter, 2002: 125–6, emphasis in original)

There are some problems with this formulation. The street seller and the pedlar may be constrained in their roles as socially marginal by their economic, social, political and cultural circumstances. So the space they occupy is striated space, even if not the mainstream path of those who buy their wares. Nevertheless, the *agoraios* is an interesting conception. She or he wanders the agora but is not constrained by it; she or he learns from it, but not necessarily the lessons it sets out to teach. At the same time, this is not the detached *flâneur* of the early twentieth century, wandering the streets as a distanced observer. As Carter notes, this is not an alienated existence. Instead, the *agoraios* engages fully with the life of the market, the café, the agora, with all the different contexts through which she or he travels. This is an embodied, engaged, communal experience. Only through such engagement can the *agoraios* perform the territorialising manoeuvres that enable her or him to construct smooth space – to think beyond the institutional, social and cultural constraints that govern everyday life.

In other words, the *agoraios* constitutes space-time not as the fixed, striated space of social and cultural institutions, but rather as a malleable space that she or he inhabits in different guises, different identities, as strategically (or tactically) required. This is a space that folds back on itself to encompass the subject (nomad, *agoraios*) who relives the same space-time in different roles – or, rather, constructs different versions of the same space-time through her or his multiple (self-)constructions. In this way, she or he constructs multiple knowledges about the world, and is not constrained by the singular logic of a particular truth-effect.

In terms of the everyday user of multimedia, we are referring to the user who is critically attuned to the assumptions of the text she or he encounters and incorporates that awareness into her or his reading practice. This is also the user who situates her or his engagement with a particular textual/reading practice within the networks of meaning-making that constitute her or his everyday environment. And we are also, therefore, referring to the critically-aware designer who appreciates the complexity of the meaning-making strategies that are involved in both the individual text and in the user's engagement with the technology that generated the text. Both user and designer are engaged in a process of meaning-formation; they bump into each other in this mutual space. However, this need not be the negative 'bumping' that Carter envisages for the agoraphobe (2002: 159). Instead, it is a space of communication in which the meaning-making practices of each are engaged. Their bumping together may not mean the same thing to each, but it will be meaningful for each.

Memory space, memory trace

This bumping together is enabled by the process of memory, which Erik Davis has theorised in terms of spatiality. Davis's work has been particularly influential in writing about digital literacy:

> We begin with a digital dream. As computers, media, and telecommunication technology continue to collect, manipulate, store, represent, and transmit an ever-increasing flux of data, they are installing nothing less than a new dimension: the space of information. This proliferating multidimensional space is virtual, densely webbed, and infinitely complex, a vast and sublime realm accessed through the mediation of our imaginative and technical representations. How powerfully we engage this information space depends on how powerfully we both manipulate and inhabit these representations, these phantasms ghosting the interface. (Davis, 1993: 586)

Davis identifies several of the spatial metaphors that have enabled our engagement with information technology, including William Gibson's cyberspace: 'Gibson's work actually created a social space, organizing the desires and intuitions of people operating in the widely disparate fields of journalism, law, media, psychedelic culture, and computer science' (Davis, 1993: 586). Davis traces the genesis of these metaphors to ancient memory practices. For example, he notes Francis Yates's description in the *Art of Memory* (1966) of the use of an imaginative space, 'usually a vast building', as a memory. Units of information, signified by specific images, are located at specific sites within the building: 'By "walking" through the phantasmic palace, one could locate the appropriate icon and then recover its store of words and information' (Davis, 1993: 589). Davis locates other spatial systems for organising data and/or information, and then goes on to discuss gnosis. He quotes Gnostic scholar, Valentinus: 'What liberates us is the knowledge of who we are, what we became, where we were, whereinto we have been thrown, whereto we speed, wherefrom we are redeemed, what birth is and what rebirth' (Davis, 1993: 604). Davis then provides his own gloss on Gnosis:

> Gnosis contains practical information as well: the 'knowledge of the way' after death, the sacramental procedures, secret names, and magic formulas that enable the soul to break through the lower spheres under demiurgic control and mount to God.
>   Gnosis also comes in the *form* of information: a sudden blast of immediate data which is identical with the abrupt recognition that such information exists. In some sense, gnosis is information about information. (1993: 604)

We can relate these different understandings of memory, space, information, data and knowledge to the ideas already discussed in this and previous chapters.

The architectural metaphor for memory relates closest to the practice of data storage, where units of data are held in their original form. We might, of course, argue that Davis's own gloss suggests that the process is/was rather more complex; that access to the stored data required a knowledge of the storage practice, a contextualising function, that transformed the data into information. This can also be read as a gloss on the practice of meaning-making, whereby the meanings of objects or events or strategies are accessed by reference to our memory of their cultural and social uses. Those remembered meanings are then deployed provisionally in relation to the multitude of (provisional) meanings offered by the whole text, from which the user draws a range of meanings and/or information.

For example, in the *HistoryWired* web site discussed above, it is likely that the use of the colours red, white and blue in the banner head signifies the USA (as against, for example, the UK which also uses these colours). In reviewing the whole site the user discovers that this site is related to the Smithsonian Museum, a major US institution, so that this provisional meaning is affirmed. However, the situation would be more complex if the colours were identified by the design(er) not just with the USA but also with the notion of parliamentary democracy. It may be that a particular user will find the explication of democracy at the site to be unconvincing, at least in the terms provided at the site. For example, if the user was only prepared to accept a parliamentary democracy in which voting was mandatory. In this case the user would be led to a more complex reading where the colours represent the USA and its self-representation as democractic, but not democracy itself. In this second example, the meanings coded into the site by the designer would not be the same as those formulated by the user. So, this is not a simple example of a meaning being stored by a particular signifier being activated unproblematically. Instead, the user contextualises that meaning in relation to her or his other cultural knowledge and reaches a different reading of the meaning of this colour – not as democracy, but as a self-representation as democratic. We might equate this to Davis's notion of the Gnostic, where 'information about information' is critical to the process of meaning-making.

Not all users are Gnostics, nor are all designers. However, critical users and readers/viewers of multimedia are Gnostics, and so are informed designers.

Yet, there is another element of complexity to add here. This model of memory – storing data in discrete conceptual or digital sites for later access – does not actually accord with current research on memory. What it does resemble, as noted earlier, is the way we instruct computers to store data – which is like storing a document in a filing cabinet. We expect to be able to retrieve that document intact from the filing cabinet at any time in the future. However, human memory does not work in this way. In a recent article in *New Scientist* John McCrone writes:

A memory is anything but static. Resurrecting a memory trace appears to render it completely fluid, as pliable and unstable as the moment it was first formed, and in need of fixing once again into the brain's circuitry. Any meddling with this fixing process could alter the trace – or even erase it completely. Simply retelling a tale may be enough to change that memory for good. Long-term memory is effectively a myth.

...

A memory trace that goes all floppy every time it gets used only seems a disaster if you believe the brain to be something like a computer where data needs to be preserved in fixed form. Fluidity, on the other hand, may be precisely what is required for memory to work as something much more organic – a living network of understanding rather than a dormant warehouse of facts. (2003: 27)

McCrone's article traces changes in scientific thinking about memory that we can relate to the understandings about meaning-making that we have developed in this chapter.

In the opening section of this chapter we discussed the way that space and time have been reconceptualised as a continuum, rather than as heterogeneous variables. So that replacing the notion of chunks of space moving through a different dimension of time, we have the notion of a field of space-time traversed by lines of force that influence the distribution of events and phenomena within the field. Further, we related this understanding of spatiality to our understanding of space(-time) as created through meaning, so that the phenomena and events we recognise and locate are situated as they are (given a space-time specificity) because of the meanings that created them.

If we now relate this understanding of meaning (and meaning-making) to memory we have a model that is closer to McCrone's 'floppy' memory trace than it is to the mechanistic notion of memory as a data storage bin. The clotting and eddying of the space-time field is another metaphor for the fluidity of the memory trace, the meaning of which is modified every time it is activated. In other words, just as we understand the space-time field as 'lumpy', or non-homogeneous, because of the fluidity of the meanings that construct it, so we can understand memory. It is not a storehouse in which a fixed representation of an event, a 'snapshot', is placed for later retrieval and activation, but an active part of the process of learning and knowledge-formation. McCrone writes:

... the real problem for the brain is not how well it can preserve the past but how successful it is at integrating new learning with old learning. Memories exist to make sense of the present – and to recognise and understand the world – and the brain needs to be able to optimise its circuits, strengthening or generalising some connections while weakening or erasing others. (2003: 28)

McCrone's model of the practice of memory is, in his words, 'essentially reconstructive' (2003: 29). Memory does not preserve a static past but reworks our understandings of the past in the process of living the present and constructing the future. So the 'past' for the brain is not retrieved, but reconstructed – made again, as an active part of our living in the world.

And again we might model the meaning-making practice of multimedia texts in this way. Textual practices – use of words, images, layout, sound, movement – can be seen as strategies for activating cultural memory traces. This is a more active model of meaning-making than the (spatial) 'storehouse' model of memory. In that (storehouse) model we are reliant on users reaching into the mental storehouse or database and retrieving a particular memory, which they then interpret in a conventional, fixed way. However, McCrone's model of memory acknowledges users as actively creating (rather than passively retrieving) meaning. This way of understanding meaning-making explains the need to effectively write the user into the narrative of a text. The user who actively generates meaning through an encounter with a text does so only if she or he is engaged by/with that text; that is, the user generates meanings by engaging with the cultural memories and their meanings, which the text activates. The user situates her or his understanding of those memories and their cultural meanings in the context of her or his own embodied experience in order to generate meanings and, subsequently, to formulate knowledge. In the *HistoryWired* example, the red, white and blue might signify the flag of the USA – but they might also cause the UK user to ponder the state of democracy in Britain, to question whether the UK would be better as a republic, to marvel at the cultural differences between the UK and a former colony, to wonder how it had become a colony of its former colony – and so on. In other words, the plasticity of human memory and its active role in enabling the individual to make sense of her or his world works against the closure of meaning in any text.

This also means that a text can be designed to maximise the engagement of users. And the basis of the design will be a detailed understanding of the culture(s) of the user groups. By this means the user's cultural knowledge (cultural memory) is engaged; she or he is thereby able to generate meanings from the text and to situate those meanings in relation to her or his everyday life. The user incorporates that text into her or his memory through the literacies that give access to shared cultural meanings. The text makes sense to the user and, furthermore, it enables him or her to use that text to make sense of the world. The text becomes part of the narrative of that user's life.

This understanding of the relationship between user, memory, meaning and knowledge is another way of positing the active role of the user in meaning-making and knowledge formation. However, it also provides a critical perspective on the relationship between human beings and machines.

Machine memory, human knowledge

As the discussion above notes, the memory faculty of machines has been configured in terms of verisimilitude. When we access a database, we expect to retrieve exactly the same data that was stored. If the data has/is changed in the process of storage and retrieval, we tend to think of this as degradation – like the decay of a book stored for years in a library. In that case we would allow for the changes, the decay, and attempt to restore the original data. In relation to an electronic database, we might make the same adjustment. We might, for example, argue that the methods of encoding and decoding data make it possible for changes in data to occur – and so we allow for the effects of encoding and decoding on the data in order to retrieve the closest possible facsimile of the original data.

Human beings don't work this way. Human memory is not a filing cabinet; it is an active practice of meaning-making that enables us to make sense of our world. However, that making of sense is not simply a matter of locating specific, objective, fixed meanings and putting them together. As Deleuze and Guattari note at the beginning of their essay, 'Rhizome', that is the most basic form of reasoning – but it is not about making meaning. Making meanings is a creative process of activating cultural memories, relating them to each other in a myriad of configurations suggested by aesthetic, ideological, political, moral, ethical, social principles, and by our embodied experience of being in the world. That embodied experience, whereby our cultural knowledges become our flesh, makes us different from machines. We may share with them some of our reasoning practices – not surprising since we designed them to reason in that way – but we differ from them fundamentally because of our embodiment.

Spaced

Spatiality is a constitutive feature of multimedia texts – web sites, performance art, museum exhibitions – and the concept of layout that we used to explore the visuality of texts is a way of studying this spatiality. However, this chapter has focused not on this intrinsic function of spatiality but instead has explored the spatial metaphors by which users have interacted with information technology, and by which contemporary theorists understand the formation of subjectivity. We began by discussing the transformation in Western conceptions of spatiality at the beginning of the twentieth century. With the publication of Einstein's *Special Theory of Relativity*, space was reconceptualised as space-time, a notion that quickly infiltrated artistic (e.g. Futurist), sociological (e.g. Lefebvre) and linguistic (e.g. Bakhtin) understandings of everyday life, and was the basis for later poststructuralist understandings of the specificity of knowledges. Essentially space was understood as created by the meaning systems we use to understand ourselves and our world (including our technology).

Cyberspace is a contemporary 'space' that may have no technical 'reality' but which is, nevertheless, 'there', engendered by the metaphors that enable us to interact with digital technologies. Similarly, the space occupied by a museum exhibition or within which a performance work takes place is understood as generated by that exhibition or work. By exploring that construction of space, we learn how the visitor or audience or user is positioned by the encounter, and so the meanings (producing that positioning) that constitute that text.

We concluded by tracing the role of spatiality in human memory, which differentiates the intertextual, constantly renegotiated, narrative human memory from the replicant memory of the machine – the embodied human subject from the robot. And yet, as contemporary culture shows us, our relations with machines are always ambiguous – marked by both possibility and dread, hope and fear. Using the key concept of connection the next chapter explores the relationship between technology and its texts and us as contemporary embodie subjects.

SEVEN

CONNECTION

In a season-linking double episode of *Star Trek: The Next Generation* Jean-Luc Picard, the captain of the *Enterprise-C,* is captured by a collective cyborg entity known as the Borg. Picard is transformed by the Borg into one of them – a cyborg with prosthetic implants surgically embedded and/or grafted to his body – so that he can operate as their mouthpiece. As Locutus he wages war on the United Federation of Planets, causing enormous loss of life. However, Picard has retained enough 'humanity' to enable him to subvert the transformation and assist the Federation. Picard/Locutus works with his crew to defeat the Borg (by putting them to sleep), Picard's prosthetic implants are removed and he returns to his normal 'human' embodiment. His human be-ing enabled Picard to defeat the Borg and yet the Borg stay with him. As later episodes (and films) reveal, Picard is changed by his encounter – his (cy)Borg identity lurking within his humanity, threatening, literally and figuratively, to erupt through his human skin.

Picard's encounter with the cyborg entity of the Borg connected him into their matrix, and he will never again be completely free of that connection. The episode dramatises a number of contemporary concerns, most obviously the relationship between human beings and technology – the effect of technology on our lives and on us as embodied beings.[1] We, too, have been changed by our interaction with information technology – by our connection to the matrix of the Internet or to the local network of a digital performance – and can never go back to our former pre-digital selves. The episode also illustrates some of the ways we have of working through these dilemmas, which include our understandings of embodiment and of connection. This chapter explores these same issues, taking us through the contextual factors that situate the textual analyses performed in the previous chapters.

I, cyBorg

In the film, *Bladerunner* (1982), humans were represented as different from cyborgs because they had memories – of childhood and of growing up; the cyborgs had a built-in obsolescence that meant long-term memories were impossible. Yet, the narrative suggests, memories could be implanted, a practice that would invalidate memory as a test to distinguish between humans and their cyborg look-alikes. In the diegetic world of the film a police department is devoted to capturing cyborgs who pose as humans. This poses for the viewer questions such as: what is it that makes humans human? what are human values? what right do humans have to use technology to enslave others? It also articulates concerns about the use of technology to invade privacy, to direct individual lives, to challenge identity.

As the argument at the end of the previous chapter claims, the difference between humans and machines is not that humans have memories and machines do not. The difference is in the practice of memory itself – or, essentially, what we define as memory. Human beings do not store memories as isolated blocks of space-time, but rather memories exist as traces that are reconstructed in the process of making sense of the present. Accordingly, memory for humans is a creative, not replicative, function. Humans narrativise their lives with the assistance of memory. Memory (the function) weaves memory traces into the individual's life narrative in order to render it meaningful. Machines, at least as they are popularly understood, do not do this. They store data in byte-size chunks and, if it changes in the storage process, that change is generally understood as decay or degradation, not narratisation and growth. So it is not that humans have memories and technological entities do not, but that human memory is qualitatively different from that of the technological entity.

Bladerunner and the Borg of *Star Trek: The Next Generation* articulate a fundamental anxiety about the relationship between human beings and technology. The premise of *Bladerunner*, however, is a technology that enables humans to build cyborgs that look and act so like human beings that they can 'pass' for human, unlike the Borg who are patently technologically-enhanced. This suggests that the concern in *Bladerunner* is as much with the issue of 'passing' as it is of technology; that is, that the cyborg operates as a figure that challenges boundaries, subverts identity, breaking through conventional categories of human selfhood or subjectivity, such as gender, sexuality, class, ethnicity, race.

Donna Haraway's cyborg does just this. This figure embraces the ambiguities inherent in the human/machine composite being. For Haraway the cyborg is a figure for the complex contemporary subject who cannot be defined by a number of strictly demarcated categories, of class (working, middle, upper), gender (male, female), sexuality (heterosexual, homosexual), race (caucasian, oriental, African), ethnicity (French, Moroccan, Indonesian, etc). Instead, this contemporary (cyborg) subject may move between many different subject-positions, her/his lack of fixity challenging the nature of each of these categories: 'a cyborg world might be about lived social and bodily realities in which people are not afraid of their joint kinship with animals and machines, not afraid of permanently partial identities and contradictory standpoints' (Haraway, 1991: 154).

Yet, this figure is also fundamentally about technology; that is, while this figure may have links with other magical or mythological figures such as the Raven, the trickster and the Fool, it is significant that one of its contemporary manifestations is technological. The cyborg can be read positively as a figure that creatively challenges boundaries, but it also articulates concerns about the interaction between humans and their technology, as did Mary Shelley's original 'cyborg' story, *Frankenstein*. Stone notes of this interaction:

> When we engage with symbolic structures of sufficient complexity, to a certain extent we synchronize our own internal symbology with those structures. ... for me prosthetic communication and the things it creates, specifically interactive entertainment software, the Internet, cyberspace, and virtual reality, are not a question of market share or even of content. In a fundamental McLuhanesque sense these things are parts of ourselves. As with all powerful discourses, their very existence shapes us. Since in a deep sense they are languages, it's hard to *see* what they do, because what they do is structure seeing. They act on the systems – social, cultural, neurological – by which we make meaning. Their implicit messages change us. (1995: 167–8)

Stone's metaphor for this process is the prosthetic, which recalls the prosthetically-enhanced Jean-Luc Picard, broadcasting to the *Enterprise* crew as Locutus:

> I am Locutus of Borg. Resistance is futile. Your life as it has been is over. From this time forward you will service us. (*The Best of Both Worlds, Part I*)

In Locutus is expressed many of the fears about the use of technology – that humans become appendages of it, rather than its master (Locutus *speaks* for the Borg); that they cannot resist it; that it changes their lives forever; that they serve it, rather than the reverse. As noted previously, the new *Matrix* films reinforce these concerns, with human beings reduced to batteries powering the machine. The anxiety we cannot evade is that raised by the technology itself – as a source of power, as potentially destructive, as changing fundamentally our understanding of ourselves as human.

There are valid precedents for these concerns, of course. Human beings have a history of using technological advantage to conquer and enslave others, human and animal. And in the process they call into question their own humanity, their self-definition. These concerns continue. The development of contemporary information and communication technologies and of new biotechnologies has exacerbated anxieties about how these technologies are used and how their use changes (technologises) us. Martin Heidegger's essay, 'The Question Concerning Technology', is read as symptomatic of that anxiety.

The section concerning technology

Heidegger's work is quoted repeatedly in debates about technology and so will form the basis of our investigation of these concerns. His writing is sometimes read as unremittingly negative, as a kind of pastoral nostalgia for pre-technological humanity. However, this seems to miss some of the most useful points in Heidegger's work. In 'The Question Concerning Technology' Heidegger outlines the problems and potentials of technology:

> So long as we represent technology as an instrument, we remain held fast in the will to master it. We press on past the essence of technology.
> When, however, we ask how the instrumental comes to presence as a kind of causality, then we experience this coming to presence as the destining of a revealing. (1977: 32)

In other words, Heidegger argues that if we adopt a purely instrumental approach to technology, then we will be trapped within that framework. We will only understand technology – and the rest of the world – within those instrumental parameters that we have created. However, if we understand that we have adopted these parameters only for instrumental reasons and so can situate those parameters within their (limited) context of use, then we are no longer bound by them or the world-view they (alone) constitute. Furthermore, we will understand our own being, since we will be able to contextualise our need for this instrumental thinking, to situate it within our ways of thinking and being in the world. So, if we understand our instrumentality as a form of causality (What is its role? What does it achieve for us?), then we come closer to the truth of our being:

> Technology is a mode of revealing. Technology comes to presence ... in the realm where revealing and unconcealment take place, where *aletheia*, truth, happens. (Heidegger, 1977: 13)

Crucial to Heidegger's rethinking of technology is his tracing of the etymology of the word, technology: '*Techne* belongs to bringing-forth, to *poiesis*; it is something poietic' (Heidegger, 1977: 13). In other words, for Heidegger technology is a way of knowing and being in the world that goes far beyond the instrumental uses that are made of it. This is not truth in Heidegger's terms, for truth requires an understanding of how that functionality came about and the part that it plays in our lives. In other words, technology is a reflexive mode of thinking and being; instrumentality lacks that reflexivity. Richard Coyne writes:

> Technologies, devices, and things have this capacity to disclose, not just simply to give us information, but to reveal something about the world in a way that presumes neither uncovering something pre-existing nor creating something new. Specific technologies, such as computers, disclose practices, and prompt us to construct narratives around such disclosures. (1998: on-line, accessed 13/12/2003)

Thus, technologies do not show us things we have overlooked or create new things; they show us the practices by which we are acting and being in the world. For example, the computer shows us the ways we have conceptualised our 'real' in order to develop and operate a digital technology. Furthermore, as Heidegger notes above, technology enhances reflexivity; in this example, it reminds us that we are thinking digitally.

Early in Heidegger's essay is an indictment of modern technology that is often cited as evidence of an anti-technology stance. Heidegger compares a simple wooden bridge over the River Rhine with a modern hydroelectric plant. The bridge, he notes, joined one bank to the other, making us aware of the meadows on either side, mutually contingent to the river. In this, it is a revealing of phenonema and of relationships. The modern plant, by contrast, is built directly into the river: 'What the river is now, namely, a water power supplier, derives from out of the essence of the power station' (Heidegger, 1977: 16). For some readers this is evidence of a kind of pastoralism in Heidegger, yearning for the days before modern technology. However, an alternative reading is possible. The problem for Heidegger, we might suggest, is the instrumentalisation of the river: it is now merely 'a water power supplier', which demonstrates instrumentalist thinking on the part of those operating the plant. This instrumentalist technology does not reveal the river or the thinking of those damming it; it constrains both.

Richard Coyne uses Heidegger's work more positively and productively. For example, he makes a Heideggerian reading of computer technologies as a 'revealing':

> Computer technologies also provide spaces in which we can dare to think what has hitherto been unthought. Similar processes are at work in what computer networks disclose about the operations of language and texts, disclosing that texts have always been interconnected, that speech is always understood in terms we use to describe texts, that the author was always an illusive concept, and that authority, authenticity, and originality have always depended on social practices and agreements, rather than notions of empirical fact, proof, or truth propositions. (Coyne, 1998: on-line)

In other words, our use of computers has prompted us to examine the ways that we think about texts because it has prompted us to think about the way we think. That thinking 'reveals' not only fundamental textual strategies such as intertextuality (how we make meanings), but also that the significance of texts is constituted not simply as a kind of eternal fact (Shakespeare is the world's greatest playwright) but as a function of our social contract (contemporary Westerners, particularly English speakers, consider Shakespeare (one of) the greatest playwright(s) in their cultural history). It does this because in using computer technology to generate texts and to communicate with others, we adapt existing modes of communication for this new medium.

Still, computer-use can also be instrumental. For some (instrumental) users, computers do not prompt reflexivity, but rather the reduction of all ways of thinking to those that accord with digital representation. This is the source of Stone's anxiety quoted above: that use of a technology may change us without our awareness. We may fall into the trap of instrumentalism, seduced by the power of the technology or simply unable to perform the kind of reflexive thought required. Heidegger warns:

> The coming to presence of technology threatens revealing, threatens it with the possibility that all revealing will be consumed in ordering and that everything will present itself only in the unconcealedness of the standing-reserve. (1977: 33)

The unreflexive use of any technology leads the user to shape her or his world in the terms of that technology; that is, in the terms she or he uses to understand that technology. Hence, the advertising campaigns for personal computers that stress their power – the most powerful personal computer ever developed, a computer that can launch the space shuttle. How often is a personal computer user actually likely to want to launch the space shuttle? Or, less facetiously, how often will the home user need that power? Yet, the lure of the 'standing-reserve' – here in the figure of the computer processor (or its human user) – is such that it serves as the focus of successive advertising campaigns. At worst, this can have disastrous consequences and it is hard not to read Heidegger's condemnation of modern technology as a response to the race for nuclear dominance between (Cold War) super-powers, which was beginning when he wrote this essay:

> The revealing that rules in modern technology is a challenging [*Herausfordern*], which puts to nature the unreasonable demand that it supply energy that can be extracted and stored as such. . . .
> This setting-upon that challenges forth the energies of nature is an expediting [*Fördern*], and in two ways. It expedites in that it unlocks and exposes. Yet that expediting is always itself directed from the beginning toward furthering something else, i.e., toward driving on to the maximum yield at the minimum expense.
> (Heidegger, 1977: 14–15)

As former New Zealand prime minister, David Lange argued, the problem of nuclear energy is the nuclear state that it creates, along with the apparatus of secrecy and control it necessitates. The problem of nuclear technology in the second half of the twentieth-century was that it created a nuclear way of thinking and being, which meant that all decisions about individual privacy and security as well as state power and control were made with reference to that technology and its development. It was an instrumental logic that enabled nuclear physicists to claim that the development of nuclear weapons was 'an interesting problem in physics' without any thought to how these weapons were deployed socially and politically. Yet, Heidegger's work allows that an alternative response is possible – that the development of nuclear technologies has the potential to challenge the ways that we think about technology, ourselves and our world. So the development of this technology may also, for example, reveal the exploitative relationship between human beings and the natural world as well as the problematic relationship between the individual and the state.

The relationship between human beings and their technologies has always been uneasy. Each new technology and the products and practices it generates involves us in a rethinking and re-situating of our selves and our world. Each technology has to be narrativised to enable us to situate it within our everyday lives; it has to be located in the narrative of our everyday lives. Heidegger's work is crucial to understandings of multimedia because it enables us to explore some of the ways that takes place – by reference to pre-existing ways of thinking and being that are (re)deployed by the technology, by analysing the motifs that recur in our cultural narratives about the technologies, and by locating new narratives created by our placement of this technology.

The mind-in-a-vat

If we refer once again to the scenario with which the chapter opened, Jean-Luc Picard as Locutus of Borg, we identify one of the key elements in our concerns about technology – its effect on embodiment. Information technology has generated a plethora of texts that deal with embodiment, from *Bladerunner* to William Gibson's *Neuromancer, The Matrix* and its sequels, the *Terminator* films, and many other examples in literature, visual arts, film and television. One of the most powerful aspects of Heidegger's analysis is also the way that embodiment is reconceptualised.

For Heidegger embodiment is fundamental to our being-in-the-world; it is a committed engagement with the world that effectively precedes even our sense of having a body. In other words, the idea that we have a body is the product of reflection that comes after, and as a result of, this fundamental embodied engagement. This is a very different understanding of embodiment than that which we find in many recent texts, and in many writings on Virtual Reality (VR), where embodiment is an encumbrance and not essential to humanity.

Many of these recent works operate with a Cartesian notion of the individual subject: 'I think, therefore I am'. The essence of the individual, they argue, is the mind. Case, of *Neuromancer*, refers to his body as 'meat' and 'wet-ware'; his 'self' or being is in his mind, particularly when it is jacked into a computer system. Many VR fantasies work from the same premise: that the body is an encumbrance that prevents the human subject from fulfilling her or his fantasies. And it is not uncommon to hear not only science fiction narrators but also real, living scientists talking about the day when they will be preserved forever, as a mind-in-a-vat. Every other part of their being, they reason, is inessential to the most vital part of themselves – the mind.

Bruno Latour addresses this notion in his essay, 'Do You Believe in Reality? News from the Trenches of the Science Wars' (2003). In this essay Latour records his amazement at being asked by a colleague whether he believed in reality. In response he argued:

> Only a mind put in the strangest position, looking at a world *from the inside out* and linked to the outside by nothing but the tenuous connection of the *gaze*, will throb in the constant fear of losing reality; only such a bodiless observer will desperately look for some absolute life-supporting survival kit. (Latour, 2003: 128, emphasis in original)

And this same bodiless observer will throb with the ecstasy of oneiric orgasms: the VR vision of 'safe sex'. Latour traces the historical development of mind- in-a-vat thinking, from Descartes to phenomenology and postmodernism. Phenomenologists, he argues, focus on the human perception of the real world – but in the process leave the real world 'out there'. Postmodernists, on the other hand, understand our perception of the real as a series of language games, with no verifiable outside real to connect with:

> The prisoners are now gagging even those who ask them to look out their cell windows; they will 'deconstruct', as they say – which means destroy in slow motion – anyone who reminds them that there was a time when they were free and when their language bore a connection with the world.
>
> Who can avoid hearing the cry of despair that echoes deep down, carefully repressed, meticulously denied in these paradoxical claims for a joyous, jubilant, free construction of narratives and stories by people forever in chains? (Latour, 2003: 129)

For Latour there is one way out of this despair – embrace our embodiment:

> Why not choose the opposite solution and forget the mind-in-a-vat altogether? Why not let the 'outside world' invade the scene, break the glassware, spill the bubbling liquid, and turn the mind into a brain, into a neuronal machine sitting inside a Darwinian animal struggling for its life? (Latour, 2003: 130)

By accepting ourselves as embodied beings we are able to interact with the world in a fully engaged way, not simply to gaze upon it – like a disembodied mind. Latour's description of the embodied being is also hybrid or cyborg – machine and animal – like the cyborgs Haraway discusses in 'A Cyborg Manifesto' (1991). Latour's cyborg is part of what he describes as 'a hybrid world made up at once of gods, people, stars, electrons, nuclear plants, and markets' (2003: 133) and he notes that it is 'our duty to turn it into either an "unruly shambles" or an "ordered whole"' (2003: 133–4):

> Once there is no longer a mind-in-a-vat looking through the gaze at an outside world, the search for absolute certainty becomes less urgent, and thus there is no great difficulty in reconnecting with the relativism, the relations, the relativity on which the sciences have always thrived. (Latour, 2003: 134)

So the disembodied thinking that Latour associates with a range of contemporary epistemologies leads to the absolutism that many of them, apparently contradictorily, appear to reject. In essence, he argues, this disembodiment created what Karl Popper identified as the 'two cultures': Science was identified as neutral and objective, a search for absolute truth; the Humanities as subjective and relativistic. This characterisation, Latour argues, damages both disciplines and led science away from the embodied engagement with the world which had been its strength. His message to both science and the humanities, as currently conceived, is one of connection:

> We tell scientists that *the more connected a science* is to the rest of the collective, *the better* it is, the more accurate, the more verifiable, the more solid ... – and this runs against all the conditioned reflexes of epistemologists. ... But, against the other camp, we tell the humanists that *the more nonhumans share existence with humans, the more humane* a collective is – and this too runs against what they have been trained for years to believe. (Latour, 2003: 134, emphasis in original)

Connection is a key term for this study. It refers to the ways in which texts generate meanings through their relationship with other texts, to the development of multimedia technologies that are characterised by their connectivity (the web, the net), and to the ways in which meanings are generated crucially by the connection between texts and their users. Latour's work identifies connection as a critical feature also of science – breaking through the barriers that constrained it within an Enlightenment rhetoric of truth and objectivity: 'we in science studies may be *the first to have found a way to free the sciences from politics* – the politics of reason, that old settlement among epistemology, morality, psychology, and theology' (Latour, 2003: 136–7, emphasis in original). The mind-in-a-vat of VR fantasy, of science (and scientist's) fiction, is the reverse – a disconnected, disembodied observer of life and so, paradoxically, unable, because of its lack of engagement, to see the relationships that activate and energise the world.

Latour re-embodies the scientist, arguing that it is only an engaged, corporeal science (and scientist) that can move beyond simplistic generalisations about the world. Latour's argument is not that the scientist actually is, or can be, disembodied but rather that the disembodied science that Latour rejects suppresses embodiment and its real world engagement. Haraway makes a similar point in her essay, 'Modest_Witness@Second_Millennium' (Haraway, 1997), where she identifies the suppressed embodiment of the 'modest witness'. Having explored the development of scientific discourse with its premise of the invisible, neutral observer, Haraway observes:

> This self-invisibility is the specifically modern, European, masculine, scientific form of the virtue of modesty. This is the form of modesty that pays off its practitioners in the coin of epistemological and social power. This kind of modesty is one of the founding virtues of what we call modernity. This is the virtue that guarantees that the modest witness is the legitimate and authorized ventriloquist for the object world, adding nothing from his mere opinions, from his biasing embodiment. (1997: 23–4)

As Haraway notes, other observers at the scientific event have been traditionally excluded from the role of scientist because their embodiment (female, working-class, non-white) is visible, unlike 'modern, European, masculine' embodiment that is 'invisible' (the neutral non-presence). This suppression of embodiment is identified by Haraway as fundamental to modern technoscience.

This is not to say that Latour and Haraway offer the same argument. Latour's argument can be seen as avoiding, often by a very engaging rhetoric, some of the critical questions raised by deconstructionist and poststructuralist writers – about the relationships between materiality, discourse, meaning and being – that Haraway does address. And Haraway writes specifically about her differences with Latour in 'Modest_Witness@Second_Millennium'. So it is significant that both reach similar conclusions about the need to acknowledge the role of embodiment in our engagement with the world. Furthermore, when Haraway argues that '[b]oth the subjects and objects of technoscience are forged and branded in the crucible of specific, located practices, some of which are global in their location' (Haraway, 1997: 35), she continues her call for the recognition of all knowledges as situated – and hence as connected. The same point is made in earlier essays such as 'Situated Knowledges' where she argues that the 'alternative to relativism is partial, locatable, critical knowledges sustaining the possibility of webs of connections called solidarity in politics and shared conversations in epistemology'

(Haraway, 1997: 191). The conversation between Haraway and Latour – both major contemporary theorists of science and technology – crucially features the terms, embodiment and connection.

We might consider now how an appreciation of embodiment impacts on our understanding of multimedia and its role in the negotiation of subjectivity and of identity. This study begins by reference to the most common textual genre of information technology – e-mail – and its role in human connection.

Virtual love

E-mail is not only the most successful on-line genre, connecting people for all kinds of reasons to do with information delivery, education, entertainment, commercial exchanges, it is also the application most often involved in discussions of that most intimate embodied practice – virtual sex.

There are many reports of people meeting on-line and conducting erotically-charged exchanges. The film, *Bridget Jones's Diary* (2001) shows Bridget beginning her relationship with her publisher-boss via flirtatious e-mails. These on-line exchanges may result in a sense of intimacy, with those involved directing each other in sexual play resulting in orgasm. The immediacy of e-mail, chat-rooms, and of communicator programs such as Messenger makes possible this relationship between strangers, between those who are geographically separated, between those who are already in real time relationships, and so on. It enables virtual flirtations, seductions, affairs without the responsibilities that attend their actual physical realisation. Further, there is a sense in which the actual sex itself cannot fail to be satisfying to some degree, since it is performed by the user – who has an intimate knowledge of her or his (own) body's pleasures. And it is not intertwined with the less glamorous realities of everyday life. This may seem to be an ideal scenario to many users – sex without responsibility. Further, it is a scenario that offers possibilities for sexual play and experimentation without the dangers that may accompany real time encounters, and that offers the possibility of sexual experience to those who for reasons such as personal choice, (dis)ability, or location may find real time experience problematic. Shannon McRae vividly describes the possibilities of netsex in her article, 'Coming Apart at the Seams' (1996):

> To be involving, netsex involves a constant phasing, simultaneous awareness of the corporeal body at the keyboard, the emoting, speaking self on the screen, and existence of another individual, real and projected, who is similarly engaged. Mind/body awareness is not split, but doubled, magnified, intermingled. (1996: 260)

For McRae the experience of sexual relationship with another person via information technology (at the end of a phone line) does not eliminate corporeality, but reinforces it. It means that the respondents are aware not only of themselves as not simply physical ('meat') but as complex emotional and intellectual, as well as physical, beings ('emoting, speaking self'), but of the other, equally complex being with whom they communicate. So, this is not analagous to pornography use, where there is no co-respondent able to interact with the user; nor is it equivalent to some of the early VR fantasies where the VR partner was a kind of animated Playboy or Playgirl centrefold. In fact, it is the connectivity of the encounter – the fact that it is an interpersonal engagement – that identifies the user as a corporeal being; which is to say that, in the act of engaging non-corporeally (via the Internet), the user is reconstituted as a corporeal being because her or his responses and her or his predictions of the responses of co-respondents depend on their identification as corporeal (physical, emotional, intellectual, spiritual) beings.

We might argue that it is not surprising if netsex – or any kind of sex – reminds us of our corporeality. Yet, again, it is the connectivity, the reciprocity, of the encounter that embodies the user, not the nature of the stimulus – which is not to say that the Internet is the contemporary answer to concerns about sex and love. If anything, it opens up as many questions as it answers, sends out as many false promises as it fulfils. Ellen Ullman's article, 'Come in, CQ: The Body on the Wire' (1996), is a nuanced account of this new encounter with our own embodiment. At one point she describes an encounter with a man she has formerly known as an e-mail respondent. During dinner at a restaurant she realises that they are communicating within their established electronic pattern:

> With a shock, I realize that we have finally gone out to dinner only to *exchange email.* I can almost see the subject headings flying back and forth. ... His face is one of my imaginings, the same serious attention, deep voice, earnest manner with an occasional smile or tease. But, in some odd way, it's as if his face is not there at all, it has so little effect on the flow of 'talk'. I look at our hands lying near each other's on the table: They might as well be typing. (Ullman, 1996: 17, emphasis in original)

The very pleasant dinner is followed by a long walk by the beach and 'we talk, talk, talk' – but no touching. Finally, each goes home alone. Next morning, the author reports feeling disappointed, until 'before noon, the email resumes'. Her friend writes of his great pleasure at their encounter and they resume their communication.

> Immediately, the body in the machine has returned us to each other. In this interchange there is the memory of the beach, its feel and smell, mentions of bed and sleep. Bed, a word we would never say in actual presence, a kind of touch by word we can only do with our machines. ... we're lucky for the email. It gives us a channel to each other, at least, an odd intimacy, but intimacy nonetheless. (Ullman, 1996: 20)

Ullman's article concludes with an anecdote that contains the essence of this notion of connection. She reports on a meeting of radio operators gathered together to mark the demise of the Morse code:

> One ten-year radioman, Petty Officer Tony Turner, talked about losing the feel of the sender. The transmission comes 'through the air, into another man's ear,' he said. The code has a personality to it, a signature in the touch and rhythm on the key. For Turner, the signature's origin is no mystery. 'It's coming from a person's *hand*,' he said. (Ullman, 1996: 20, emphasis in original)

Ullman here identifies the corporeal connection created by the (embodied) users of the technology. A common assumption might be that the technology itself is neutral; that it carries only the meaning of the words that it transmits. However, the radio operator's testimony belies this. Even a communication system as basic as the Morse code (a series of short and long bursts of transmission that is represented as dot and dash) is imbued with the corporeality of the particular operator. To gloss Ullman's quote: the receiver of a Morse code communication did not simply decode a mechanical signal; he felt on his ear the caress of the sender's hand. How much more compelling, then, is the digital address of an e-mail correspondent whose message, as well as transmission practice, is imbued with (embodied) being?

The embodied reality of on-line communication reverberates through our understanding and analysis of information technology and its products, and its consequences are both textual and ethical. Individual users incorporate this technology, and its texts, into their everyday lives and it is only by understanding the relationship with the technology as fully incorporated that we can begin to understand and assess its meanings for users – the meanings it offers, the ethics it embodies.

Seduction

The 'anonymous sex' – the orgy dream – of VR is challenged by the corporeality of the user. In her article, 'Of Bonding and Bondage: Cults, Culture, and the Internet' (2001), Denise Caruso records a comment by science fiction writer, Bruce Sterling: 'One of his best friends is getting a divorce because he's literally spending all his time in a virtual world, with virtual people' (Caruso, 2001: 215). Sterling's friend experiences the consequences of his on-line experience not just in a virtual world removed from everyday reality; it reverberates critically through his everyday life, causing the breakdown of his marriage with all its attendant grief and disturbances. In other words, communication on-line doesn't only happen in Case's hallucination of cyberspace – it also happens in real time, in the embodied being of users.

And we might argue further that this is, after all, what all successful communication is about – an embodied engagement with a text or event or person. So when a visitor walks into the multimedia space of a museum or art gallery or shopping mall or logs on to a web site, we do not envisage that visitor as leaving their body at the door or the keyboard. On the contrary, designers work with all available resources to engage that visitor, which commonly means deploying all possible sensory, as well as intellectual, resources. The designer's work is seduction – whether the end is aesthetic, educational, commercial, interpersonal – and seduction is a whole body affair.

The previous chapters – on writing, visuals, sound, movement and space – all deal with aspects of seduction of and by the multimedia text. And here it is necessary to deal with the complex ethics of this seduction. Baudrillard's writing on seduction reflects the complexity and ambiguity of this relationship. In the first place it confirms that this interaction is, indeed, a relationship – not simply a matter of a passive user positioned to receive a message or direction:

> ... the enchantment of seduction puts an end to every libidinal economy, every sexual and psychological contract, substituting in its place a staggering openness of possible responses. It is never an investment but a risk; never a contract but a pact; never individual but dual; never psychological but ritual; never natural but artificial. It is no one's strategy, but a destiny. (Baudrillard, 2001: 161–2)

In other words, seduction is not an economic exchange or a contract whereby the roles of each party are regulated and an exchange formalised in particular terms – sexual or psychological. Instead, it involves a continual interrelationship between two parties, for both of whom the exchange is part of their being. In other words, this relationship cannot be contained within the rules of contract; each party is engaged in a communication that is multiple, allusive, intertextual – open to multiple and shifting meanings and so to constant renegotiation. Rex Butler glosses Baudrillard's notion of seduction in this way:

> ... seduction is the idea that the other cannot be forced to follow, that in any such forcing there is always an ambiguity, a resistance possible by the other. Seduction is the idea that we cannot have a relationship without this undecidability, without it being impossible to determine whether it is we who lead the other or the other who leads us. (1999: 72–3)

It is this understanding of seduction that describes the user–text interactions described elsewhere in this study; that is, a relationship between the multimedia text and the user marked by multiple and shifting meanings and meaning-making, in which neither user nor text is identifiable as wholly determining the exchange.

Again, neither site nor user can control the generation of meanings. Meaning-making is ritualised, in that it involves the generation of meanings through textual strategies that are meaningful through their relationship with other textual strategies, rather than because of any inherent 'natural' meaning. This is Baudrillard's second register of objects (the non-functional or subjective), equivalent to the paradigmatic axis in descriptions of language function, and, more pertinently in this study, to Bakhtin's notion of heteroglossia. So a user reads elements or properties of the site through their familiarity with other similar elements or properties: a colour means as it does because of its positioning within a particular culturally-specific colour system or network; a sound takes its meaning from its positioning within its acoustic environment and the systems or networks through which it is heard. It is also ritualised in that the user's meaning-making is ritualised; it is culturally-learned rather than individual or idiosyncratic. So a user 'reads' a web site through her or his (learned) understanding of web sites as a genre of text and mode of communication, rather than through any idiosyncratic or individual perception of web sites.

As the chapters on different meaning-making strategies have indicated, this reading and its seductions involve the senses (sight, hearing, spatiality, kinesics) as well as the intellect of the user. They are seductive, in Baudrillard's sense, in that they attempt to lead the user to a particular conclusion/meaning/action – yet they are also, by nature, indeterminate and so involve the user in a play of meaning(-making) that neither seducer nor seducee can control. For those involved in designing and analysing multimedia this leads to a number of conclusions. Firstly, that the user relationship has to be seen as fundamentally dual or reciprocal. There is simply no point to the 'stupid user' accusation (not uncommon in IT circles) since it positions the user as passive consumer, rather than active producer of meaning and partner in the process of (textual) seduction. Secondly, acknowledging the user's role in meaning-making means more than a narrow and prescriptive reading of user literacy. It means exploring different user groups for their (different) literacies – and acknowledging these in the design of a site. Furthermore, it means acknowledging the complex cultural history of meaning-making or literacy skills so that a design may make use of the richest mesh of potential meanings in its design. So the designer works with a number of parameters: the cultural history of specific meaning-making strategies, their deployment by specific user groups at a particular space/time, the cultural history of the text-type (web site, museum exhibition) and its relationship with specific user groups.[2] And the user works with a similar set of literacies and potential meanings. Both may be more or less consciously informed about the meanings of particular textual strategies, beyond their inclusion in a particular design – yet nevertheless (unconsciously) deploy that history of meanings in the generation of meaning at the site. So a conscious knowledge of meaning-making strategies assists both to identify and proliferate meanings – to engage with the seducer and also to resist persuasion.

Betrayal

Baudrillard not only identifies the seductiveness of the text; he warns against it. For Baudrillard seduction is a manipulation of weakness, not a test/play of strengths:

> To seduce is to weaken. To seduce is to falter. We seduce with weakness, never with strong powers and strong signs. In seduction we enact this weakness, and through it seduction derives its power. (2001: 162)

Baudrillard uses the qualifiers strong and weak to distinguish between 'challenge' (a contest based on strengths) and seduction, which he identifies with weakness. Endemic to this argument is the same mistrust of the body and reification of mind that we identified in many writings on technology, and which has been a constant in Western thinking. Seduction, as a holistic appeal to the senses as well as intellect, is commonly viewed as a corruption of the seduced – an overwhelming of her or his better judgment (mind) by the stimulation of the senses (body).

Of course, this may happen; a user may be so enchanted by a web site, or a viewer by a film, or an audience member by an exhibition or performance, that her or his critical judgment is diminished. But we all deal with this seductiveness daily. When Plato excluded writers from his *Republic*, was he not responding to this same danger – the seductive sensuousness of fiction? This seductiveness is a feature of any communication; any attempt to address another in terms most likely to influence the other person to accept the communication in our terms. Further, as Baudrillard argues, it is both a fundamental feature of all simulation and it is mutual: the seducer and the seducee are locked in a relationship of mutual influence. Thus, one answer to this conundrum may be an increased awareness of the meanings of those sensory appeals – the textual strategies by which our senses are stimulated and so we are directed to make certain meanings/readings. And that involves recognising the fundamental imbrication of mind and body; that both are involved in thinking and in judgment – in which case seduction becomes an embodied challenge, not a simple attempt to control and corrupt. The seducee is not only influenced conceptually and corporeally by the text – and so liable to make particular meanings; she or he also responds corporeally and conceptually to the text, generating meanings that relate specifically to her or his cultural history and literacies.

Baudrillard writes that:

To be seduced is to be diverted from one's truth. To seduce is to divert the other from his truth. The truth then becomes the secret that escapes him. (2001: 160)

We might respond by noting that any communication (with another – person or text) involves a negotiation of one's truth, since it is always different from that of any other. The diversion from one's current understanding of truth is a part of the subsequent renegotiation of one's own truth, which is a continual state of being. Baudrillard constitutes the power of the text/object to divert the individual from truth as greater than we are allowing – since we argue that the individual responds to this seduction with her or his embodied being, which is not so easily betrayed.

Again, the seductiveness of the text/object/simulation is a function of the designer's awareness of the seductive power of strategies used in the composition of the text. It is also a function of the user's awareness of how those strategies impact on her or his truth. This awareness may be conscious or it may be implicit in the design and/or use of a text. The purpose of this study has been to show how a critical awareness of these strategies can assist both designers and users in their meaning-making. This means that seduction can be viewed as an invigorating and mutual exchange, rather than manipulation and betrayal.

Threat

Yet, there are at least two kinds of seduction involving the user of information technology – the seduction of and by the text, and the seduction of and by the technology. The rapturous responses of many scientists and technicians to information technology reveal the latter kind of seduction, which leads the seducee to forget that the purpose of much IT is communication. This is Heidegger's reserve army, the accumulation of power for its own sake.

The blogger often evinces this kind of rhapsody – the joy of sharing one's thoughts with the world, by way of a technology that is (potentially) global. Though perhaps the blogger's response also has something of what John Hartley described in relation to television as 'frottage' (Hartley, 1989) – the joy of experiencing the virtual community of viewers. Hartley uses this term to describe the enjoyment that viewers derive from watching their favourite programme as part of a community of others, even when that community is not physically present. In a similar way, the blogger experiences her- or himself as part of a virtual community, sharing thoughts about a topic of mutual interest. This may be an event like the war in Iraq conducted by Bush Senior, and Salam Pax's sharing of his experience of the war with those outside Iraq. Or, it may be the shared musing of a fan about the source of her or his fan loyalty. In both cases, information technology makes this communication possible, and this is communication – connection – on a scale and with an immediacy not previously possible, particularly for individuals.

In this case, perhaps the seduction of the technology is to think that this connection is, in itself, proof of the democratic nature of the medium. Yet, surely, we might argue, the early proponents of mail, telegraph, and telephone technologies thought the same – that the greater speed and coverage of communication offered by their technology equalled greater democracy. Howard Rheingold (1992, 1993, 2000) has long argued the democratising power of information technology, and Salam Pax's blogs on the Iraq war seem to support this claim. Yet there is another argument, of course, about how this same technology was instrumental in the planning and management of the war. Perhaps the argument that the technology benefits democracy is a reflex of its threat to democracy – through both the information it makes accessible to those who would wage war and the access it offers to personal information.

No technology is neutral. Each technology bears the marks of its development and implementation. Each technology changes the society in which it is developed and the individuals that constitute that society. Steam power irrevocably changed early nineteenth-century Europe – the nature of that society, the cultures and individuals that comprised it. The novel, *Wuthering Heights,* by nineteenth-century English writer, Emily Brontë, is a fictional depiction of that kind of technological change and of its affective significance for those living through it. It shows the demise of a class, the yeomanry, and their replacement by the new capitalist land-owning class – who owned the land but did not work the land. The trauma of that change is articulated in the love story of Catherine and Heathcliff, torn between classes and allegiances and dying along with the world in which they had grown up.

Contemporary information and communication technologies have changed the nature of contemporary societies just as fundamentally. They have led to the demise of some earlier technologies – such as typesetting – and to fundamental changes in work practices and skills. And they have impacted in all kinds of ways on cultures, people and whole societies: for example, changing the access to isolated cultures, the skills and literacies required by individuals and the economic base of most Western societies. Yet that impact is not simply or entirely positive or negative. As Heidegger argued, a technology can enslave in that it can lead to a way of thinking determined by that technology or it can lead us to question ourselves: the kind of society and people that have generated a particular technology, and how the use of that technology inevitably influences the nature of the society and its people.

Information technology has the potential to enslave, just as did the steam engine. It threatens in a number of specific ways, most obviously through its use as a surveillance mechanism. The speed of information management that makes IT so attractive to users also makes it a major tool of surveillance. Information stored on individuals, whether accurate or not, can be rapidly accessed and transmitted from one source to another – or to many, unless clear legal limits are placed on this (ab)use of information. When the stored information is inaccurate, the consequences can be devastating for the individual: for example, inaccurate financial information can lead to individuals being refused a range of financial products. Equally, however, there are concerns about the management of data. Visual technologies have a history of use as weapons of social control – delineating social and cultural norms that can be used to demonise individuals and groups. It is not a long way from the phrenologists of the nineteenth century who classified individuals according to the shape of their heads, to the mug shots of the late twentieth and early twenty-first century and the classification of individuals into sub-cultural groups – 'a youth of Middle Eastern appearance'.

Concerns about electronic shadowing continue, with countries developing legislation to deal with issues of privacy (vs surveillance). As commentators have noted, the collection of individual data by the German government was subsequently used by the Nazi party in their genocidal campaign against Jewish people, Travellers and others. The collection of data on individuals in our own time – via information technology – is even more prolific, with individual choices about purchasing able to be tracked in a number of ways (point of sale transactions, credit cards, register data, cookies), and with the interactions of individuals with institutions and corporations (government departments, courts, share market, banks) able to be collected and collated rapidly. And here the distinction between data, information and knowledge becomes important – as we consider the effect of forms of data storage and collation on the profiling of individual social subjects.

Here is a simple example: a single male who has never been married, lives alone, dresses well, attends the opera regularly and keeps in shape at the gym might well fit a Western stereotype of the homosexual man. If data on individuals is collated via a program that unconsciously reproduces this stereotype, then an individual whose profile accords with the stereotype might well be constituted as homosexual – or as likely to be so. This is not necessarily a problem unless those in charge of the data collation are also homophobic and have the power to influence negatively the lives of people classified as homosexual. The point about this case is that the individuals involved have not self-identified in terms of their sexuality – as we often do in terms of gender, ethnicity, religion, etc. Instead, their sexuality has been constituted via a collation of signifiers – which may be correct or not – and then used as the basis of actions towards them. In the same way, the purchase of particular kinds of books, attendance at particular events and contribution to particular charities may constitute an individual as having a particular political orientation – according to the assumptions of the programmer who wrote the software. And again the result may be that this individual is marked out for persecution. Recent events in Western countries such as Australia and the USA, in which individuals of Arab background have been singled out for surveillance and/or interrogation, demonstrate that this kind of stereotyping already afflicts the collation of data, and the subsequent construction of information on individuals.

Information is an interpretation of data, not a matter of fact – and yet the power of this technology to rapidly collate information may lead users to assume that the interpretation built into its software delivers fact. Further, the notion of knowledge as a situated practice, located in terms of its space/time and the social and cultural assumptions inherent within it, may also be lost in the adrenalin rush of its immediacy. So, our concern is not only the accuracy of stored data, but also its subsequent collation via uncritical and unselfconscious programs that may be used as the basis of social and cultural control. This is one of the ways in which 'connection' may be negative – and the democratising potential of the technology is perverted into a threat.

Much has also been written about the threat of the global pervasiveness of technologies such as television and information technologies. These technologies spread the cultural assumptions of the society that produced them to other societies with which they come in contact and, in that sense, are seen as imperialistic. Yet, it must also be noted that the societies these technologies enter do not passively receive them, but recontextualise them in relation to local conditions. Like individual users, they do not passively receive the (texts of that) technology but situate those (texts and) technologies within their local cultures in ways that are meaningful to local inhabitants. This is not to say that these technologies are not influential. Arguably, the strong government controls on Internet use in countries such as China and Singapore argue that exposure to the Internet is effective in challenging cultural values; in other words, the exposure to other cultures is an implicit challenge to the values of one's own culture; whether the individual simply replaces her/his former values with those of a new technology and its texts is another matter.

Tactics

Technologies and their texts may be seductive, but that seduction necessarily involves dialogue and indeterminacy. New technologies may be employed by old cultures to affirm their cultural value and continuing role in contemporary society – as Australian Aboriginal cultures use television and the Internet. What is at issue here is the appropriate response to these threats – rather than a Luddite dream of dismantling the technology. The technology itself is in a state of rapid change and development, with convergence of different systems a continuing source of interest. Mobile/cell phones are a major example of this – with their relatively recent incorporation of visual technologies and Internet links. One constant feature of all this development is connection – that this technology is all about ways of people connecting to other people. As noted earlier, the 'killer ap' so desired by the tech jocks turned out to be e-mail, the on-line successor to the humble letter. What it enabled was rapid communication and that was prized above all the flashy software the industry could offer.

This study focuses on the multimedia texts that can be generated via new technologies, by individuals, institutions, corporations, governments. There are many other aspects of this technology that demand ongoing study, including some of the threats discussed briefly above – its deployment in surveillance, its use as a means of social and cultural control, its role in globalisation. Each of these threats is also an opportunity to rethink our society and its values, and to determine the kind of society we want in the future. Each threat requires responses that, in themselves, can be part of the problem – as was/is the secrecy that attended the development of nuclear technology. Or, we can respond by examining the role we want surveillance to play in the life of the individual, or by challenging the process of globalisation and the institutions that support it. And we can use this technology and its potential to create connections as our means of discussing these issues and of creating tactical allegiances – as anti-globalisation groups have used the Internet to organise demonstrations. In the final chapter I attempt to bring together the insights from this and the preceding chapters, and so suggest some of the ways this study offers for creating those critical connections.

Notes

1   I explored the significance of Picard's transformation in an essay, 'The erotics of the (cy)Borg: authority and gender in the sociocultural imaginary', published in *Future Females, the Next Generation: New Voices and Velocities in Feminist Science Fiction*, ed. Marleen Barr (Rowman and Allenheld, 2000), pp. 145–63.

2   This is not to say that the designer cannot introduce new meanings, by using familiar meaning practices in different ways. The fact that the user expects the familiar meaning and finds something different is what generates the new meaning. This new meaning may be temporary, and fashionable, characterising a particular space/time (as paisley characterised the 1960s in the West) or it may have a longer or more profound effect on cultural meaning systems. In either case it is part of the cultural history of its society (so while paisley clothing characterises the 1960s, paisley has a much longer history, bound up with cultural exchange and with imperialism, as well as its role in fabric design).

EIGHT

SYNAESTHESIA

Sign-aesthesia

This final chapter is an attempt to bring together, to synthesise, the materials in the previous chapters about textuality and about users. These chapters attempt to open up for analysis the different meaning-making practices available to designers of multimedia – to explore the ways in which they communicate with users and how they can be manipulated to make particular meanings. This is, in this sense, a study of the aesthetics of the sign, where aesthetics is understood not simply as a matter of 'taste', but as a co-articulation of the poetic, the cultural, and the political in the text.

There has been a move in text analysis over the last two decades to focus not on the meaning-making practice of the text, but on what readers, viewers or users actually 'do' with the text – what kinds of meanings they make in relation to texts. This work was prompted, at least in part, by the tendency of previous forms of text analysis to be prescriptive in relation to what a text 'said' and how it 'said' it. Those earlier forms of text analysis were characteristically unreflective and unreflexive about the assumptions they read into their own reading and critical practice; about how those assumptions shaped the reading they prescribed. They neglected the cultural and political aspects of the aesthetic and fetishised the poetic – which they then constituted as above or beyond or without cultural or political specificity. In doing so they failed to acknowledge how the cultural or political specificity of their reading practice might disadvantage or disempower a reader from a different cultural or political positioning who might not make the same reading of a text. Furthermore, the conservatism of their own cultural and political positioning (which was accepted by mainstream institutions or instrumentalities as transparent and unproblematic since it was the same as their own) enabled them to claim a disinterested position in relation to their reading, which they equated with objectivity or neutrality or 'truth'.

One response to this prescriptive reading and critical practice has been to focus on the reader or user – to explore the meanings mobilized by different readers by doing ethnographic research on those readers. This work has been enormously productive in opening up a range of issues about how readers/users interact with texts, how they are incorporated into people's everyday lives, how that process of situating texts in relation to the everyday determines, at least in part, the meanings that individuals make in their readings.

Yet it has also, to some extent, led us away from the practice of meaning-making. It is as if an art school were to focus on a study of why people bought artworks for their homes and then taught art practice entirely in those terms. Whilst this study of people's use of artwork would be immensely informative, it could not be all that is taught. We would also expect students to be taught the basic meaning-making practices of their art-form (for example, we would expect painters to learn about drawing and composition, colour and brushwork) as well as its history (so that they could situate their own work in relation to its tradition). And we might further expect students to learn the contemporary cultural and political significance of their work; how their work characterises their specific time and place, rather than an earlier time and different society.

We ask the same of multimedia designers. They too have specific meaning-making practices that are characteristic of their work, which include their use of a number of different meaning systems characteristic of earlier forms of communication, as well as meanings that are endemic to their own form of text production and distribution. We want multimedia designers to understand those meaning-making practices not only technically (as the art student understands how to handle a paintbrush or charcoal) but also aesthetically – which means poetically, culturally and politically. We want designers to think about the choices they make in a design in relation to both the overall composition of the design, and the cultural and political meanings of their work. This is another way of saying that we want designers to understand how their work impacts on the everyday lives of the people who come into contact with it.

Considered in this way the study of (multimedia) textual practice is not simply a prescriptive mechanism for ensuring that people read, write and think the same way – eliding and repressing cultural and political differences; instead, it is a way of opening up these issues of difference, of situating a text in relation to different audiences and user groups (so ensuring that the textual practice used is most appropriate to the desired user group) and of understanding the meanings those users might generate from the text.

De-signing and re-signing the text

Teasing out the history and contemporary cultural and political meanings of each of the modalities used with multimedia begins the process of relating textual practice to users: what kinds of meanings can multimedia texts convey to users? how can designers utilise the potentials – existing and new – in these meaning systems to make new kinds of texts for these new kinds of readers/viewers whom we call users? And when in the previous chapter we looked at the technology used to produce and interact with multimedia texts, we are asking how this textual/technological practice directly affects the user, as an embodied social subject. In each case we offered some ways of understanding and analysing these textual strategies and technology – for their (potential) meanings, and how they work to position the contemporary subject/user.

Anahid Kassabian, in her study of film music, *Hearing Film* (2001), distinguishes between competence and literacy:

> Competence is based on decipherable codes learned through experience. As with language and visual image, we learn through exposure what a given tempo, series of notes, key, time signature, rhythm, volume, and orchestration are meant to signify. (2001: 23)

Literacy, on the other hand, is a more specialist knowledge of a particular musical discourse:

> Competence in [institutionalised music studies] ... is what I'm calling here literacy. It has a specific ideological history of its own, and has created a situation in which music can be spoken of only in terms of its intramusical features: form, harmonic language, orchestration, etc. The discourse of musical analysis has, in other words, interiorised itself, so that only trained musicians and music scholars are literate, are permitted to speak about music – and never in terms of the extramusical associations that nonprofessionals generally understand as the music's meaning. (Kassabian, 2001: 21)

Each of the modalities studied in the chapters of this book has its practitioners, each of whom has developed their own specialist discourses. The problem with this specialisation is that it can be used, as Kassabian notes of music, to silence those who are non-professionals; who are not trained in that speciality. Yet, we all use multimedia in our everyday lives, so have developed our own ways of understanding the meanings generated by these meaning-systems. One of the arguments of this study, as of Kassabian's, is that we non-specialists also need to be acknowledged as having a voice; as being capable of commenting on the way the meaning-system operates in the text, just as the author/producer/designer/composer of the text relies on our ability to understand and generate meanings from the text.

Kassabian goes on to argue that the film music she studies is a semiotic code and 'should be subjected to various semiotic and cultural studies methods, such as discourse analysis and ideology critique' (2001: 36). This study is an attempt to do just this for multimedia and its many constitutive modalities. The aim of this book has been to show that all modalities are susceptible to discourse analysis (which includes what Kassabian calls 'ideology critique') and that the contribution of non-specialists should be a valued part of the analysis of (multimedia) texts. Further, it may be that in developing a non-specialist analysis for multimedia, we develop a language for discussing and analysing these texts that can be shared by many of those involved in both their production and their use.

The analyses performed in the book have relied on a number of concepts – genre, intertextuality, discourse, subjectivity – that work across a range of meaning systems. Each meaning system also has its own specific properties, and these are deployed as particular textual strategies: for example, colour and layout with visuals, tonality and loudness with sound, vectors with movement, and so on. In each case, we are working to develop terms and concepts that can be used by non-specialists – so, for example, sound can be explored without the training of a musicologist or sound engineer, but with a terminology that enables us to describe the function of particular sound strategies in our everyday lives. And the role and effect of each of these strategies in a multimedia text then depends on the particular type or genre of text – and its social and cultural purpose and function; its ways of generating meanings and of positioning users or audiences.

In Chapter 3 (Visuals) we discussed the web site as a textual genre, noting that a range of (sub-)genres of web site have already developed, defined by their social and cultural function. This function, in turn, defines their use of particular textual strategies. So, for example, it was noted that government web sites in Western societies are unlikely to use Hello Kitty graphics on their home page as this would be interpreted as lacking authority. However, they might use these graphics on pages directed to audiences for whom these graphics might invite engagement; for example, young teenage girls. In making these kinds of judgments, the designer positions the text, and its genre, in relation to a range of roles and functions.

The diagram in Figure 8.1 represents some of the factors that influence the making of a particular web site. Its composition will, for example, be influenced by the kind of web site it is; that is, the (sub-)genre of web site in which it is likely to be positioned by users. So, again, if it is a government site, users will expect certain strategies to be used, that convey particular meanings – about authority, power, reliability. If it is a fan site, the expectations will be quite different and the site can 'look' and function quite differently. The textual strategies employed at the site are directly influenced by the kind of site it is. And as designers experiment with the use of textual strategies, their designs become part of the history of that genre, and influence its development.

Another influence on the particular site will be the history of representation of the product or information or entertainment it communicates – which also influences the web site genre. Again, the information conveyed by governments to their citizens is conventionally presented in a way that stresses qualities such as authority, power and reliability; however, its presentation may incorporate other factors such as engagement, responsibility, friendliness or approachability. Democratic governments, for example, commonly want to be considered 'popular' in that they are responsible, and responsive, to people (individual citizens). So when conveying information to people, they often attempt to incorporate those qualities into the way the material is conveyed. In written form that might mean attempts to be accessible to all kinds of people (with different levels of literacy, for example, or speaking different languages); visually it may mean using images that convey accessibility and

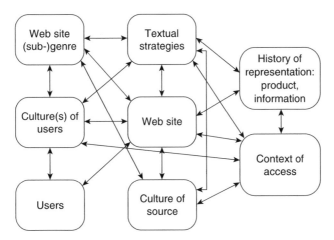

FIGURE 8.1   Matrix of influences: web site

friendliness. Furthermore, different levels of government often deploy these qualities to different degrees – with federal or commonwealth governments less 'friendly' and more authoritative than state or county governments, and local governments more 'friendly' and accessible still. Just as printed information from these different sources reflects their particular approach to the information they convey – and its means of communication – so, too, will their web sites.

The same set of interrelated factors is traceable to the source of the site, and its culture. This source culture is discussed above in relation to its communication with users. For governments, it means appearing to be powerful, authoritative, reliable, but also accessible, friendly, responsive. And this is qualified by noting that different levels of government may have different priorities, with local governments stressing accessibility, friendliness and responsiveness far more than federal governments, which focus on power, authority and reliability. In other words, we can draw a discursive profile of the source, locating the attitudes, values and beliefs that motivate its culture and reflecting on how these are conveyed by the text that represents it (web site or other). For example, we may be dealing with a multimedia performance (see Figure 8.2), rather than a government web site.

In this case the particular performance will be responsive to the body of work characterised as performance art, to the strategies it employs, to the ways it addresses particular issues and to the source culture, which we might characterise as the arts or culture industries. In each case the performance, like the web site, works not only within the conventions of its conventional representation, but also contributes to the ongoing development of those conventions. A government web site may do this in a relatively unobtrusive way, since its principal aim is to communicate information directly to citizens;

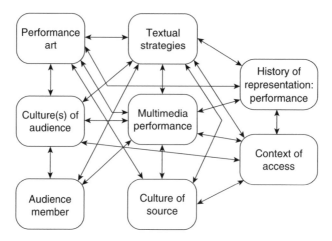

FIGURE 8.2   Matrix of influences: multimedia performance artwork

a multimedia performance piece, on the other hand, may foreground its textual strategies, since the nature of its textual or artistic practice is often a major subject of performance art. So, when a performance artist such as Stelarc manipulates a prosthetic limb as part of a performance, the audience is meant to see the technology – to understand what it says about the ways in which contemporary technologies are incorporated (literally and conceptually) into our everyday lives.

The culture – or cultures – of the user or audience are also anticipated by the designer or artist. Many audiences and user groups are complex, of course, and comprise a number of different cultural groups, and also include individuals who are members of several different cultural groups. So, for example, a government web site has to be accessible to all citizens, though separate departments and institutions will be able to specify some major user groups: the Department of Defence might reasonably predict that it needs to cater to members of the different forces (Army, Navy, Air Force); the Department of Education might identify major user groups as educationists, students and their parents, and so on. Similarly, a performance artist might reasonably assume an audience literate in the arts, with some audience members familiar with performance art as a genre. Their texts will reflect this knowledge in their modes of address and the extent to which they accommodate to the audience. If they make no accommodation to audience or user, then they risk losing those who are unfamiliar with the textual practices they deploy. Or, they may find that audiences read those practices very differently. This is very familiar from exhibitions in which challenging performance artworks are placed in the same venue as more conventional pieces. Many audience members cannot 'read' the work, other than as deliberately and self-consciously provocative and so reject it and its (other) potential meanings. More usually, however, multimedia texts (like all texts) are addressed within a known context, which alerts the audience to the kinds of strategies it may be using. Accordingly, their participation indicates that they are prepared to address the text in its own terms.

In the same way, designers and artists of multimedia works address their audiences with respect for their cultures. Where a text addresses one specific user group or audience, the designer is able to use their knowledge of that group to constitute the text in terms that are accessible or entertaining or informative or educational – or all of these. Where the audience is more complex, then the text may offer different pathways or different possibilities for different groups. We saw this with the *Documenting a Democracy* web site, which addressed casual visitors as well as specialist historians. Similarly, a performance artwork may incorporate features that make its textual practice accessible to the novice, as well as to the experienced visitor.

Considering the culture of the user or visitor means more than allowing for different literacies, however; it also means being aware of the discursive formation that characterises that culture. We noted in Chapter 3 that the professional historians who visited the *Documenting a Democracy* site might be more engaged by its implicit questioning of the practice of history than the casual visitor or school student. That is because part of every discipline involves the reflexive challenge to its own practice; history is always, to some extent, not only about the study of the past but also about how we study the past. Every cultural group that can be identified as a distinct formation has its own ideas, values and beliefs – discourses – that identify it. To be accessible and attractive to that group, the multimedia text employs textual strategies that acknowledge those discourses (whether they totally affirm them or not). In order to do that, the designer or artist needs to understand the discursive significance of textual strategies that might be used to compose a text; which means knowing both the meanings historically associated with particular strategies and their contemporary significance for the target culture(s). For example, the colour 'green' has a range of historical associations including freshness, Spring, jealousy and envy, and Irish Catholicism, but for most contemporary teens 'green' would primarily be associated with the environmental movement. Its use in a particular text might include one, some or many of these meanings – but that will also depend on the projected audience. Basing a text around the use of this colour to signify Irish Catholicism is likely to be lost on an audience who did not grow up with the 'orange and green' controversies of the mid-twentieth century. On the other hand, deploying this colour in texts intended for contemporary child or teenage audiences, who have been raised with an awareness of and sympathy for environmental concerns, is likely to appeal to these audiences – particularly when the use of this colour is strategically associated with positive issues or ideas for this audience. So, the culture of the user group or audience for a text is also important for the designer or artist in that it identifies their values, beliefs and attitudes – which the text may subsequently challenge or support.

The embodied user is another influence on the text, whether this means the user of information technology, the visitor to the museum or art gallery or the audience at a multimedia performance. In each case the corporeal presence of the user is a factor in the composition of the text and the meanings it may generate. So museums may deploy the corporeal presence of the visitor in the composition of an exhibition in a number of ways, such as interactive exhibits and defined pathways. Information technology is currently working to utilise the sensory abilities of embodied human subjects – manipulating haptic capacities to enable a more direct engagement between individuals and between individuals and objects; enabling individuals to feel what they are looking at may bring about more accurate distant diagnoses, medical and scientific. In these different ways multimedia acknowledges the corporeality of users and audiences as an integral part of their engagement with the world – with texts, events and other people.

At a more basic level multimedia designers need also to be aware of the physical limitations of their users and audiences, so that they do not exclude those who may have problems physically negotiating the text and its technology – whether that be the fine motor control and visual access required for web site access, or the mobility and vision assumed by many exhibitions and performances. So web sites now have standards that ensure their text is accessible via cursor to the visually impaired, though the fact that it has developed as a visually-based technology suggests that it cannot generate the same meanings for those who do not 'read' it visually.

The user's and audience's negotiation of subjectivity as they generate meanings from a text is also an ethical concern for multimedia (as for other forms of textuality). For some multimedia authors this may be a critical feature of the textual engagement; that is, their work is intended to influence the formation of subjectivity by positioning the user/audience to engage with particular ideas or values or beliefs. Of course, texts that have no direct political or cultural purpose also position audiences to engage with the ideas, values and beliefs they articulate. This means that texts that are intended for vulnerable cultural groups – such as children – are encouraged to examine the values they articulate. It also means that text strategies cannot be conceived as neutral or value-free in themselves; their meanings must also be considered in the context of their prospective users and audiences. This, in turn, means that literacy is more than a set of skills; it is a discursive practice. For example, we have noted already the way in which Western narrative encodes ideas, beliefs and values about causality and progress. That narrative trajectory is not value-free or neutral; it encodes a fundamental way of thinking that individuals in Western societies need to understand in order to function effectively in this society. They do not need to agree with that structure, or to use it in all their own production; but they need to know what it is in order to understand much everyday communication.

This raises the issue of access, which is related to many of the concerns discussed above. The culture of a user or audience may or may not be a means of access to a text, depending on whether it provides the individual with an understanding of the genre and its meanings. Or, the user's or audience's embodiment may make access to a work more or less difficult. Access (or not) may be physical, technical, conceptual, political, ethical, affective, cultural, social. In a sense, access is an issue that we have already considered in relation to each of the areas already discussed – but it bears repetition. Without access a text is useless – a voice crying in a heteroglossic wilderness, without contextualising voices to give it meaning. Designers, artists and performers must always be aware of issues of access. They may choose to make their work not easily accessible – for political or cultural reasons – but need to be aware of the reasons for this, and of the ethics in which their work is embedded. Many writers and performers, for example, consider the effort needed to make meaning from a work to be a vital part of the work itself; that, in inducing the audience to engage in this labour, they are displacing them from preconceived ideas, values and beliefs and (potentially) opening up new ways of thinking and being. Each text has its own ethics, of which accessibility is a key feature.

This matrix of practices, environments and being in which the individual text is embedded constitutes its heteroglossia. It is through the interactions between user, text and all of these practices and forces that meanings are generated. A designer or author who understands the meanings associated with each of these interactions (the meanings generated by: textual practices; the cultures of users and audiences; the culture of the source (which may be her or his own or those of the entity articulated by the text); the issues of access and how they influence meaning-making; the genre of text itself and its intertextual referents; and by the complex issue of embodiment and its constitution of meaning) has more chance of positioning an audience to understand the meanings she or he wishes to communicate. Equally, users and audiences who are aware of the complex practices by which they generate meanings from texts will have more chance of situating that meaning in relation to their own being and beliefs – which is not to preclude the ability of a text to cause the user to alter or modify her or his beliefs, but rather to enable the user to understand the change and her or his production of new knowledge.

Resemioticisation

Another issue that arises in the examination of complex multimedia texts is their composition, their coarticulation of a range of meaning-systems (verbal, visual, aural, kinesic and so on). There are two different ways to approach this issue: one is that it is not new, just newly obvious; the other is to look at other contexts in which similar issues are being raised.

In the first case, we might note that – as has been pointed out throughout the study – texts have long been multimedia, if not digitally multimedia. In other words, we have a tradition of texts and practices that involve different meaning systems working together to generate meanings. One simple example was the visuality of written text, where visual conventions of layout are used to signify the modality of a text – as prose, poetry, drama. When we interact with someone in conversation, we also commonly mobilise more than one meaning system. The conversation is much more than the words transcribed; it also involves vocal qualities, body language and facial expressions. We learn by experience how these different meaning-making (textual) strategies work (in the genre of everyday conversation) and use them to achieve the kind of communication we wish. With the multimedia texts in our study we do the same thing. We learn the meanings of textual strategies used in these texts – what meanings they communicate, and to which cultural groups. Some of these meanings are derived from older uses; some are new to the digital medium. In some cases their deployment in the new medium adds to or modifies their meanings. In each case our concern is to explore the meaning potential of both new textual strategies and older or familiar textual strategies deployed in the new medium – in order to develop a repertoire of meaning-making abilities (as both designer/author and user/audience).

Another approach is to focus on what Rick Iedema calls in another context 'resemioticization' (Iedema, 2003). Iedema explores the different meanings a particular strategy may have when it is adapted to a different discipline, with a different set of material and semiotic constraints. His particular focus of study was the dialogue between medical professionals, bureaucrats and architects in the design of a new medical facility. He was intrigued by the kinds of (mis)communications that could occur as the values of one group confronted those of another – and with how these had subsequently to be converted into material practices (constructing a building). There is a sense in which Bolter and Grusin's (1999) 'hypermediation' exemplifies the fascination with the technology of such a transformation.

In our study the new uses of familiar textual strategies in multimedia texts partook of this same sense of resemioticisation. The material practice they encounter is a (virtual) technology and the reality it gives the text. That multimedia text is the reality that users and audiences encounter, and by which they make meanings of themselves and their lives. My redeployment of terms such as genre, intertextuality, discourse, embodiment and subjectivity in this study has been an attempt to discuss this resemioticisation – the interrelation of meaning systems that have previously been held in different disciplinary areas (language and literary studies, visual arts, musicology and audiology, performance, architecture). By providing a common basic language for the meaning-making functions of these different systems of meaning it is possible to discuss their meaning-making practice in a holistic way. In a sense what this strategy avoids is the pigeon-holing of specific practices that has bedeviled the analysis of film sound – and that militated against the development of Walter Murch's conception of the sound designer for film (Murch, 2003).

Instead, we can range across meaning-systems and talk about the ways their different meanings are coarticulated in the complex practice that is the multimedia text.

Internal resonance

Yet, those meanings do not simply erupt out of the surface of the text; they are generated through the interaction of the text with a user or audience, without whom no production of meaning takes place. The term, 'internal resonance' captures the individual's interactions with both texts and technologies. Mark Hansen evokes the term, 'internal resonance' (as theorised by French philosopher, Gilbert Simondon), to explain how the individual makes order from the chaos of forces in which she or he is situated in order to 'maintain the metastability that is the precondition of ongoing individuation' (Hansen, 2002: 349); that is, in order to maintain the sense that she or he is, at any one time-space, a coherent, individual subject. In Hansen's terms again: 'internal resonance permits a system to maintain its life-giving "communication" with the metastability of the material flux while at the same time giving the mechanism for a system to individuate itself – that is, to achieve a certain degree of autonomy vis-à-vis that metastability' (Hansen, 2002: 349).

In relation to texts, this can be understood as the individual's ability to enter into the rule-governed meaning systems used to compose a text and allow her or his resonance with those systems to generate particular meanings. In relation to technology, the same reasoning can apply, as the individual mobilises new ways of interfacing with the world that are compatible with that technology. Again, this adaptation by the individual enables her or him to enter into the logic of that technology and generate meanings – and knowledge – through that encounter. At the same time, the individual converts these encounters into communication with her or his own existing meaning-making capacities and knowledge, so that she or he is able to maintain an ongoing sense of self. The value of this term is that it captures the fully embodied nature of this relationship. This is not a mental game pursued by a disembodied brain. Instead the embodied subject quivers with the energy generated by this dialogue, momentarily decentred by her or his participation in the flux of forces over which she or he has no power. Yet, the individual is able – through this process of dialogue and incorporation – to re-establish the metastability that is her or his ongoing and ever-changing autonomy. This is another way of arguing Hayles's (2002) point that the human body and human consciousness do not pre-exist this interface with technologies and meaning systems but are generated through this exchange. Or, as Bernadette Wegenstein has recently argued:

> … the body and all of its organs not only serve as a medium of expression through appearance to the outer world, but have themselves adopted the appearance of a medium. The discourse of getting under the skin

was necessary to 'free' the strata of a given hierarchy. The skin and the other organs, thus freed, have taken on the role of pure mediation, of flat screen, of the sur-face on which the body as such is produced. (2002: 221–259)

The exploration of multimedia – and of the human be-ing – generated by our use of multimedia has just begun; it is an exciting time. I leave the last word to designer, Bob Aufuldish:

What makes multimedia so interesting is its digital nature, because a given project is, in a sense, never 'final', never finished; it's eternally editable and transmutable. (1997: 99)

APPENDIX: SOUND ANALYSIS

The Day the Earth Stood Still (Robert Wise, 1951)

1 Opening scenes

Visuals	Words	Voice	Music	Sound FX
Titles over stars, nebulae, planets, cloud [trajectory to Earth]			Orchestral score, including theremin: light piano/deep wind juxtaposed	
View over ocean – US radar station – map – British radar station – Taj Mahal – Indian broadcaster reading in 'Indian' – people listening to French broadcast – woman in taxi – petrol attendant – people in shop – on porch – in pool hall – outside radio shop – US broadcast – Washington radio broadcast – Washington tourist sites …	Many voices describing the appearance of the saucer – first on radar screens (navy people), then in broadcasts – then 'Drew Pearson' takes over, describing 'scenes of normalcy' in Washington – tourists visiting sites	Voices: US navy – British navy – Indian broadcast – French broadcast – British broadcast – US broadcaster: many different accents, tones; US finally dominates	Light and dark staccato piano	
Tourist sites with small saucer above – picnickers fleeing – baseball park from above – saucer lands				Humming noises of craft in flight; lots of reverb; wind up sound as it settles
Busy road, man running and shouting – police cars emerging from underground car park – army police vehicles – police cars and bikes – troops in	'They've landed'	Male voice calling out		Sounds of busy traffic: sirens, jeep noise, more sirens, heavier transport (APCs)

(Continued)

(Continued)

Visuals	Words	Voice	Music	Sound FX
jeeps – APCs – army man on phone – row of switchboard operators – newspaper printing press – man asks to speak to President – broadcaster, Drew Pearson – radio and TV – in studio, camera operators, Drew Pearson at desk, wearing hat, TV monitor beside him, intercut with scenes from around saucer – army taking position, sightseers, including African-American woman … then Pearson announces …	'Get me the Chief of Staff'	Male voice to phone	Music over voices: staccato piano – not Pearson	Machinery noises: switchboard, press
	You'll have to interrupt him'	Male voice to phone		
		Pearson's professional broadcaster voice		
	Pearson's introduction … 'wait a minute, ladies and gentlemen …'			
Saucer starts to open – ramp extends – repeated shots between troops, onlookers and saucer intercut with: Klaatu emerges in			High and low tones, lots of reverb	Voices in background – hubbub – Sound of guns being cocked – Crowd noise – hubbub
spacesuit – speaks – begins to descend ramp – long shot, medium shot, close up	Klaatu: 'we come in peace'	Klaatu's voice: deep, magnified and distorted by helmet		
Klaatu in close-up takes out gift – soldier shoots – Klaatu struggles to rise – gift lies broken – soldiers gather around				Guns being cocked
Klaatu – soldiers look up in horror Gort descends ramp – crowd flees – soldiers retreat – Gort			Gort theme: deep music, reverb, theremin	Crowd panic voices

(Continued)

Visuals	Words	Voice	Music	Sound FX
stops as saucer closes up – Gort helmet – troops in b/ground, Klaatu on ground (Gort's point of view)				
Gort's visor opens – ray melts rifles, gun emplacements, APCs or tanks – Klaatu struggles up and addresses Gort – visor closes – Klaatu speaks to soldiers – soldiers gather around Klaatu – officer arrives and tells them to take Klaatu to Walter Read hospital	K: [addresses Gort] K: It was a gift for your president. With this he could have studied life on the other planets. Officer: Get that ambulance over here. Take him to Walter Read Hospital right away. Soldier: Yes, sir.	K's reverberating voice, distorted by helmet as it magnifies his voice for Gort. K's voice, deep, resonant. Officer's voice: flat Soldier's voice: flattened affect	Music down as visor opens ... continues as background throughout scene	'Ziiipppp' sound to signify 'ray gun' Squeal of tyres as officer's car arrives
Ante-room outside Klaatu's hospital room – gathering of men – Mr Harley from the White House arrives. Is shown to Klaatu's room. Turns as he is about to knock. Then knocks and enters.	Soldier: Mr Harley, sir, from the White House. Harley: General. General: Right in there, Mr Harley	Soldier's voice: pleasant General: affect-flattened military voice. Harley: voice of the bureaucrat – minimal affect	[none]	Footsteps Knock on door

(Continued)

(Continued)

Visuals	Words	Voice	Music	Sound FX
			[none]	
Harley enters Klaatu's room – Klaatu in shadow profile – eerie. Greets Klaatu	Harley: My name is Harley, Secretary to the President. I've been told you speak our language and that your name is Mr … Klaatu?	Harley's voice: pleasant, fairly flat		
	Klaatu: Just Klaatu.			
	Harley: The president asked me to convey his deepest apologies for what has happened.	Klaatu's deep resonant voice		
	Klaatu: Sit down, Mr Harley			
who invites him to sit down	Harley: Thank you [sits down] I'm sure I need hardly point out that your arrival was something of a surprise. Have you been travelling long?			Scrape of chair on floor [no carpet]
We then see Klaatu front on	Klaatu: About five months. Your months.			
	Harley: You must have come a long way.			
	Klaatu: About 250 million of your miles.			
	Harley: Naturally we're very curious to know where it is you come from.			
	Klaatu: From another planet. Let's just say that we're neighbours.			

2 *Klaatu's escape*

Visuals	Words	Voice	Music	Sound FX
Harley leaves and Klaatu hears a key turn in the lock of his room. Smiles wryly. Image fades over later scene as nurse walks towards his door with a tray, accompanied by soldier. When the soldier goes to unlock the door, he finds it open.	[none]			key turns in lock
They open the door and see no one is there. Soldier checks the bathroom and then runs out. Tells desk soldier that Klaatu has escaped. Man in charge phones. Scenes of soldiers running		Soldier: Captain, sir, the man from the spaceship has got away.	Music – urgent	
Soldiers driving off. Soldiers around desk – summit. People buying newspapers. Close up on headline: "Man from Mars" escapes'. Radio announcer. Husband and wife sitting next to radio, looking worried, with drink. Another radio announcer. Man sitting in car, another next to him, listening to car radio. Another radio announcer. Family around the dinner table. Mother gathers in two children from outside		Captain: What? Get every available man.	Klaatu theme: piano (light) over wind Back to urgent theme with elements of other world …	
			Fade down	

(Continued)

(Continued)

Visuals	Words	Voice	Music	Sound FX
Klaatu walking along footpath – from back	Radio announcer #1: The authorities at Walter Read hospital refuse to comment on how he managed to escape or what measures may be taken to apprehend him.	Professional radio voice	[none]	
	Announcer #2: ... creature have been denounced by police chief, Walter Baxter. He's not eight feet tall, as reported, nor does he have tentacles.	Professional radio voice		Muted footsteps
	Announcer #3: There's no denying that there is a monster at large; that we are dealing with forces beyond our knowledge and power. The public is advised to take ordinary precautions and to remain calm as we await the president's ... Mix of voices.	Professional radio voice		
Klaatu stops. Puts down the suitcase	Announcer #4: ... come to the inescapable conclusion that this ship and its occupants have come from some other planet. Thus far scientists have refused to	Professional radio voices		Suitcase put down on footpath

(Continued)

Visuals	Words	Voice	Music	Sound FX
Klaatu adjusts sleeves and notices dry cleaning label, which we then see in close-up. Label shows owner is Major Carpenter. Klaatu smiles. Throws away label. Notices 'Room to rent' sign at boarding house. Picks up suitcase which we see in close up has initials LMC printed on it. Walks on	speak officially on just which planet until they've had an opportunity to study the ship. They seem to agree however that either Venus or Mars is the most likely possibility. Not only are these the closest planets to earth but all ... meagre knowledge ...			
Group watching television. Drew Pearson is discussing spaceman. Close up on TV set (DP in hat). Medium shot of TV viewers with set in background. Bobbie turns to speak to his mother and notices something behind them	Pearson on the visitor ... on the need to be vigilant, but also noting that he may be an enemy or a new-found friend ... Bobbie: Mum, do you think I could ... hey, who's that?	Pearson's professional announcer's voice Bobbie: light tenor	[none]	[none]
All turn around. Klaatu standing in shadow. All stand, except Mrs Benson. Klaatu puts down suitcase and moves forward. Landlady turns off set and comes forward to turn on lamp. Puts all in light, including Klaatu	Pearson: ... this is no ordinary manhunt. We may be up against powers that are beyond our control. Landlady: What is it you want? Klaatu: My name is Carpenter. I'm looking for a room.	Pearson's professional announcer's voice Landlady's voice Klaatu's resonant voice	[none]	[none]

BIBLIOGRAPHY

Adorno, Theodor W. (1988) *Introduction to the Sociology of Music*. New York: Continuum.

Adorno, Theodor W. (1991) *The Culture Industry*. London and New York: Routledge.

Albrecht, Donald and Lupton, Ellen (eds) (2000) *Design Culture Now*. London: Lawrence King.

Anderson, Benedict (1983) *Imagined Communities: Reflections on the Origin and Spread of Nationalism*. London: Verso.

Architectural Theory Review (2002) 7 (1).

Arnold, Matthew (1994) *Culture and Anarchy*. Sam Lipman. (ed.) New Haven and London: Yale University Press.

Aronowitz, Stanley, Martinsons, Barbara, Menser, Michael and Rich, Jennifer (eds) (1996) *Technoscience and Cyberculture*. New York and London: Routledge.

Attali, Jacques (1985) *Noise: The Political Economy of Music*. Trans. Brian Massumi. Minneapolis: University of Minnesota Press.

Aufuldish, Bob (1997) '[Interview]', in Steven Heller and Daniel Drennan, *The Digital Designer: The Graphic Artist's Guide to the New Media*. New York: Watson-Guptill, pp. 97–100.

Aufuldish, Bob (2001) 'Gestures in TypeSpace', in Steven Heller (ed.), *The Education of an E-Designer*. New York: Allworth, pp. 48–9.

Axtell, Roger E. (1991) *Gestures: The Do's and Taboos of Body Language around the World*. New York: Wiley.

Bachelard, Gaston (1994) *The Poetics of Space*. Trans. Maria Jolas. Boston: Beacon Press.

Baggerman, Lisa (2001) *Web Design That Works: Secrets for Successful Web Publishing*. Gloucester, MA: Rockport Publishing.

Bakhtin, M.M. (1968) *Rabelais and his World*. Trans. H. Iswolsky. Cambridge, MA: MIT Press.

Bakhtin, M.M. (1981) *The Dialogic Imagination: Four Essays*. Trans. C. Emerson and M. Holquist. (ed.) M. Holquist. Austin: University of Texas Press.

Bakhtin, M.M. (1984) *Problems of Dostoyevsky's Poetics*. (ed.) and trans. C. Emerson. Introd. W.C. Booth. Manchester: Manchester University Press.

Bakhtin, M.M. (1986) *Speech Genres and Other Late Essays*. Trans. Vern McGee. (ed.) C. Emerson and M. Holquist. Austin: University of Texas Press.

Baldry, Anthony (ed.) (2000) *Multimodality and Multimediality in the Distance Learning Age: Papers in English Linguistics*. Campobasso: Palladino Editore.

Baldwin, Sandy (2002) 'On Speed and Ecstasy: Paul Virilio's "Aesthetics of Disappearance" and the Rhetoric of Media', *Configurations* 10: 129–48.

Balla, Giacomo (1912) *Dynamism of a Dog on a Leash,* viewed at http://www.usc.edu/schools/annenberg/asc/projects/comm544/library/images/286.html

Balsamo, Anne (1996) *Technologies of the Gendered Body: Reading Cyborg Women*. Durham: Duke University Press.

Bandt, Ros (2001) *Sound Sculpture: Intersections in Sound and Sculpture in Australian Artworks.* Sydney: Craftsman House.

Barr, Marleen (ed.) (2000) *Future Females, the Next Generation: New Voices and Velocities in Feminist Science Fiction.* Lantham, MD: Rowman and Littlefield.

Barthes, Roland (1977) *Image/Music/Text: Essays.* Sel. and trans. Stephen Heath. London: Fontana.

Baudrillard, Jean (2001) *Selected Writings.* (ed.) and introd. Mark Poster. Cambridge: Polity.

Benjamin, Walter (1973) *Illuminations.* Trans. Harry Zohn. (ed.) Hannah Arendt. Glasgow: Fontana.

Bennett, Tony (1995) *The Birth of the Museum: History, Theory, Politics.* London: Routledge.

Bennett, Tony (1998) *Culture: A Reformer's Science.* St Leonards: Allen and Unwin.

Bolter, Jay David and Grusin, Richard (1999) *Remediation: Understanding New Media.* Cambridge, MA: MIT Press.

Bosseur, Jean-Yves (1993) *Sound and the Visual Arts: Intersections between Music and Plastic Arts today.* Collab. Alexandre Broniarski. Trans. Brian Holmes and Peter Carrier. Paris: Dis Voir.

Bourdieu, Pierre (1990a) *In Other Words: Essays Towards a Reflexive Sociology.* Trans. Matthew Adamson. Cambridge: Polity.

Bourdieu, Pierre (1990b) *The Logic of Practice.* Trans. Richard Nice. Cambridge: Polity.

Boylan, P. (ed.) (1992) *Museums 2000: Politics, People, Professionals and Profit.* London: Museums Association/Routledge.

Bronte, Emily (1996) *Wuthering Heights.* Koln: Konemann.

Bukataman, Scott (1993) *Terminal Identity: The Virtual Subject in Postmodern Science Fiction* (Durham: Duke University Press).

Bull, Michael (2000) *Sounding Out the City: Personal Stereos and the Management of Everyday Life.* Oxford and New York: Berg.

Burbules, Nicholas C. (1997) 'Rhetorics of the web: hyperreading and critical literacy', in Ilana Snyder (ed.), *Page to Screen: Taking Literacy into the Electronic Era.* St Leonards: Allen and Unwin. pp. 102–22.

Burnett, Robert and Marshall, David P. (2003) *Web Theory: An Introduction.* London: Routledge.

Butler, Judith (1990) *Gender Trouble: Feminism and the Subversion of Identity.* New York and London: Routledge.

Butler, Judith (1993) *Bodies That Matter: On the Discursive Limits of 'Sex'.* New York: Routledge.

Butler, Rex (1999) *Jean Baudrillard: The Defence of the Real.* London: Sage.

Butterick, Matthew (2001) 'Type is Dead: Long Live Type', in Steven Heller and Philip B. Meggs (eds), *Texts on Type: Critical Writings on Typography.* New York: Allworth Press. pp. 39–41.

Bynum, Caroline Walker (1992) *Fragmentation and Redemption: Essays on Gender and the Human Body in Medieval Religion.* New York: Zone.

Carter, Paul (2002) *Repressed Spaces: The Poetics of Agoraphobia.* London: Reaktion Books.

Caruso, Denise (2001) 'Of Bonding and Bondage: Cults, Culture and the Internet', in Steven Heller (ed.), *The Education of an E-Designer.* New York: Allworth Press. pp. 214–218.

Casimir, Jon (2002) 'So happy together', *The Sydney Morning Herald*, August 2 25, pp. 4–5.

Cherny, Lynn and Weise, Elizabeth Reba (eds) (1996) *Wired Women: Gender and New Realities in Cyberspace.* Seattle: Seal Press.

Chesher, Chris (1997) 'The ontology of digital domains', in David Holmes (ed.), *Virtual Politics: Identity and Community in Cyberspace.* London: Sage. pp. 79–92.

Chion, Michel (1994) *Audio-Vision: Sound on Screen* (ed.) and trans. Claudia Gorbman. New York: Columbia University Press.

Chion, Michel (1999) *The Voice in Cinema* (ed.) and trans. Claudia Gorbman. New York: Columbia University Press.

Cloninger, Curt (2002) *Fresh Styles for Web Designers: Eye Candy from the Underground.* Indianapolis: New Riders Publishing.

Connah, Roger (2001) *How Architecture Got Its Hump.* Cambridge, MA: MIT Press.

Coyle, Karen (1996) 'How Hard Can It Be?', in Lynn Cherny and Elizabeth Reba Weise (eds), *Wired Women: Gender and New Realities in Cyberspace.* Seattle, Washington: Seal Press. pp. 42–55.

Coyle, Rebecca (ed.) (1998) *Screen Scores: Studies in Contemporary Australian Film Music.* Sydney: Australian Film, Television and Radio School.

Coyle, Rebecca (2002) 'Scoring Australia. Film music and Australian identities in *Young Einstein, Strictly Ballroom* and *The Adventures of Priscilla, Queen of the Desert*'. PhD thesis, Department of Critical and Cultural Studies, Macquarie University, Sydney.

Coyne, Richard (1998) 'Cyberspace and Heidegger's Pragmatics', *Information Technology and People*, 11 (4): 338–50.

Cranny-Francis, Anne (1992) *Engendered Fiction: Analysing Gender in the Production and Reception of Texts.* Sydney: NSW University Press.

Cranny-Francis, Anne (1994) *Popular Culture.* Geelong: Deakin University Press.

Cranny-Francis, Anne (1995) *The Body in the Text.* Melbourne: Melbourne University Press.

Cranny-Francis, Anne (2000a) 'The erotics of the (cy)Borg: authority and gender in the sociocultural imaginary', in Marleen Barr (ed.), *Future Females, the Next Generation: New Voices and Velocities in Feminist Science Fiction.* Lantham, MD: Rowman and Littlefield. pp. 145–63.

Cranny-Francis, Anne (2000b) 'Connexions', in D. Gibbs and K. Krause (eds), *Cyberlines: The Languages of Cyberspace.* Albert Park, Vic.: James Nicholas Publishers. pp. 123–48.

Cubitt, Sean (1998) *Digital Aesthetics.* London: Sage.

Davis, Colin (1996) *Levinas: An Introduction.* Cambridge: Polity.

Davis, Erik (1993) 'Techgnosis: magic, memory, and the angels of information', in Mark Dery (ed.), *Flame Wars: The Discourse of Cyberculture,* special issue of *Southern Atlantic Quarterly*, 92 (4): 585–616.

Davis, Erik (1998) *Techgnosis: Myth, Magic and Mysticism in the Age of Information.* London: Serpent's Tail.

De Certeau, Michel (1984) *The Practice of Everyday Life.* Trans. Steven Rendall. Berkeley: University of California Press.

De Lauretis, Teresa (1986) 'Feminist studies/critical studies: issues, terms, and contexts', in de Lauretis (ed.) *Feminist Studies/Critical Studies.* Bloomington: Indiana University Press. pp. 1–19.

De Lauretis, Teresa (1987) *Technologies of Gender: Essays on Theory, Film and Fiction.* Bloomington and Indianapolis: Indiana University Press.

Dean, David (1994) *Museum Exhibition: Theory and Practice.* London and New York: Routledge.

Deck, Barry http://www.barrydeck.com

Deleuze, Gilles and Guattari Félix (1983a) 'Rhizome', in *On the Line,* trans. John Johnston. New York: Semiotext(e), pp. 1–65.

Deleuze, Gilles and Guattari Félix (1983b) *Anti-Oedipus: Capitalism and Schizophrenia.* Trans. R. Hurley, M. Steen and H.R. Lane. Minneapolis: University of Minnesota Press. [Fr 1972].

Deleuze, Gilles and Guattari Félix (1987) *A Thousand Plateaus: Capitalism and Schizophrenia.* Trans. Brian Massumi. Minneapolis and London: University of Minnesota Press.

Deleuze, Gilles (1986) *Cinema 1: The Movement-Image.* Trans. Hugh Tomlinson and Barbara Habberjam. Minneapolis: University of Minnesota Press.

Deleuze, Gilles (1989) *Cinema 2: The Time-Image.* Trans. Hugh Tomlinson and Robert Galeta. Minneapolis: University of Minnesota Press.

DeNora, Tia (2000) *Music in Everyday Life.* Cambridge: Cambridge University Press.

Derrida, Jacques (1974) *Of Grammatology.* Trans. Gayatri Chakravorty Spivak. Baltimore and London: Johns Hopkins University Press.

Derrida, Jacques (1978) *Writing and Difference.* Trans. and introd. Alan Bass. London: Routledge and Kegan Paul.

Derrida, Jacques (1980) 'La loi du genre/The Law of Genre', *Glyph,* 7: 176–232.

Dery, Mark (ed.) (1993) *Flame Wars: The Discourse of Cyberculture,* special issue of *Southern Atlantic Quarterly* 92 (4).

Documenting a Democracy (2002) Online. http://www.foundingdocs.gov.au (25 August 2002).

Douglas, Mary (1966) *Purity and Danger.* London: Routledge and Kegan Paul.

Dyer, Richard (1997) *White.* London and New York: Routledge.

Eagleton, Terry (1983) *Literary Theory: An Introduction.* Oxford: Basil Blackwell.

Everard, Michele (1996) '"So please stop, thank you": Girls Online', in Lyna Cherny and Elizabeth Reba Weise (eds), *Wired Women: Gender and New Realities in Cyberspace.* Seattle, WA: Seal Press. pp. 188–204.

Featherstone, Mike and Burrows, Roger (1995) *Cyberspace/cyberbodies/cyberpunk: Cultures of Technological Embodiment.* London: Sage.

Feenberg, Andrew and Hannay, Alastair (eds) (1995) *Technology and the Politics of Knowledge.* Bloomington: Indiana University Press.

Ferré, Frederick (1995) *Philosophy of Technology.* Athens and London: University of Georgia Press.

Figgis, Mike (2003) 'The absence of sound', in Larry Sider, Diane Freeman and Jerry Sider (eds), *Soundscape: The School of Sound Lectures, 1998–2001.* London and New York: Wallflower Press. pp. 1–14.

Finlay, Victoria (2002) *Colour: Travels Through the Paintbox.* London: Hodder and Stoughton.

Fiske, John (1989) *Understanding Popular Culture.* Boston: Hyman Unwin.

Fleming, Jennifer (1998) *Web Navigation: Designing the User Experience.* Sebastopol, CA: O'Reilly.

Foucault, Michel (1977) *Language, Counter-Memory, Practice: Selected Essays and Interviews.* Trans. Donald F. Bouchard and Sherry Simon. (ed.) Donald F. Bouchard. Oxford: Basil Blackwell.

Foucault, Michel (1980) *Power/Knowledge.* New York: Pantheon.

Foucault, Michel (1981) *The History of Sexuality Volume 1: An Introduction.* Trans. Robert Hurley. Harmondsworth: Penguin.

Fried, Geoffrey (2001) 'The wrong horse?', in Steven Heller (ed.), *Education of an E-Designer.* New York: Allworth Press. pp. 10–13.

Fuller, Gillian (2002) 'The arrow – directional semiotics: wayfinding in transit', *Social Semiotics,* 12 (3): 231–44.

Gage, John (1993) *Colour and Culture: Practice and Meaning from Antiquity to Abstraction.* London: Thames and Hudson.

Gage, John (1999) *Colour and Meaning: Art, Science and Symbolism.* London: Thames and Hudson.

Gibbs, Donna and Krause, Kerri-Lee (eds) (2000) *Cyberlines: Languages and Cultures of the Internet.* Albert Park: James Nicholas Publishers.

Gibson, William (1986) *Neuromancer.* London: Grafton.

Giger, H.R. *GigersAlien* viewed at www.hrgiger.com.

Gillard, P. (2002) 'Cruising through HistoryWired'. Paper presented at the Museums and the Web Conference, Boston, 17 April.

Gillard, P. (2002) 'Museum visitors as audiences: innovative research for online museums', in M. Balnaves, T. O'Regan and J. Sternberg (eds), *Mobilising the Audience.* St Lucia: University of Queensland Press. pp. 168–87.

Gillard, Patricia and Cranny-Francis, Anne (2002) 'Evaluation for effective web communication: an Australian example', *Curator: the Museum Journal,* 45 (1): 35–49.

Gilster, Paul (1997) *Digital Literacy.* New York: John Wiley.

Girard, René (2000) 'From ritual to science', *Configurations,* 8: 171–85.

Gomringer, Eugen (1971) 'Silencio', *New Poetry: Magazine of the Poetry Society of Australia,* 19 (3): 11.

Gorbman, Claudia (1987) *Unheard Melodies: Narrative Film Music.* Bloomington: Indiana University Press.

Gray, Chris Hables (1995) *The Cyborg Handbook.* New York and London: Routledge.

Grodin, Debra and Lindlof, Thomas R. (1996) *Constructing the Self in a Mediated World.* Thousand Oaks: Sage.

Grosz, Elizabeth (2001) *Architecture from the Outside: Essays on Virtual and Real Space.* Cambridge, MA: MIT Press.

Guattari, Félix (1995) *Chaosmosis: An Ethico-aesthetic Paradigm.* Trans. Paul Bains and Julian Pefanis. Sydney: Power Publications.

Gunn, Aeneas (1908) *We of the Never Never.* London: Hutchinson.

Hall, Stuart (1992) 'The question of cultural identity', in Stuart Hall, David Held and Tony McGrew (eds), *Modernity and its Futures.* Cambridge: Polity Press. pp. 273–325.

Hanna, Judith Lynne (2001) 'The Language of Dance', *The Journal of Physical Education, Recreation and Dance,* 72 (4).

Hansen, Mark B. (2002) 'Wearable Space', *Configurations,* 10.2: 321–70.

Haraway, Donna (1991) *Simians, Cyborgs and Women: The Reinvention of Nature.* New York: Routledge.

Haraway, Donna (1997) *Modest_Witness@Second_Millennium.FemaleMan©_Meets_OncoMouse™* New York and London: Routledge.

Hardin, C.L. and Maffi, Luisa (1997) *Color Categories in Thought and Language.* Cambridge and New York: Cambridge University Press.

Hartley, John (1989) 'Continuous pleasures in marginal places: TV, continuity and the construction of communities', in John Tulloch and Graeme Turner (eds), *Australian Television: Programmes, Pleasures and Politics*. Sydney: Allen and Unwin. pp. 139–57.

Hawisher, Gail E. and Selfe, Cynthia L. (eds) (2000) *Global Literacies and the World Wide Web*. London and New York: Routledge.

Hayles, N. Katherine (1999) *How We Became Posthuman: Virtual Bodies in Cybernetics, Literature, and Informatics*. Chicago: University of Chicago Press.

Hayles, Katherine N. (2002) 'Flesh and metal: reconfiguring the mindbody in virtual environments', *Configurations*, 10: 297–320.

Hays, K. Michael (ed.) (1998) *Architecture Theory since 1968*. Cambridge, MA and London: MIT Press.

Hayward, Philip (1997) 'Danger! Retro-Affectivity! The cultural career of the theremin', *Convergence: The Journal of Research into New Media Technologies*, 3 (4): 38.

Heidegger, Martin (1977) *The Question Concerning Technology and Other Essays*. Trans. William Lovitt. New York: Harper and Row.

Heinicke, Elisabeth (2002) *Web Tricks and Techniques: Layout. Fast Solutions for Hands-On Design*. Gloucester, MA: Rockport.

Heller, Steven and Drennan, Daniel (1997) *The Digital Designer: The Graphic Artist's Guide to the New Media*. New York: Watson-Guptill.

Heller, Stephen (2001a) 'Designing hate: Is there a graphic language of vile emotion?', in Steven Heller and Philip B. Meggs (eds), *Texts on Type: Critical Writings on Typography*. New York: Allworth Press. pp. 42–4.

Heller, Steven (ed.) (2001b) *The Education of an E-Designer*. New York: Allworth Press.

Heller, Steven (2002) *The Graphic Design Reader*. New York: Allworth Press.

Herman, Andrew and Swiss, Thomas (eds) (2000) *The World Wide Web and Contemporary Cultural Theory*. New York and London: Routledge.

HistoryWired. http://historywired.si.edu

Holmes, David (ed.) (1997) *Virtual Politics: Identity and Community in Cyberspace*. London: Sage.

Hooper-Greenhill, Eilean (1992) *Museums and the Shaping of Knowledge*. London and New York: Routledge.

Howard, S. (ed.) (1998) *Wired-up. Young People and the Electronic Media*. London: UCL Press.

Idhe, Don (1990) *Technology and the Lifeworld: From Garden to Earth*. Bloomington: Indiana University Press.

Iedema, Rick (2003) 'Multimodality, resemioticization: extending the analysis of discourse as multi-semiotic practice', *Social Semiotics*, 2 (1): 29–57.

Ihde, Don (1993a) *Philosophy of Technology: An Introduction*. New York: Paragon House.

Ihde, Don (1993b) *Postphenomenology: Essays in the Postmodern Context*. Evanston, IL: Northwestern University Press.

Jacka, E. (1994) 'Researching audiences: a dialogue between cultural studies and social science', *Media Information Australia*, 73: 45–51.

Jacobson, Robert (ed.) (2000) *Information Design*. Cambridge, MA: MIT Press.

Jameson, Fredric (1981) *The Political Unconscious: Narrative as a Socially Symbolic Act*. London: Methuen.

Jenkins, Henry (1991a) 'Star Trek rerun, reread, rewritten: fan writing as textual poaching', in Constance Penley, Elisabeth Lyon, Lynn Spigel and Janet Bergstrom (eds), *Close Encounters: Film, Feminism, and Science Fiction*. Minneapolis: University of Minnesota Press. pp. 171–204.

Jenkins, Henry (1991b) '"If I could speak with your sound": textual proximity, liminal identification, and the music of the science fiction community', *Camera Obscura*, 23 (May): 149–76.

Jenkins, Henry (1992) *Textual Poachers: Television Fans and Participatory Culture*. New York: Routledge.

Kalinak, Kathryn (1992) *Setting the Score: Music and the Classical Hollywood Film*. Madison: University of Wisconsin Press.

Karp, Ivan and Lavine, Steven D. (eds) (1991) *Exhibiting Cultures: The Poetics and Politics of Museum Display*. Washington: Smithsonian Institution Press.

Kassabian, Anahid (2001) *Hearing Film: Tracking Identifications in Contemporary Hollywood Film Music*. New York and London: Routledge.

Kirkup, Gill (ed.) (2000) *The Gendered Cyborg: A Reader*. London and New York: Routledge and Oxford University Press.

Kitzinger, Sheila (1988) *Freedom and Choice in Childbirth: Making Pregnancy Decisions and Plans*. Harmondsworth: Penguin.

Kotler, N. and Kotler, P. (1998) *Museum Strategy and Marketing*. San Francisco: Jossey-Bass.

Kress, Gunther and van Leeuwen, Theo (1996) *Reading Images: The Grammar of Visual Design*. London and New York: Routledge.

Kress, Gunther (1997) 'Visual and verbal modes of representation in electronically mediated communication: the potentials of new forms of text', in Ilana Snyder (ed.), *Page to Screen: Taking Literacy into the Electronic Era*. St Leonards: Allen and Unwin. pp. 53–79.

Kruger, Barbara (1981) *Untitled (Your gaze hits the side of my face)*, viewed at www.usc.edu/schools/anneberg/asc/projects/comm544/library/images/541.html

Kuhn, Thomas (1962) *The Structure of Scientific Revolutions*. Chicago: University of Chicago Press.

Kwinter, Stanford (1998) 'La citta nuova: modernity and continuity', in K. Michael Hays (ed.), *Architecture Theory since 1968*. Cambridge, MA and London: MIT Press. pp. 588–612.

Lafranchi, Guy (1999) *A.R.C.H.O.N.P.O.I.S.O.N.* New York and Wien: Springer.

Lamb, Trevor and Bourriau, Janine (eds) (1995) *Colour: Art and Science*. Cambridge: Cambridge University Press.

Landow, George P. (1994) 'What's a critic to do?: Critical theory in the age of hypertext', in George P. Landow (ed.), *Hyper/Text/Theory*. Baltimore and London: The Johns Hopkins University Press. pp. 1–48.

Lang, Fritz (dir.) (1926) *Metropolis*, viewed at http://www.celtoslavica.de/chiaroscuro/films/metropolis/metro.html

Langton, Marcia (1993) ' "Well, I heard it on the radio and I saw it on the television" ...: An essay for the Australian Film Commission on the politics and aesthetics of filmmaking by and about Aboriginal people and things'. North Sydney: Australian Film Commission.

Latour, Bruno (1993) *We Have Never Been Modern*. Trans. Catherine Porter. Cambridge, MA: Harvard University Press.

Latour, Bruno (2003) 'Do you believe in reality? News from the trenches of the science wars', in Robert C. Scharff and Val Dusek (eds), *Philosophy of Technology: The Technological Condition. An Anthology*. Oxford: Blackwell. pp. 126–37.

Leach, N. (1997) *Rethinking Architecture: A Reader in Cultural Theory*. London and New York: Routledge.

Leahy, James (2003) 'A slap of sea and tickle of sand: echoes of sounds past', in Larry Sider, Diane Freeman and Jerry Sider (eds), *Soundscape: The School of Sound Lectures 1998–2001*. London and New York: Wallflower Press. pp. 54–72.

Lefebvre, Henri (1998) 'From *The Production of Space*', in K. Michael Hays (ed.), *Architecture Theory since 1968*. Cambridge, MA and London: MIT Press. pp. 178–88.

Levinas, Emmanuel (1998) *Otherwise Than Being Or Beyond Essence*. Trans. Alphonso Lingis. Pittsburg: Duquesne University Press.

Levinas, Emmanuel (2000) *God, Death, and Time*. Trans. Bettina Bergo. Stanford: Stanford University Press.

Lindsay, Jack (1985) *Turner: The Man and His Art*. London: Granada.

Loomis, Ross J. (1987) Museum visitor evaluation: New tool for management. American Association for State and Local History. Nashville, TN.

Lumley, Robert (ed.) (1988) *The Museum Time-Machine*. London and New York: Comedia/Routledge.

Lynch, David (2003) 'Action and Reaction', a video interview, in Larry Sider, Diane Freeman and Jerry Sider (eds), *Soundscape: The School of Sound Lectures, 1998–2001*. London and New York: Wallflower Press. pp. 49–53.

Mama, Amina (1995) *Beyond the Masks: Race, Gender and Subjectivity*. London: Routledge.

Manovich, Lev (2001) *The Language of New Media*. Cambridge, MA: MIT Press.

Mansfield, Nick (2000) *Subjectivity: Theories of the Self from Freud to Haraway*. St Leonards: Allen and Unwin.

Marcus, Julie (1999) *A Dark Smudge Upon the Sand: Essays on Race, Guilt and the National Consciousness*. Canada Bay, NSW: LHR Press.

Marinetti, F.T. (1973) 'Founding and Manifesto of Futurism 1909', in Umbro Apollonio (ed.), *Futurist Manifestos*. London: Thames and Hudson. pp. 19–24.

Martin, Paul (1999) *Popular Collecting and the Everyday Self: The Reinvention of Museums?* London and New York: Leicester University Press.

Mauss, Marcel (1992) 'Techniques of the Body', in Jonathan Crary and Stanford Kwinter (eds), *Incorporations*. New York: Zone Books. pp. 455–77. [1934].

McClary, Susan (1986) 'A musical dialectic from the Enlightenment: Mozart's Piano Concerto in G Major, K. 453, Movement 2', *Cultural Critique*, 4: 129–70.

McClary, Susan (1991) *Feminine Endings: Music, Gender, and Sexuality*. Minnesota and Oxford: University of Minnesota Press.

McClintock, Anne (1995) *Imperial Leather: Race, Gender and Sexuality in the Colonial Contest*. New York: Routledge.

McCrone, John (2003) 'Not-so Total Recall', *New Scientist*, 178 (2393): 26–9.

McGovern, Gerry and Norton, Rob (2002) *Content Critical: Gaining Competitive Advantage Through High-Quality Web Content*. Harlow: Pearson Education.

McRae, Shannon (1996) 'Coming Apart at the Seams', in Lynn Cherny and Elizabeth Reba Weise (eds), *Wired Women: Gender and New Realities in Cyberspace*. Seattle, WA: Seal Press. pp. 242–64.

Melville, Herman (1995) *Moby Dick or The Whale*. Köln, Könemann.

Merlau-Ponty, Maurice (1962) *Phenomenology of Perception*. Trans. Colin Smith. Routledge and Kegan Paul, London.

Michaels, Eric (1987) *For a Cultural Future: Francis Jupurrurla makes TV at Yuendumu*. Malvern, Vic.: Artspace.

Michaels, Eric (1994) *Bad Aboriginal Art: Tradition, Media and Technological Horizons*. St Leonards: Allen and Unwin.

Mirzoeff, Nicholas (ed.) (1998) *The Visual Culture Reader*. London and New York: Routledge.

Mirzoeff, Nicholas (1999) *An Introduction to Visual Culture*. London and New York: Routledge.

Mitchell, William J. (1995) *City of Bits: Space, Place and the Infobahn*. Cambridge, MA: MIT Press.

Moore, Kevin (1997) *Museums and Popular Culture*. London and Washington: Cassell.

Murch, Walter (2003) 'Touch of silence', in Larry Sider, Diane Freeman and Jerry Sider (eds), *Soundscape: The School of Sound Lectures, 1998–2001*. London and New York: Wallflower Press. pp. 83–102.

National Archives of Australia (2002) On-line. http://www.naa.gov.au (25 August 2002).

National Inquiry into the Separation of Aboriginal and Torres Strait Islander Children from their Families (1997) *Bringing them home: report of the National Inquiry into the Separation of Aboriginal and Torres Strait Islander Children from their Families (Australia)/Commissioner: Ronald Wilson*. Sydney: Human Rights and Equal Opportunities Commission.

Nattiez, Jean-Jacques (1990) *Music and Discourse: Toward a Semiology of Music*. Trans. Carolyn Abbate. Princeton: Princeton University Press.

Neill, Sean and Caswell, Chris (1993) *Body Language for Competent Teachers*. London and New York: Routledge.

Niederhelman, Melissa (2001) 'Interactivity is not an elective', in Steven Heller (ed.), *Education of an E-Designer*. New York: Allworth Press. pp. 14–19.

Nielsen, Jakob (2000) *Designing Web Usability: The Practice of Simplicity*. Indianapolis: New Riders.

Nightingale, V. (1966) *Studying Audiences. The Shock of the Real*. New York: Routledge.

Ong, Walter (1982) *Orality and Literacy: The Technologizing of the Word*. London: Methuen.

Palumbo, Maria Luisa (2000) *New Wombs: Electronic Bodies and Architectural Disorders*. Basel: Birkhauser.

Patton, Paul (2000) *Deleuze and the Political*. London and New York: Routledge.

Paulin, Tom (2003) 'The despotism of the eye', in Larry Sider, Diane Freeman and Jerry Sider (eds), *Soundscape: The School of Sound Lectures, 1998–2001*. London and New York: Wallflower Press. pp. 35–48.

Pearce, Susan M. (1992) *Museums, Objects, and Collections: A Cultural Study*. Washington: Smithsonian Institution Press.

Pearson, David (2001) *New Organic Architecture: The Breaking Wave*. London: Gaia Books.

Penley, Constance (1991) 'Brownian motion: women, tactics and technology', in Constance Penley and Andrew Ross (eds), *Technoculture*. Minneapolis: University of Minnesota Press. pp. 135–61.

Penley, Constance (1992) 'Feminism, psychoanalysis, and the study of popular culture', in Lawrence Grossberg, Cary Nelson and Paula A. Teichler (eds), *Cultural Studies*. New York: Routledge. pp. 479–500.

Pérez-Gomez, Alberto and Parcell, Stephen (1996) *Chora: Volume Two*. Montreal and Kingston: McGill-Queen's University Press.

Periera, Suvendrini (ed.) (1995) *Asian and Pacific Inscriptions: Identities, Ethnicities, Nationalities*. Bundoora, Vic.: Meridian.

Perloff, Marjorie (2000) '"Multiple Pleats": Some Applications of Michael Serres's Poetics', *Configurations* 8: 187–200.

Postman, Neil (1993) *Technopoly*. New York: Vintage.

Poyner, Rick (2001) 'American Gothic', in Steven Heller and Philip B. Meggs (eds), *Texts on Type: Critical Writings on Typography*. New York: Allworth Press. p. 51.

Price, Jonathan and Price, Lisa (2002) *Hot Text: Web Writing That Works*. Indianapolis: New Riders.

Raman, Pattabi G. and Richard Coyne 'The production of architectural criticism', *Architectural Theory Review*, 5 (1): 83–103.

Rasekoala, Elizabeth (2002) 'Opinion interview', *New Scientist*, 173 (2333): 44–7 (1).

Rheingold, Howard (1992) *Virtual Reality*. London: Mandarin.

Rheingold, Howard (1993) *Virtual Community: Homesteading on the Electronic Frontier*. Reading, MA: Addison-Wesley.

Rheingold, Howard (2000) *Tools for Thought: The History and Future of Mind-Expanding Technology*. Cambridge, Mass and London: MIT Press.

Roberts, Lisa C. (1997) *From Knowledge to Narrative: Educators and the Changing Museum*. Washington and London: Smithsonian Institution Press.

Rosenfeld, Louis and Morville, Peter (1998) *Information Architecture for the World Wide Web*. Sebastopol, CA: O'Reilly.

Said, Edward (1978) *Orientalism*. London: Penguin.

Sand, Darrell (1996) *Designing Large-Scale Web Sites: A Visual Design Methodology*. New York: John Wiley.

Schafer, R. Murray (1969) *The New Soundscape: A Handbook for the Modern Music Teacher*. Don Mills, Ontario: BMI Canada.

Schafer, R. Murray (1977) *The Tuning of the World: Toward a Theory of Soundscape Design*. New York: Knopf.

Schafer, R. Murray (1994) *The Soundscape: Our Sonic Environment and the Tuning of the World*. Rochester, VT: Destiny.

Scharff, Robert C. and Dusek, Val (eds) (2003) *Philosophy of Technology: The Technological Condition. An Anthology*. Oxford: Blackwell.

Schwarz, David, Kassabian, Anahid and Siegel, Lawrence (eds) (1997) *Keeping Score: Music, Disciplinarity, Culture*. Charlottesville: University Press of Virginia.

Seed, David (1999) *American Science Fiction and the Cold War: Literature and Film*. Edinburgh: Edinburgh University Press.

Severini, Gino (1973) 'The plastic analogies of dynamism – Futurist Manifesto 1913', in Umbro Apollonio (ed.), *Futurist Manifestos*. London: Thames and Hudson. pp. 118–25.

Shelley, Mary (1982) *Frankenstein or The Modern Prometheus* (ed.) Maurice Hindle. Harmondsworth: Penguin [1818].

Shepherd, John (1991) *Music as Social Text*. Cambridge: Polity.

Shneiderman, Ben (1987) *Designing the User Interface: Strategies for Effective Human-Computer Interaction*. Reading, MA: Addison-Wesley.

Shuker, Roy (1998) *Key Concepts in Popular Music*. London and New York: Routledge.

Sider, Larry, Freeman, Diane and Sider, Jerry (eds) (2003) *Soundscape: The School of Sound Lectures 1998–2001*. London and New York: Wallflower Press.

Silverman, Kaja (1988) *The Acoustic Mirror: The Female Voice in Psychoanalysis and Cinema*. Bloomington and Indianapolis: Indiana University Press.

Simondon, Gilbert (1992) 'The genesis of the individual', in Jonathan Crary and Stanford Kwinter (eds), *Incorporations*. New York: Zone Books. pp. 455–77.

Singh, Amrit and Rabindra. http://www.twinstudio.supanet.com.

Smith, Valerie (ed.) (1997) *Representing Blackness: Issues in Film and Video*. London: Athlone Press.

Snyder, Ilana (ed.) (1997) *Page to Screen: Taking Literacy into the Electronic Era.* St Leonards: Allen and Unwin.

Sobchak, Vivian (1987) *Screening Space: The American Science Fiction Film.* New York: Ungar.

Sobel, Dava (1996) *Longitude: The True Story of a Lone Genius Who Solved the Greatest Scientific Problem of His Time.* Fourth Estate: London.

Spool, Jared M., Scanlon, Tara, Schroeder, Will, Snyder, Carolyn and DeAngelo, Terri (1999) *Web Site Usability: A Designer's Guide.* San Francisco: Morgan Kaufmann.

Springer, Claudia (1996) *Electronic Eros: Bodies and Desire in the Postindustrial Age.* Austin: University of Texas Press.

Stone, Allucquère Rosanne (1995) *The War of Desire and Technology at the Close of the Mechanical Age.* Cambridge, MA and London: MIT Press.

Sturken, Marita and Cartwright, Lisa (2001) *Practices of Looking: An Introduction to Visual Culture.* Oxford: Oxford University Press.

Template Gothic (1995–2004) Viewed at http://www.emigre.com/EF.php?fid=125

Tennyson, Alfred, Lord (1970) *Poems of Alfred, Lord Tennyson.* Sel. and introd. Charles Tennyson. London: Collins.

Thom, Randy (2003) 'Designing a movie for sound', in Larry Sider, Diane Freeman and Jerry Sider (eds), *Soundscape: The School of Sound Lectures, 1998–2001.* London and New York: Wallflower Press. pp. 121–37.

Thomas, Nicholas (1995) *Possessions: Indigenous Art, Colonial Culture.* London: Thames and Hudson.

Thurstun, J. (2000) 'Screenreading: challenges of the new literacy', in D. Gibbs and K. Krause (eds), *Cyberlines: Languages and Cultures of the Internet.* Albert Park: James Nicholas Publishers. pp. 61–78.

Todorov, Tzevetan (1984) *Mikhail Bakhtin: The Dialogical Principle.* Trans. Wlad Godzich. Manchester: Manchester University Press.

Tolkien, J.R.R. (1991) *The Lord of the Rings.* London: HarperCollins.

Tonks, Paul (2001) *Film Music.* Harpenden, Herts: Pocket Essentials.

Trend, David (ed.) (2001) *Reading Digital Culture.* Oxford: Blackwell.

Tschumi, Bernard (1998) 'The architectural paradox', in K. Michael Hays (ed.), *Architecture Theory since 1968.* Cambridge, MA and London: MIT Press. pp. 218–28.

Turkle, Sherry (1995) *Life on the Screen: Identity in the Age of the Internet.* London: Phoenix.

Ullman, Ellen (1996) 'Come in, CQ: the body on the wire', in Lynn Cherny and Elizabeth Reba Weise (eds), *Wired Women: Gender and New Realities in Cyberspace.* Seattle, Washington: Seal Press. pp. 3–23.

Van Leeuwen, Theo (1989) 'Changed times, changed tunes: music and the ideology of the news', in J. Tulloch and G. Turner (eds), *Australian Television: Programmes, Pleasures, and Politics.* Sydney: Allen and Unwin. pp. 172–86.

Van Leeuwen, Theo (1999) *Speech, Music, Sound.* London: Macmillan.

Virilio, Paul (1991) *Lost Dimension.* Trans. Daniel Moshenberg. New York: Semiotext(e).

Virilio, Paul (1995) *The Art of the Motor.* Trans. Julie Rose. Minneapolis, MN: University of Minnesota Press.

Virilio, Paul (2000) *Polar Inertia.* Trans. Patrick Camiller. London: Sage.

Wegenstein, Bernadette (2002) 'Getting under the skin, or, how faces have become obsolete', *Configurations* 10: 221–59.

Weis, Elisabeth and Belton, John (eds) (1985) *Film Sound: Theory and Practice* New York: Columbia University Press.

Welchman, John C. (1996) *Rethinking Borders*. Minneapolis, MN: University of Minnesota Press.

Weller, Richard (2002) 'Mapping the nation', in Dimity Reed (ed.), *Tangled Destinies*. Mulgrave, Vic: Images Publishing Group. pp. 124–37.

White, Michael (2002) *Rivals: Conflict as the Fuel of Science*. London: Vintage.

Wigley, Mark (1997) *The Architecture of Deconstruction: Derrida's Haunt.* Cambridge, MA: MIT Press.

Winograd, Terry and Flores, Fernando (1986) *Understanding Computers and Cognition: A New Foundation for Design.* Norwood, NJ: Ablex.

Wise, Richard (2000) *Multimedia: A Critical Introduction*. London and New York: Routledge.

Woodhead, David (1995) ' "Surveillant gays": HIV, Space and the constitution of identities', in David Bell and Gill Valentine (eds), *Mapping Desire: Geographies of Sexualities*. London and New York: Routledge. pp. 231–44.

Wordig (web site): http://www.wordig.com.2004

Yates, Francis A. (1966) *The Art of Memory*. London and Henley: Routledge and Kegan Paul.

Zurbrugg, Nicholas (ed.) (1994) 'Electronic arts in Australia', special edition: *Continuum*, 8 (1).

FILMS AND TELEVISION

Arnold, Jack (dir.) (1953) *It Came from Outer Space*. Universal Studios.

Cameron, James (dir.) (1984) *The Terminator*. Orion/Hemdale/Pacific Western.

Cameron, James (dir.) (1986) *Aliens*. TCF/Brandywine.

Cameron, James (dir.) (1990) *Terminator 2: Judgment Day*. Pacific Western.

Donen, Stanley and Kelly, Gene (dirs) (1952) *Singin' in the Rain*. MGM.

Fincher, David (dir.) (1992) *Alien 3*. TCF/Brandywine.

Fowler, Gene (dir.) (1958) *I Married a Monster from Outer Space*. Paramount/ Gene Fowler Jr.

Haskin, Byron (dir.) (1953) *War of the Worlds*. Paramount.

Hawks, Howard (dir.) (1951) *The Thing*. RKO/Winchester.

Hitchcock, Alfred (dir.) (1945) *Spellbound*. Anchor Bay Entertainment.

Howard, Ron (dir.) (1988) *Willow*. UIP/MGM.

Hunter, Paul (dir.) (2003) *Bulletproof Monk*. MGM.

Huston, John (dir.) (1956) *Moby Dick*. MGM/UA.

Jackson, Peter (dir.) (1994) *Heavenly Creatures*. Miramax.

Jackson, Peter (dir.) (2001) *The Lord of the Rings: The Fellowship of the Ring*. New Line.

Jackson, Peter (dir.) (2002) *The Lord of the Rings: The Two Towers*. New Line.

Jackson, Peter (dir.) (2003) *The Lord of the Rings: The Return of the King*. New Line.

Kazdan, Lawrence (dir.) (1983) *The Big Chill*. Columbia/Tristar.

Lang, Fritz (dir.) (1926) *Metropolis*. UFA (Erich Pommer).

Lee, Ang (dir.) (2000) *Crouching Tiger, Hidden Dragon*. Columbia/Tristar.

Lucas, George (dir.) (2000) *Star Wars I: The Phantom Menace*. TCF/Lucasfilm.

Maguire, Sharon (dir.) (2001) *Bridget Jones's Diary*. Miramax.

Meyer, Nicholas (dir.) (1982) *Star Trek II: The Wrath of Khan*.

Neuman, Kurt (dir.) (1950) *Rocketship X-M*. Image Entertainment.

Nimoy, Leonard (dir.) (1984) *Star Trek III: The Search for Spock*. Paramount/Cinema Group Venture.

Scott, Ridley (dir.) (1979) *Alien*. TCF/Brandywine.

Scott, Ridley (dir.) (1982) *Bladerunner*. Warner/Ladd/Bladerunner Partnership.

Scott, Ridley (dir.) (1985) *Legend*. TCF/Universal.

Sears, Fred F. (dir.) (1956) *Earth Versus the Flying Saucers*. Columbia.

Siegel, Don (dir.) (1956) *Invasion of the Body Snatchers*. Superscope/Allied Artists/Walter Wagner.

Siodmark, Robert (dir.) (1946) *The Spiral Staircase*. Anchor Bay Entertainment.

Spielberg, Steven (dir.) (1984) *Indiana Jones and the Temple of Doom*. Paramount/ Lucasfilm.

Spielberg, Steven (dir.) (2002) *Minority Report*. TCF/Dreamworks/Amblin.

Star Trek: The Next Generation (1988–94) Paramount Pictures Corporation.

Tarantino, Quentin (dir.) (2003) *Kill Bill*. Volume I. Miramax.

Tarkovsky, Andrei (dir.) (1972) *Solaris*. Sovcolor/Scope Mosfilm.

Wachoski, Larry and Wachoski, Andy (dirs) (1999) *The Matrix*. Village Roadshow/ Silver.

Wachoski, Larry and Wachoski, Andy (dirs) (2003) *The Matrix Reloaded*. Village Roadshow/Silver.

Wachoski, Larry and Wachoski, Andy (dirs) (2003) *The Matrix Revolutions*. Village Roadshow/Silver.

Wilcox, Fred M. (dir.) (1956) *Forbidden Planet*. MGM.

INDEX